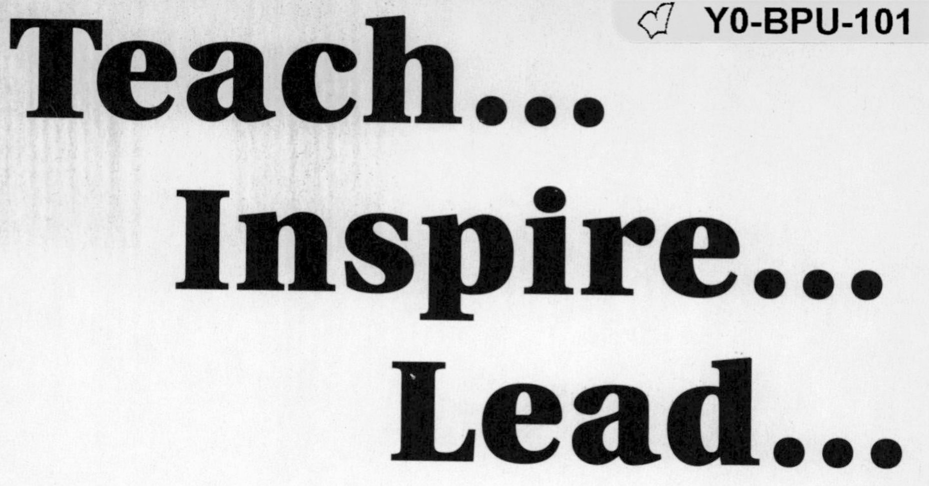
Teach...
Inspire...
Lead...

Research & Education Association

The Best Teachers' Test Preparation for the

WEST–B™

Washington Educator Skills Test–Basic™

With CD-ROM for Windows®
REA's **TEST***ware*® for the WEST–B™

Staff of
Research & Education Association

Visit our Educator Support Center at:
www.REA.com/teacher

Research & Education Association
61 Ethel Road West
Piscataway, New Jersey 08854
E-mail: info@rea.com

The Best Teachers' Test Preparation for the WEST–B™
(Washington Educator Skills Test–Basic™)
With TEST*ware*® on CD-ROM

Printed in the United States of America

Library of Congress Control Number 2005935934

International Standard Book Number 0-7386-0158-6

J05-0101

CONTENTS

About Research & Education Association

Founded in 1959, Research & Education Association is dedicated to publishing the finest and most effective educational materials—including software, study guides, and test preps—for students in middle school, high school, college, graduate school, and beyond.

REA's Test Preparation series includes books and software for all academic levels in almost all disciplines. Research & Education Association publishes test preps for students who have not yet completed high school, as well as for high school students preparing to enter college. Students from countries around the world seeking to attend college in the United States will find the assistance they need in REA's publications. For college students seeking advanced degrees, REA publishes test preps for many major graduate school admission examinations in a wide variety of disciplines, including engineering, law, and medicine. Students at every level, in every field, with every ambition can find what they are looking for among REA's publications.

REA's practice tests are always based upon the most recently administered exams and include every type of question that you can expect on the actual exams.

REA's publications and educational materials are highly regarded and continually receive an unprecedented amount of praise from professionals, instructors, librarians, parents, and students. Our authors are as diverse as the fields represented in the books we publish. They are well-known in their respective disciplines and serve on the faculties of prestigious high schools, colleges, and universities throughout the United States and Canada.

Today, REA's wide-ranging catalog is a leading resource for teachers, students, and professionals.

We invite you to visit us at *www.rea.com* to find out how "REA is making the world smarter."

Acknowledgments

We would like to thank REA's Larry B. Kling, Vice President, Editorial, for supervising development; Pam Weston, Vice President, Publishing, for setting the quality standards for production integrity and managing the publication to completion; John Paul Cording, Vice President, Technology, for coordinating the design, development, and testing of REA's TEST*ware*® software; Christine Reilley, Senior Editor, for project management and preflight editorial review; Diane Goldschmidt, Associate Editor, for post-production quality assurance; Project Managers Heena Patel and Reena Shah for their tireless software testing efforts; Jeremy Rech, Graphic Artist, for interior page design; Christine Saul, Senior Graphic Artist, for cover design; and Jeff LoBalbo, Senior Graphic Artist, for post-production file mapping.

We gratefully acknowledge David M. Myton, Ph.D., Renay M. Scott, Ph.D., Karen Bondarchuck, M.F.A., John A. Lychner, Ph.D., Janet E. Rubin, Ph.D., Ellen R. Van't Hof, M.A., Nelson Maylone, Ph.D., and Ginny Muller, Ph.D., for providing foundational material for this book. We also thank Al Davis, M.A., M.S. for editing this book.

We also gratefully acknowledge the team at Publication Services for editing, proofreading, and page composition.

Teach...
Inspire...
Lead...

With this book in hand, you've taken an important step toward becoming a certified teacher in the state of Washington. REA's all-new **WEST–B** teacher certification test prep is designed to help you get into a Washington classroom. The instructive chapters in this book provide complete coverage of the **WEST–B** with in-depth reviews of every topic and area you can expect to encounter on exam day. A full-length practice test carefully modeled after the actual WEST–B exam will hone your test-taking skills. All practice test questions are explained in thorough detail to provide you with a greater understanding of the exam's content and difficulty. When you finish preparing with this book, you will be well equipped with all the knowledge, practice, and strategies needed to succeed on this important exam.

ABOUT THE TESTS

What is the WEST–B used for?

The WEST–B, or Washington Educator Skills Test–Basic, is one part of the teacher certification process in Washington state. Passing the WEST–B alone is not sufficient to earn a teaching certificate in the Evergreen State. You must possess a bachelor's degree from a regionally accredited college or university, and you are required to complete a teacher preparation program. You must also pass a background check conducted by the Washington State Patrol and the FBI. Once the Washington State Certification Office verifies that you have met all these requirements, you will be issued your teaching certificate.

The WEST–B is aligned with standards established by the Washington Professional Educator Standards Board (PESB). Teachers in public and private schools in Washington state are required to hold a teaching certificate.

Information about who must be tested and which tests must be taken can be found in the WEST–B Registration Bulletin, located online at *http://www.west.nesinc.com*. The registration bulletin and website also contain test dates and information that can assist you in determining which tests must be successfully completed.

Am I required to take this test if I hold a teaching certificate from another state?

If applying from out of state for a residency certificate, applicants must pass a basic skills test within 12 months of receiving their first temporary permit. Those who have a passing score on the

CBEST, Praxis I: PPST, or computerized Praxis I: PPST may submit official score reports in lieu of the WEST–B. For information on test registration and administration, contact National Evaluation Systems at (800) 784-4999. Online registration is available at *http://www.west.nesinc.com*.

How is the test content determined?

The WEST–B is criterion referenced and objective based. A criterion-referenced test is designed to measure a candidate's knowledge and skills in relation to an established standard, rather than in relation to the performance of other candidates. The explicit purpose of the WEST–B is to help identify those candidates with the required level of basic skills to perform successfully in an educator preparation program or as a teacher in a public school classroom.

Washington state legislation authorizes the Professional Educator Standards Board to set the passing score on the assessments for prospective teachers. The PESB established a standards-setting process to get recommendations from Washington educators regarding an appropriate passing score. Through this process, educators examined the content of the test, the difficulty of the questions, and the examinees' performance to determine the level of performance needed to pass the basic skills test.

Who administers the WEST–B?

The WEST–B is administered by National Evaluation Systems, Inc., a private testing group.

When is the WEST–B test offered? How long is the testing time?

The WEST–B test is offered up to six times a year. Test session reporting time is 8:30 A.M. The session ends at approximately 1:30 P.M. The actual testing time is four and one-half hours. To receive more information, consult the WEST–B registration bulletin.

Additional information is available from the Washington Office of Public Education, to which NES is under contract. The department can be contacted as follows:

Washington Office of Public Education
Old Capitol Building
P.O. Box 47200
Olympia, WA 98504-7200
Phone: (360) 725-6000
TTY: (360) 664-3631
Website: *www.k12.wa.us/certification/teacher/teacherinformation.aspx*

Is there a registration fee?

Yes. In fact, there are several fees. There is a nonrefundable registration processing fee, a Reading Subtest fee, a Mathematics Subtest fee, and a Writing Subtest fee. Additional service fees are added for late registration, emergency registration, and changes in registration. Check with NES for fees and payment options.

HOW TO USE THIS BOOK AND TESTware®

What do I study first?

We recommend beginning your study with the comprehensive chapter reviews. It is important to read over each review, noting crucial test-taking suggestions and insights. By studying each review thoroughly, you will reinforce basic skills that are vital to performing well on the WEST–B. After reviewing, take the practice tests. This will familiarize you with the actual exam's format, procedures, and level of difficulty. An added bonus to taking these practice tests is knowing what to expect on exam day.

Apart from the book itself, we give you the full-length practice test (comprised of three subtests) on CD-ROM. **We strongly suggest that you begin your preparation with the TEST*ware*® practice test.** The software provides the added benefits of automatic scoring and enforced time conditons.

Wisely scheduling your study time is also a key component to your success on the WEST–B. To best utilize your study time, follow our flexible WEST–B study schedule found at the end of this chapter. The schedule is based ideally on a seven-week program, but can be condensed if needed.

When should I start studying for the WEST–B test?

It is never too early to start studying for your WEST–B test. Time is your ally here. The earlier you begin, the more time you will have to sharpen your skills and focus your efforts. Do not procrastinate! Cramming is not an effective way to study, since it does not allow you enough time to learn what will be required of you. It takes time to learn the tested areas and test format. Make the most of your time while you have it. Use it well to master the essentials necessary to pass.

FORMAT OF THE WEST–B TEST

What is the basic format of the WEST–B?

The WEST–B contains three separate subtests: Reading, Mathematics, and Writing. The Reading and Mathematics Subtests each consist of approximately 60 multiple-choice questions. The Writing Subtest consists of approximately 50 multiple-choice questions and two writing prompts.

About the Subject Reviews

The subject reviews in this book are designed purposefully to provide you critical insight into the content and form of the WEST–B. For smarter study, we break down this part of test preparation into more manageable "chunks." Before you begin reviewing, it is important to note that your own schooling experience has taught you most of what is needed to answer the questions on the actual WEST–B. Our review is written to help you fit and shape information acquired over the years into a context ideally suited for taking the WEST–B.

You may also be taking test preparation classes for the WEST–B or have purchased other study guides and textbooks. Reviewing class notes and textbooks along with our subject reviews will provide you with an even better foundation for passing the WEST–B.

SCORING THE WEST–B

To pass the WEST–B, you must pass all three subtests. A passing score is 240 for each subtest. A 240 score for each subtest is defined as:

- 63% of the READING multiple-choice questions
- 63% of the MATHEMATICS multiple-choice questions
- 62% of the WRITING multiple-choice questions and a score of 11 of 16 points on two writing tasks

Unofficial scores for the WEST–B test will be available on the internet by 5:00 P.M., Pacific time on the official examinee score report mailing date. Refer to the test registration schedule on the back cover of the WEST–B Registration Bulletin for further information. Unofficial scores are available on the internet for approximately two weeks. To access your unofficial scores, go to www.west.nesinc.com and follow the score retrieval instructions.

All essays for the Writing Subtest of the WEST–B are scored according to standardized procedures during scoring sessions held after a test's administration. As part of the scoring process, written responses are scored by more than one scorer.

If you do not achieve a passing score on the practice test, review the detailed explanations for the questions you answered incorrectly. Note which types of questions you answered wrong, and re-examine the corresponding review. After further review, you may want to retake the practice tests.

And finally, if you do not do well on test day, don't panic! The test can be taken again, so you can work on improving your score on your next WEST–B. A score on the WEST–B that does not match your expectations does not mean you should change your plans about teaching.

Test-Taking Strategies

Although you may not be familiar with tests like the WEST–B, this book will help acquaint you with this type of exam and help alleviate test-taking anxieties. Here are the key ways you can more easily get into an WEST–B state of mind:

Become comfortable with the format of the WEST–B. Practice tests are the best way to learn the format of the WEST–B. When you take a practice test, try to simulate the environmental conditions of the actual testing facility. Remember, you are in training for the WEST–B, and simulated testing conditions will only help you perform better. Stay calm and pace yourself. After simulating a test even once, you boost your chances of doing well, and you will be able to sit down for the actual WEST–B with much more confidence.

Read all the possible answers. Examine each answer choice to ensure that you are not making a mistake. Jumping to conclusions without considering all the answers is a common test-taking error.

Use the process of elimination. GUESS if you do not know. If you do not know the answer immediately after reading the answer choices, try to eliminate as many of the answers as possible. Eliminating just one or two answer choices gives you a far better chance of selecting the right answer.

Do not leave an answer blank. There is no penalty for wrong answers, and you might even get it right if you had to guess at the answer.

Familiarize yourself with the test's directions and content. Familiarizing yourself with the directions and content of the WEST–B not only saves you valuable time, but can also aid in reducing anxiety before the test. Many mistakes are caused by anxiety. It's simply better to go in knowing what you will face.

Score it right! Be sure that the answer oval you mark corresponds to the appropriate number in the test booklet. The test is multiple-choice and is graded by machine. Marking just one answer in the wrong place can throw off the rest of the test. Correcting an error like this can take away many minutes of precious test time.

After the Test

When you finish your test, hand in your materials and you will be dismissed. Then, you are free. Go home and relax. Meet with friends. Go out to dinner. Or go shopping. Whatever you do, make it a great day! After all you have done to get this far, you deserve it!

WEST–B Study Schedule

The following study schedule allows for thorough preparation to pass the Washington Educator Skills Test–Basic (WEST–B). This is a suggested seven-week course of study. This schedule can, however, be condensed if you have less time available to study or expanded if you have more time. Whatever the length of your available study time, be sure to keep a structured schedule by setting aside ample time each day to study. Depending on your schedule, you may find it easier to study throughout the weekend. No matter which schedule works best for you, the more time you devote to studying for the WEST–B, the more prepared and confident you will be on the day of the test.

Week	Activity
1	Take the practice test on CD-ROM as a diagnostic exam. Your score will indicate where your strengths and weaknesses lie. Try to take the test under simulated exam conditions, and review the explanations for the questions you answered incorrectly.
2	Study the WEST–B test objectives to get a better idea of the content on which you will be tested. You should make a list of the objectives that you know you will have the most trouble mastering so that you can concentrate your study on those areas.
3	Study *The Best Teachers' Test Preparation for the WEST–B*. Take notes on the sections as you work through them, as writing will aid in your retention of information. Keep a list of the subject areas for which you may need additional aid.
4	Identify and review references and sources. Textbooks for college composition and mathematics courses will help in your preparation for the Basic Skills areas. You may also want to consult the Washington curriculum website at *www.k12.wa.us.*
5	Condense your notes and findings. You should develop a structured outline detailing specific facts. You may want to use index cards to aid you in memorizing important facts and concepts.
6	Test yourself using the index cards. You may want to have a friend or colleague quiz you on key facts and items. Then, retake the drills and tests. Review the explanations for the questions you answered incorrectly.
7	Study any areas you consider to be your weaknesses by using your study materials, references, and notes. You may want to retake some tests.

INSTALLING REA's TEST*ware*®

SYSTEM REQUIREMENTS

Pentium 75 MHz (300 MHz recommended) or a higher or compatible processor; Microsoft Windows 98 or later; 64 MB Available RAM; Internet Explorer 5.5 or higher.

INSTALLATION

1. Insert the WEST–B TEST*ware*® CD-ROM into the CD-ROM drive.
2. If the installation doesn't begin automatically, from the Start Menu choose the RUN command. When the RUN dialog box appears, type d:\setup (where D is the letter of your CD-ROM drive) at the prompt and click OK.
3. The installation process will begin. A dialog box proposing the directory "Program Files\REA\WESTB" will appear. If the name and location are suitable, click OK. If you wish to specify a different name or location, type it in and click OK.
4. Start the WEST–B TEST*ware*® application by double-clicking on the icon.

REA's WEST–B TEST*ware*® is **EASY** to **LEARN AND USE**. To achieve maximum benefits, we recommend that you take a few minutes to go through the on-screen tutorial on your computer. The "screen buttons" are also explained here to familiarize you with the program.

TECHNICAL SUPPORT

REA's TEST*ware*® is backed by customer and technical support. For questions about **installation or operation of your software**, contact us at:

Research & Education Association
Phone: (732) 819-8880 (9 a.m. to 5 p.m. ET, Monday–Friday)
Fax: (732) 819-8808
Website: http://www.rea.com
E-mail: info@rea.com

Note to Windows XP Users: In order for the TEST*ware*® to function properly, please install and run the application under the same computer administrator-level user account. Installing the TEST*ware*® as one user and running it as another could cause file-access path conflicts.

WEST–B

Washington Educator
Skills Test–Basic

Review

Chapter

1

Reading

The reading portion of the WEST–B asks the test taker to utilize critical reading and reading comprehension skills. The objectives for this section of the test are to understand the main ideas of the passage based on the supporting evidence or details and to understand the author's purpose, point of view, and/or intended meaning.

Test takers will be asked to read a passage and answer questions about the material included in that passage. The reading section is entirely multiple choice. It will be to your benefit to read the questions about the particular passage first. This will give you an idea of what to look for and focus on as you are reading. It is also crucial that you understand the passage as a whole and comprehend the overall intention, meaning, or main idea of the material you have read.

This review was developed to prepare you for the reading section of the WEST–B. You will be guided through a step-by-step approach to attacking reading passages and questions. Also included are tips to help you quickly and accurately answer the questions that will appear in this section. By studying this review, you will greatly increase your chances of achieving a good score on the reading section of the WEST–B.

Fast Facts

The more you know about the skills tested, the better you will perform on the test.

Remember, the more you know about the skills tested, the better you will perform on the test. In this section, the objectives you will be tested on are contained in the following list:

0001 Understand the main idea and supporting details of a reading selection.

The following are examples of content that may be covered under this objective.

- Identify the explicit or implicit main idea, theme, or message of a reading selection.
- Recognize explicit and implicit information, facts, and details that support, illustrate, or elaborate on the main idea of a reading selection.
- Determine whether particular statements strengthen or weaken the main idea of a reading selection.

0002 Analyze the relationships among ideas or information within one or more reading selections.

The following are examples of content that may be covered under this objective.

- Predict outcomes, make generalizations, and draw conclusions inductively or deductively from ideas or information presented within one or more reading selections.
- Identify similarities, differences, and implied relationships between or among ideas or information within one or more reading selections.
- Recognize implications of ideas or information presented within one or more reading selections.
- Identify the sequence of steps or events within a reading selection.
- Select solutions to problems based on ideas or information presented within one or more reading selections.

0003 Use critical reasoning skills to evaluate a reading selection.

The following are examples of content that may be covered under this objective.

- Recognize stated or implied assumptions on which the validity of an argument depends.
- Determine the relevance of specific facts, examples, or graphic data to a writer's argument.
- Recognize fallacies in the logic of a writer's argument.
- Recognize qualifying language, and distinguish between fact and opinion in a reading selection.
- Assess the credibility, objectivity, or bias of the writer of a reading selection or of the writer's sources.

0004 Analyze the writer's purpose, intent, and point of view in a reading selection.

The following are examples of content that may be covered under this objective.

- Recognize the writer's stated or implied purpose for writing (e.g., to persuade, to describe) in a reading selection.

- Determine the appropriateness of a writer's choice of words or language for various purposes or audiences.
- Identify the attitude, opinion, or point of view expressed by the writer of a reading selection.

0005 Determine the meaning of words and phrases in context.

The following are examples of content that may be covered under this objective.

- Determine the meaning of words using context clues, syntax, and/or structural analysis.
- Recognize the correct use of commonly misused words (e.g., to/too/two, their/they're/there, your/you're) in a reading selection.
- Determine the meaning of figurative or colloquial language in a reading selection.
- Identify appropriate synonyms or antonyms for words in a reading selection.

0006 Apply study skills to aid in understanding reading selections, graphs, tables, and charts.

The following are examples of content that may be covered under this objective.

- Identify an accurate summary, outline, or graphic representation of a reading selection.
- Interpret information presented in charts, graphs, or tables.
- Identify where to find specified information using a table of contents, section headings, or an index.

To help you master these skills, we present examples of the types of questions you will encounter and explanations of how to answer them.

THE PASSAGES

The reading passages in the reading section are designed to be on the level of the type of material encountered in college textbooks. They will present you with very diverse subjects. Although you will not be expected to have prior knowledge of the information presented in the passages, you will be expected to know the fundamental reading comprehension techniques presented in this chapter. Only your ability to read and comprehend material will be tested.

THE QUESTIONS

Each passage will be followed by a number of questions. The questions will ask you to make determinations based on what you have read. You will commonly encounter questions that will ask you to:

- Determine which of the given answer choices best expresses the main idea of the passage.

- Determine the author's purpose in writing the passage.
- Determine which fact best supports the writer's main idea.
- Know the difference between fact and opinion in a statement.
- Organize the information in the passage.
- Determine which of the answer choices best summarizes the information presented in the passage.
- Recall information from the passage.
- Analyze cause-and-effect relationships based on information in the passage.
- Determine the definition of a word as it is used in the passage.
- Answer a question based on information presented in graphic form.
- Answer a question based on an excerpt from a table of contents or an index.

Strategies for the Reading Section

The following is a recommended plan of attack to follow when answering the questions in the reading section.

When reading the passage,

Step 1: Read quickly while keeping in mind that questions will follow.
Step 2: Uncover the main idea or theme of the passage. Many times it is contained within the first few lines of the passage.
Step 3: Uncover the main idea of each paragraph. Usually it is contained in either the first or last sentence of the paragraph.
Step 4: Skim over the detailed points of the passage while circling key words or phrases. These are words or phrases such as *but, on the other hand, although, however, yet,* and *except.*

When answering the questions,

Step 1: Approach each question one at a time. Read it carefully.
Step 2: Uncover the main idea or theme of the passage. Many times it is contained within the first few lines of the passage.
Step 3: If the question is asking for an answer that can only be found in a specific place in the passage, save it for last since this type of question requires you to go back to the passage and therefore takes more of your time.

ADDITIONAL TIPS

- Read over the questions before reading the passage. This will give you an idea of what you are reading for.
- Look over all the passages first and then attack the passages that seem easiest and most interesting.
- Identify and underline what sentences are the main ideas of each paragraph.
- If a question asks you to draw inferences, your answer should reflect what is implied in the passage, rather than what is directly stated.
- Use the context of the sentence to find the meaning of an unfamiliar word.
- Identify which sentences are example sentences and label them with an "E." Determine whether or not the writer is using facts or opinions.
- Circle key transitions and identify dominant patterns of organization.
- Make your final response and move on. Don't dawdle or get frustrated by the really troubling passages. If you haven't gotten answers after two attempts, answer as best you can and move on.
- If you have time at the end, go back to the passages that were difficult and review them again.

A Four-Step Approach

When you take the reading section of the WEST–B, you will have two tasks: to read the passage, and to answer the questions.

Of the two, carefully reading the passage is the more important; answering the questions is based on an understanding of the passage. What follows is a four-step approach to reading:

Step 1: preview
Step 2: read actively
Step 3: review the passage
Step 4: answer the questions

You should study the following exercises and use these four steps when you complete the reading section of the WEST–B.

STEP 1: PREVIEW

A preview of the reading passage will give you a purpose and a reason for reading; previewing is a good strategy to use when taking a test. Before beginning to read the passage (usually a four-minute activity if you preview and review), you should take about thirty seconds to look over the passage and questions. An effective way to preview the passage is to quickly read the first sentence of each paragraph, the concluding sentence of the passage, and the questions—but not the answers—following the passage. A passage follows; practice previewing the passage by reading the first sentence of each paragraph and the last line of the passage.

A preview of the reading passage will give you a purpose and a reason for reading.

Fast Facts

Passage

That the area of obscenity and pornography is a difficult one for the Supreme Court is well documented. The Court's numerous attempts to define obscenity have proven unworkable and left the decision to the subjective preferences of the justices. Perhaps Justice Stewart put it best when, after refusing to define obscenity, he declared, but "I know it when I see it." Does the Court literally have to see it to know it? Specifically, what role does the fact-pattern, including the materials' medium, play in the Court's decision?

Several recent studies employ fact-pattern analysis in modeling the Court's decision making. These studies examine the fact-pattern or case characteristics, often with ideological and attitudinal factors, as a determinant of the decision reached by the Court. In broad terms, these studies owe their theoretical underpinnings to attitude theory. As the name suggests, attitude theory views the Court's attitudes as an explanation of its decisions.

These attitudes, however, do not operate in a vacuum. As Spaeth explains, "the activation of an attitude involves both an object and the situation in which that object is encountered." The objects to which the court directs its attitudes are litigants. The situation—the subject matter of the case—can be defined in broad or narrow terms. One may define the situation as an entire area of the law (e.g., civil liberties issues). On an even broader scale, the situation may be defined as the decision to grant certiorari or whether to defect from a minimum-winning coalition.

Defining the situation with such broad strokes, however, does not allow one to control for case content. In many specific issue areas, the cases present strikingly similar patterns. In examining the Court's search and seizure decisions, Segal found that a relatively small number of situational and case characteristic variables explain a high proportion of the Court's decisions.

Despite Segal's success, efforts to verify the applicability of fact-pattern analysis in other issue areas and using broad-based factors have been slow in forthcoming. Renewed interest in obscenity and pornography by federal and state governments as a result of lobbying campaigns by fundamentalist groups, the academic community, and other antipornography interest groups pro and con indicate the Court's decisions in this area deserve closer examination.

The Court's obscenity and pornography decisions also present an opportunity to study the Court's behavior in an area where the Court has granted significant decision-making authority to the states. In *Miller v. California* (1973) the Court announced the importance of local community standards in obscenity determinations. The Court's subsequent behavior may suggest how the Court will react in other areas where it has chosen to defer to the states (e.g., abortion).

Questions

1. The main idea of the passage is best stated in which of the following?

   A. The Supreme Court has difficulty convicting those who violate obscenity laws.

   B. The current definitions for obscenity and pornography provided by the Supreme Court are unworkable.

   C. Fact-pattern analysis is insufficient for determining the attitude of the Court toward the issues of obscenity and pornography.

   D. Despite the difficulties presented by fact-pattern analysis, Justice Segal found the solution in the patterns of search and seizure decisions.

2. The main purpose of the writer in this passage is to

   A. convince the reader that the Supreme Court is making decisions about obscenity based on their subjective views alone.

   B. explain to the reader how fact-pattern analysis works with respect to cases of obscenity and pornography.

   C. define obscenity and pornography for the layperson.

   D. demonstrate the role fact-pattern analysis plays in determining the Supreme Court's attitude about cases in obscenity and pornography.

3. Of the following, which fact best supports the writer's contention that the Court's decisions in the areas of obscenity and pornography deserve closer scrutiny?

   A. The fact that a Supreme Court Justice said, "I know it when I see it."

   B. Recent studies that employ fact-pattern analysis in modeling the Court's decision-making process.

   C. The fact that attitudes do not operate in a vacuum.

   D. The fact that federal and state governments, interested groups, and the academic community show renewed interest in the obscenity and pornography decisions by the Supreme Court.

4. Among the following statements, which states an opinion expressed by the writer rather than a fact?

   A. It is well documented that the area of obscenity and pornography is a difficult one for the Supreme Court.

   B. The objects to which a court directs its attitudes are the litigants.

   C. In many specific issue areas, the cases present strikingly similar fact-patterns.

   D. The Court's subsequent behavior may suggest how the Court will react in other legal areas.

5. The group of topics in the list that follows that best reflects the organization of the topics of the passage is

A. I. The difficulties of the Supreme Court
II. Several recent studies
III. Spaeth's definition of *attitude*
IV. The similar patterns of cases
V. Other issue areas
VI. The case of *Miller v. California*

B. I. The Supreme Court, obscenity, and fact-pattern analysis
II. Fact-pattern analyses and attitude theory
III. The definition of *attitude* for the Court
IV. The definition of *situation*
V. The breakdown in fact-pattern analysis
VI. Studying Court behavior

C. I. Justice Stewart's view of pornography
II. Theoretical underpinnings
III. A minimum-winning coalition
IV. Search and seizure decisions
V. Renewed interest in obscenity and pornography
VI. The importance of local community standards

D. I. The Court's numerous attempts to define obscenity
II. Case characteristics
III. The subject matter of cases
IV. The Court's proportion of decisions
V. Broad-based factors
VI. Obscenity determination

6. Which paragraph among those that follow is the best summary of the passage?

   A. The Supreme Court's decision-making process with respect to obscenity and pornography has become too subjective. Fact-pattern analyses used to determine the overall attitude of the Court reveal only broad-based attitudes on the part of the Court toward the situations of obscenity cases. But these patterns cannot fully account for the Court's attitudes toward case content. Research is not conclusive on whether fact-pattern analyses work when applied to legal areas. Renewed public and local interest suggests continued study and close examination of how the Court makes decisions. Delegating authority to the states may reflect patterns for Court decisions in other socially sensitive areas.

   B. Though subjective, the Supreme Court decisions are well documented. Fact-pattern analyses reveal the attitude of the Supreme Court toward its decisions in cases. Spaeth explains that an attitude involves both an object and a situation. For the Court, the situation may be defined as the decision to grant certiorari. Cases present strikingly similar patterns, and a small number of variables explain a high proportion of the Court's decisions. Segal has made an effort to verify the applicability of fact-pattern analysis with some success. The Court's decisions on obscenity and pornography suggest weak Court behavior, such as in *Miller v. California*.

   C. To determine what obscenity and pornography mean to the Supreme Court, we must use fact-pattern analysis. Fact-pattern analysis reveals the ideas that the Court uses to operate in a vacuum. The litigants and the subject matter of cases are defined in broad terms (such as an entire area of law) to reveal the Court's decision-making process. Search and seizure cases reveal strikingly similar patterns, leaving the Court open to grant certiorari effectively. Renewed public interest in the Court's decisions proves how the Court will react in the future.

   D. Supreme Court decisions about pornography and obscenity are under examination and are out of control. The Court has to see the case to know it. Fact-pattern analyses reveal that the Court can only define cases in narrow terms, thus revealing individual egotism on the part of the Justices. As a result of strikingly similar patterns in search and seizure cases, the Court should be studied further for its weakness in delegating authority to state courts, as in the case of *Miller v. California*.

7. Based on the passage, the rationale for fact-pattern analyses arises out of what theoretical groundwork?

   A. Subjectivity theory

   B. The study of cultural norms

   C. Attitude theory

   D. Cybernetics

8. Based on data in the passage, what would most likely be the major cause for the difficulty in pinning down the Supreme Court's attitude toward cases of obscenity and pornography?

   A. The personal opinions of the Court Justices

   B. The broad nature of the situations of the cases

   C. The ineffective logistics of certiorari

   D. The inability of the Court to resolve the variables presented by individual case content

9. In the context of the passage, *subjective* might be most nearly defined as

   A. personal.

   B. wrong.

   C. focused.

   D. objective.

By previewing the passage, you should have read the following:

- It is well documented that the areas of obscenity and pornography are difficult ones for the Supreme Court.
- Several recent studies employ fact-pattern analysis in modeling the Court's decision making.
- These attitudes, however, do not operate in a vacuum.
- Defining the situation with such broad strokes, however, does not allow one to control for case content.
- Despite Segal's success, efforts to verify the applicability of fact-pattern analysis in other issue areas and using broad-based factors have been slow in coming.
- The Court's obscenity and pornography decisions also present an opportunity to study the Court's behavior in an area where the Court has granted significant decision-making authority to the states.
- The Court's subsequent behavior may suggest how the Court will react in other areas where it has chosen to defer to the states (e.g., abortion).

These few sentences tell you much about the entire passage. As you begin to examine the passage, you should first determine the main idea of the passage and underline it so you can easily refer to it if a question requires you to do so (see question 1). The main idea should be found in the first paragraph of the passage, and may even be the first sentence. From what you have read thus far, you now know that the main idea of this passage is that the Supreme Court has difficulty in making static decisions about obscenity and pornography.

In addition, you also know that recent studies have used fact-pattern analysis in modeling the Court's decision. You have learned that attitudes do not operate independently and that case content is important. The feasibility of using fact-pattern analysis in other areas and broad-based factors have not been quickly verified. To study the behavior of the Court in an area in which they have granted significant decision-making authority to the states, one has only to consider the obscenity and pornography decisions. In summary, the author suggests that the Court's subsequent behavior may suggest how the Court will react in those other areas in which decision-making authority has previously been ceded to the states. As you can see, having this information will make the reading of the passage much easier.

You should have also looked at the stem of the question in your preview. You do not necessarily need to spend time reading the answers to each question in your preview. The stem alone can help to guide you as you read.

The stems in this case are

1. The main idea of the passage is best stated in which of the following?

2. The main purpose of the writer in this passage is to _______?

3. Of the following, which fact best supports the writer's contention that the Court's decisions in the areas of obscenity and pornography deserve closer scrutiny?

4. Among the following statements, which states an opinion expressed by the writer rather than a fact?

5. The group of topics in the list that follows that best reflects the organization of the topics of the passage is _______.

6. Which paragraph among those that follow is the best summary of the passage?

7. Based on the passage, the rationale for fact-pattern analyses arises out of what theoretical groundwork?

8. Based on data in the passage, what would most likely be the major cause for the difficulty in pinning down the Supreme Court's attitude toward cases of obscenity and pornography?

9. In the context of the passage, *subjective* might be most nearly defined as _______.

STEP 2: READ ACTIVELY

After your preview, you are now ready to read actively. This means that, as you read, you will be engaged in such things as underlining important words, topic sentences, main ideas, and words denoting the tone of a passage. If you think underlining can help you save time and help you remember the main ideas, feel free to use your pencil.

Read the first sentence of each paragraph carefully, since this often contains the topic of the paragraph. You may wish to underline each topic sentence.

During this stage, you should also determine the writer's purpose in writing the passage (see question 2), as this will help you focus on the main points and the writer's key points in the organization of a passage.

You can determine the author's purpose by asking yourself whether the relationship between the writer's main idea and evidence the writer uses answer one of the following four questions:

- What is the writer's primary goal or overall objective?
- Is the writer trying to persuade you by proving or using facts to make a case for an idea?
- Is the writer trying only to inform and enlighten you about an idea, object, or event?
- Is the writer attempting to amuse you? To keep you fascinated or laughing?

Read these examples and see whether you can decide what the primary purpose of the statements that follow might be.

(A) Jogging too late in life can cause more health problems than it solves. I will allow that the benefits of jogging are many: lowered blood pressure, increased vitality, better cardiovascular health, and better muscle tone. However, an older person may have a history of injury or chronic ailments that makes jogging counterproductive. For example, the elderly jogger may have hardening of the arteries, emphysema, or undiscovered aneurysms just waiting to burst and cause stroke or death. Chronic arthritis in the joints will only be aggravated by persistent irritation and use. Moreover, for those of us with injuries sustained in our youth—such as torn Achilles tendons or knee cartilage—jogging might just make a painful life more painful, cancelling out the benefits the exercise is intended to produce.

(B) Jogging is a sporting activity that exercises all the main muscle groups of the body. That the arms, legs, buttocks, and torso voluntary muscles are engaged goes without question. Running down a path makes you move your upper body as well as your lower body muscles. People do not often take into account, however, how the involuntary muscle system is also put through its paces. The heart, diaphragm, and even the eye and facial muscles take part as we hurl our bodies through space at speeds up to five miles per hour over distances as long as twenty-six miles and more for some.

(C) It seems to me that jogging styles are as identifying as fingerprints! People seem to be as individual in the way they run as they are in personality. Here comes the Duck, waddling down the track, little wings going twice as fast as the feet in an effort to stay upright. At about the quarter-mile mark, I see the Penguin, quite natty in the latest jogging suit, body stiff as a board from neck to ankles and the ankles flexing a mile a minute to cover the yards. And down there at the half-mile post—there goes the Giraffe—a tall fellow in a spotted electric yellow outfit, whose long strides cover about a dozen yards each, and whose neck waves around under some old army camouflage hat that may have served its time in a surplus store in the Bronx or in the Arabian desert. If you see the animals in the jogger woods once, you can identify them from miles away just by seeing their gait. And, by the way, be careful whose hoof you're stepping on, it may be mine!

In (A) the writer makes a statement that a number of people would debate and which isn't clearly demonstrated by science or considered common knowledge. In fact, common wisdom usually maintains the opposite thesis. Many would say that jogging improves the health of the aging—even to the point of slowing the aging process. As soon as you see a writer point to or identify *an issue open to debate* that stands in need of proof, he or she is setting out to persuade you that one side or the other is the more justified position. You'll notice, too, that the writer in this case takes a stand here. It's almost as if he or she is saying, "I have concluded that . . ." But a thesis or arguable idea is only a *hypothesis* until evidence is summoned by the writer to prove it. Effective arguments are based on serious, factual, or demonstrable evidence, not merely opinion.

In (B) the writer is just stating a fact. This is not a matter for debate. From here, the writer's evidence is to *explain* and *describe* what is meant by the fact. This is accomplished by *analyzing* (breaking down into its constituent elements) the way the different muscle groups come into play or do work when jogging, thus explaining the fact stated as a main point in the opening sentence. The assertion that jogging exercises all the muscle groups is not in question or a matter of debate. Besides taking the form of explaining how something works or what parts it comprises (for example, the basic parts of a bicycle are . . .), writers may show how the idea, object, or event functions. A writer may use this information to prove something. But if the writer doesn't argue to prove a debatable point one way or the other, then the purpose must be either to inform (as here) or to entertain.

In (C) the writer is taking a stand yet not attempting to prove anything; a lighthearted observation is made instead and nothing more. In addition, all of the examples used to support the statement are fanciful, funny, odd, or peculiar to the writer's particular vision. Joggers aren't *really* animals, after all.

Make sure to examine all the facts that the author uses to support the main idea. This will allow you to decide whether or not the writer has made a case, and what sort of purpose it supports. Look for supporting details—facts, examples, illustrations, the testimony or research of experts—that are relevant to the topic in question and show what the writer says is so. In fact, paragraphs and theses consist of *show* and *tell*. The writer *tells* you something is so or not so and then *shows* you facts, illustrations, expert testimony, or experiences to back up whatever is assertedly the case or is not the case. As you determine where the author's supporting details are, you may want to label them with an "S" so that you can refer back to them easily when answering questions (see question 3).

It is also important for you to be able to recognize the difference between the statements of fact presented versus statements of the author's opinion. You will be tested on this skill in this section of the test (see question 4). Look at the following examples. In each case ask yourself whether you are reading a fact or an opinion.

1. Some roses are red.

2. Roses are the most beautiful flower on Earth.

3. After humans smell roses, they fall in love.

4. Roses are the worst plants to grow in your backyard.

Item 1 is a fact. All you have to do is look at the evidence. Go to a florist. You will see that item 1 is true. A fact is anything that can be demonstrated to be objectively true in reality or which has been demonstrated to be true in reality and is documented by others. For example, the moon is orbiting about 250,000 miles from the Earth.

Item 2 is an opinion. The writer claims this as truth, but since it is a subjective quality (beauty), it remains to be seen. Others may hold different opinions. This is a matter of taste, not fact.

Item 3 is an opinion. There is probably some time-related coincidence between these two, but there is no verifiable, repeatable, or observable evidence that this is always true—at least not the way it is true that if you throw a ball into the air, it will come back down to Earth if left on its own without interference. Opinions have a way of sounding absolute; they are held by the writer with confidence, but are not facts that provide evidence.

Item 4, though perhaps sometimes true, is nevertheless a matter of opinion. Many variables contribute to the health of a plant in a garden: soil, temperature range, amount of moisture, and number and kinds of bugs. This is a debatable point for which the writer would have to provide evidence.

As you read, you should note the structure of the passage. There are several common structures for the passages. Some of these structures are described below.

MAIN TYPES OF PARAGRAPH STRUCTURES

1. The structure is a main idea plus supporting arguments.

2. The structure is a main idea plus examples.

3. The structure includes comparisons or contrasts.

4. There is a pro and a con structure.

5. The structure is chronological.

6. The structure has several different aspects of one idea.

For example, a passage on education in the United States in the 1600s and 1700s might first define education, then describe colonial education, then give information about separation of church and state, and then outline the opposing and supporting arguments regarding taxation as a source of educational funding. Being able to recognize these structures will help you recognize how the author has organized the passage.

Examining the structure of the passage will help you answer questions that ask you to organize (see question 5) the information in the passage or to summarize (see question 6) the information presented in that passage.

For example, if you see a writer using a transitional pattern that reflects a sequence moving forward in time, such as "In 1982 . . . Then, in the next five years . . . A decade later, in 1997, the . . .," chances are the writer is telling a story, history, or the like. Writers often use transitions of classification to analyze an idea, object, or event. They may say something like, "The first part . . . Secondly . . . Thirdly . . . Finally . . ." You may then ask yourself what the analysis is for. Is it to explain or to persuade you of something? These transitional patterns may also help reveal the relationship of one part of a passage to another. For example, a writer may be writing, "On the one hand . . . On the other hand . . ." This should alert you to the fact that the writer is comparing two things or contrasting them. What for? Is one better than the other? Worse?

By understanding the *relationship* among the main point, transitions, and supporting information, you may more readily determine the pattern of organization as well as the writer's purpose in a given piece of writing.

As with the paragraph examples above showing the difference among possible purposes, you must look at the relationship between the facts or information presented (that's the show part) and what the writer is trying to point out to you (that's the tell part) with that data. For example, in the data given earlier, in item 6, the discussion presented about education in the 1600s might be used

- to prove that it was a failure (a form of argument).
- to show that it consisted of these elements (an analysis of the status of education during that time).
- to show that education during that time was silly.

To understand the author's purpose, the main point and the evidence that supports it must be considered together to be understood. In item 6, no statement appears that controls these disparate areas of information. To be meaningful, a controlling or main point is needed. You need to know that that main point is missing. You need to be able to distinguish between the writer showing data and the writer making a point.

In the two paragraphs that follow, consider the different relationship between the same data above and the controlling statement, and how that controlling statement changes the discussion from explanation to argument.

(A) Colonial education was different than today's education and consisted of several elements. Education in those days meant primarily studying the three "R's" (Reading, 'Riting, and 'Rithmetic) and the Bible. The church and state were more closely aligned with one another—education was, after all, for the purpose of serving God better, not to make more money.

(B) Colonial "education" was really just a way to create a captive audience for churches. Education in those days meant studying the three "R's" in order to learn God's word—the Bible—not commerce. The churches and the state were closely aligned with one another, and what was good for the church was good for the state—or else you were excommunicated, which kept you out of Heaven for sure.

The same informational areas are brought up in both cases, but in (A) the writer treats it more analytically ("consisted of several elements"), not taking as debatable a stand on the issue. However, the controlling statement in (B) puts forth a more volatile hypothesis, and then uses the same information to support that hypothesis.

STEP 3: REVIEW THE PASSAGE

After you finish reading actively, take ten or twenty seconds to look over the main idea and the topic sentences that you have underlined, and the key words and phrases you have marked. Now you are ready to enter Step 4 and answer the questions.

STEP 4: ANSWER THE QUESTIONS

In Step 2, you gathered enough information from the passage to answer questions dealing with main idea, purpose, support, fact vs. opinion, organization, and summarization. Let's look again at these questions.

MAIN IDEA QUESTIONS

Looking back at the questions that follow the passage, you should see that question 1 is a *main idea* question.

1. The main idea of the passage is best stated in which of the following?

   A. The Supreme Court has difficulty convicting those who violate obscenity laws.

   B. The current definitions for obscenity and pornography provided by the Supreme Court are unworkable.

   C. Fact-pattern analysis is insufficient for determining the attitude of the Court toward the issues of obscenity and pornography.

   D. Despite the difficulties presented by fact-pattern analysis, Justice Segal found the solution in the patterns of search and seizure decisions.

In answering the question, you see that answer choice C is correct. The writer uses the second, third, fourth, and fifth paragraphs to show how fact-pattern analysis is an ineffective determinant of the Supreme Court's attitudes toward obscenity and pornography.

Choice A is incorrect. Nothing is ever said directly about *convicting* persons accused of obscenity, only that the Court has difficulty defining it.

Choice B is also incorrect. Though the writer states it as a fact, it is only used as an effect that leads the writer to examine how fact-pattern analysis does or does not work to reveal the "cause" or attitude of the Court toward obscenity and pornography.

Also, answer choice D is incorrect. The statement is contrary to what Segal found when he examined search and seizure cases.

PURPOSE QUESTIONS

In examining question 2, you see that you must determine the author's purpose in writing the passage:

2. The main purpose of the writer in this passage is to

   A. convince the reader that the Supreme Court is making decisions about obscenity based on their subjective views alone.

   B. explain to the reader how fact-pattern analysis works with respect to cases of obscenity and pornography.

   C. define obscenity and pornography for the layperson.

   D. demonstrate the role fact-pattern analysis plays in determining the Supreme Court's attitude about cases in obscenity and pornography.

Looking at the answer choices, you should see that choice D is correct. Though the writer never states it directly, the data is consistently summoned to show that fact-pattern analysis only gives us part of the picture, or "broad strokes" about the Court's attitude, but cannot account for the attitude toward individual cases.

Choice A is incorrect. The writer doesn't try to convince us of this fact, but merely states it as an opinion resulting from the evidence derived from the "well-documented" background of the problem.

B is also incorrect. The writer not only explains the role of fact-pattern analysis but also rather shows how it cannot fully apply.

The passage is about the Court's difficulty in defining these terms, not the man or woman in the street. Nowhere do definitions for these terms appear. Therefore, choice C is incorrect.

SUPPORT QUESTIONS

Question 3 requires you to analyze the author's supporting details.

3. Of the following, which fact best supports the writer's contention that the Court's decisions in the areas of obscenity and pornography deserve closer scrutiny?

   A. The fact that a Supreme Court Justice said, "I know it when I see it."

   B. Recent studies that employ fact-pattern analysis in modeling the Court's decision-making process.

   C. The fact that attitudes do not operate in a vacuum.

   D. The fact that federal and state governments, interested groups, and the academic community show renewed interest in the obscenity and pornography decisions by the Supreme Court.

Look at the answer choices to answer this question. Choice D must be correct. In the fifth paragraph, the writer states that the "renewed interest"—a real and observable fact—from these groups "indicates the Court's decisions . . . deserve closer examination," another way of saying scrutiny.

Choice A is incorrect. The writer uses this remark to show how the Court cannot effectively define obscenity and pornography, relying on "subjective preferences" to resolve issues.

In addition, choice B is incorrect because the writer points to the data in D, not fact-pattern analyses, to prove this. C, too, is incorrect. Although it is true, the writer makes this point to show how fact-pattern analysis doesn't help clear up the real-world situations in which the Court must make its decisions.

FACT VS. OPINION QUESTIONS

By examining question 4, you can see that you are required to know the difference between fact and opinion.

4. Among the following statements, which states an opinion expressed by the writer rather than a fact?

   A. It is well documented that the area of obscenity and pornography is a difficult one for the Supreme Court.

   B. The objects to which a court directs its attitudes are the litigants.

   C. In many specific issue areas, the cases present strikingly similar fact-patterns.

   D. The Court's subsequent behavior may suggest how the Court will react in other legal areas.

Keeping in mind that an opinion is something that is yet to be proven to be the case, you can determine that choice D is correct. It is the only statement among the four for which evidence is yet to be gathered. It is the writer's opinion that this may be a way to predict the Court's attitudes.

A, B, and C are all derived from verifiable data or documentation, and are therefore incorrect.

ORGANIZATION QUESTIONS

Question 5 asks you to organize given topics to reflect the organization of the passage.

5. The group of topics in the list that follows that best reflects the organization of the topics of the passage is

A. I. The difficulties of the Supreme Court
II. Several recent studies
III. Spaeth' s definition of *attitude*
IV. The similar patterns of cases
V. Other issue areas
VI. The case of *Miller v. California*

B. I. The Supreme Court, obscenity, and fact-pattern analysis
II. Fact-pattern analyses and attitude theory
III. The definition of *attitude* for the Court
IV. The definition of *situation*
V. The breakdown in fact-pattern analysis
VI. Studying Court behavior

C. I. Justice Stewart's view of pornography
II. Theoretical underpinnings
III. A minimum-winning coalition
IV. Search and seizure decisions
V. Renewed interest in obscenity and pornography
VI. The importance of local community standards

D. I. The Court's numerous attempts to define obscenity
II. Case characteristics
III. The subject matter of cases
IV. The Court's proportion of decisions
V. Broad-based factors
VI. Obscenity determination

After examining all of the choices, you will determine that choice (B) is the correct response. These topical areas lead directly to the implied thesis that the "role" of fact-pattern analysis is insufficient to determine the attitude of the Supreme Court in the areas of obscenity and pornography.

Choice A is incorrect because the first topic stated in the list is not the topic of the first paragraph. It is too global. The first paragraph is about the difficulties the Court has with defining obscenity and how fact-pattern analysis might be used to determine the Court's attitude and clear up the problem.

C is incorrect because each of the items listed in this topic list represents supporting evidence or data for the real topic of each paragraph. (See the list in B for correct topics.) For example, Justice Stewart's statement about pornography is only cited to indicate the nature of the problem the Court has with obscenity. It is not the focus of the paragraph itself.

Finally, D is incorrect. As with choice C, these are all incidental pieces of information or data used to support broader points.

SUMMARIZATION QUESTIONS

To answer question 6, you must be able to summarize the passage.

6. Which paragraph among those that follow is the best summary of the passage?

   A. The Supreme Court's decision-making process with respect to obscenity and pornography has become too subjective. Fact-pattern analyses used to determine the overall attitude of the Court reveal only broad-based attitudes on the part of the Court toward the situations of obscenity cases. But these patterns cannot fully account for the Court's attitudes toward case content. Research is not conclusive on whether fact-pattern analyses work when applied to legal areas. Renewed public and local interest suggests continued study and close examination of how the Court makes decisions. Delegating authority to the states may reflect patterns for Court decisions in other socially sensitive areas.

   B. Though subjective, the Supreme Court decisions are well documented. Fact-pattern analyses reveal the attitude of the Supreme Court toward its decisions in cases. Spaeth explains that an attitude involves both an object and a situation. For the Court, the situation may be defined as the decision to grant certiorari. Cases present strikingly similar patterns, and a small number of variables explain a high proportion of the Court's decisions. Segal has made an effort to verify the applicability of fact-pattern analysis with some success. The Court's decisions on obscenity and pornography suggest weak Court behavior, such as in *Miller v. California*.

   C. To determine what obscenity and pornography mean to the Supreme Court, we must use fact-pattern analysis. Fact-pattern analysis reveals the ideas that the Court uses to operate in a vacuum. The litigants and the subject matter of cases are defined in broad terms (such as an entire area of law) to reveal the Court's decision-making process. Search and seizure cases reveal strikingly similar patterns, leaving the Court open to grant certiorari effectively. Renewed public interest in the Court's decisions proves how the Court will react in the future.

   D. Supreme Court decisions about pornography and obscenity are under examination and are out of control. The Court has to see the case to know it. Fact-pattern analyses reveal that the Court can only define cases in narrow terms, thus revealing individual egotism on the part of the Justices. As a result of strikingly similar patterns in search and seizure cases, the Court should be studied further for its weakness in delegating authority to state courts, as in the case of *Miller v. California*.

The paragraph that best and most accurately reports what the writer demonstrated based on the implied thesis is answer choice C, which is correct.

Choice A is incorrect because, while it reflects some of the evidence presented in the passage, the passage does not imply that all Court decisions are subjective, just the ones about pornography and obscenity. Similarly, the writer does not suggest that ceding authority to the states (as in *Miller v. California*) is a sign of some weakness, but merely that it is worthy of study as a tool for predicting or identifying the Court attitudes.

Response B is also incorrect. The writer summons information over and over to show how fact-pattern analysis cannot pin down the Court's attitude toward case content.

D is incorrect. Nowhere does the writer say or suggest that the justice system is "out of control" or that the justices are "egotists," only that they are liable to be reduced to being "subjective" rather than having a cogent and identifiable shared standard.

At this point, the three remaining question types must be discussed: recall questions (see question 7), cause/effect questions (see question 8), and definition questions (question 9). They are as follows.

RECALL QUESTIONS

To answer question 7, you must be able to recall information from the passage.

7. Based on the passage, the rationale for fact-pattern analyses arises out of what theoretical groundwork?

   A. Subjectivity theory

   B. The study of cultural norms

   C. Attitude theory

   D. Cybernetics

The easiest way to answer this question is to refer back to the passage. In the second paragraph, the writer states that recent studies using fact-pattern analyses "owe their theoretical underpinnings to attitude theory." Therefore, we can conclude that response C is correct.

Answer choices A, B, and D are incorrect, as they are never discussed or mentioned by the writer.

CAUSE/EFFECT QUESTIONS

Question 8 requires you to analyze a cause-and-effect relationship.

8. Based on data in the passage, what would most likely be the major cause for the difficulty in pinning down the Supreme Court's attitude toward cases of obscenity and pornography?

   A. The personal opinions of the Court Justices

   B. The broad nature of the situations of the cases

   C. The ineffective logistics of certiorari

   D. The inability of the Court to resolve the variables presented by individual case content

Choice D is correct, as it is precisely what fact-pattern analyses cannot resolve.

Response A is incorrect because no evidence is presented for it; all that is mentioned is that they do make personal decisions. Answer choice B is incorrect because it is one way in which fact-pattern analysis can be helpful. Finally, C is only a statement about certiorari being difficult to administer, and this was never claimed about them by the writer in the first place.

DEFINITION QUESTIONS

Returning to question 9, we can now determine an answer.

9. In the context of the passage, *subjective* might be most nearly defined as

   A. personal.

   B. wrong.

   C. focused.

   D. objective.

Choice A is best. By taking in and noting the example of Justice Stewart provided by the writer, we can see that Justice Stewart's comment is not an example of right or wrong. Most of the time, if we are talking about people's "preferences," they are usually about taste or quality, and they are usually not a result of scientific study or clear reasoning, but arise out of personal taste, idiosyncratic intuitions, et cetera. Thus, A is the most likely choice.

C is incorrect because the Court's focus is already in place: on obscenity and pornography. Choice B is incorrect. Nothing is implied or stated about the tightness or wrongness of the decisions themselves. Rather it is the definition of obscenity that seems "unworkable." D is also incorrect. Objective is an antonym of subjective in this context. To reason based on the object of study is the opposite of reasoning based upon the beliefs, opinions, or ideas of the one viewing the object, rather than the evidence presented by the object itself, independent of the observer.

You may not have been familiar with the word subjective, but from your understanding of the writer's intent, you should have been able to figure out what was being sought. Surrounding words and phrases almost always offer you some clues in determining the meaning of a word. In addition, any examples that appear in the text may also provide some hints.

INTERPRETATION OF GRAPHIC INFORMATION QUESTIONS

Graphs, charts, and tables may play a large part on the WEST–B, and you should be familiar with them. More than likely, you will encounter at least one passage that is accompanied by some form of graphic information. You will then be required to answer any question(s) based on the interpretation of the information presented in the graph, chart, or table.

Graphs are used to produce visual aids for sets of information. Often, the impact of numbers and statistics is diminished by an overabundance of tedious numbers. A graph helps a reader rapidly visualize or organize irregular information, as well as trace long periods of decline or increase. The following is a guide to reading the three principal graphic forms that you will encounter when taking the WEST–B.

LINE GRAPHS

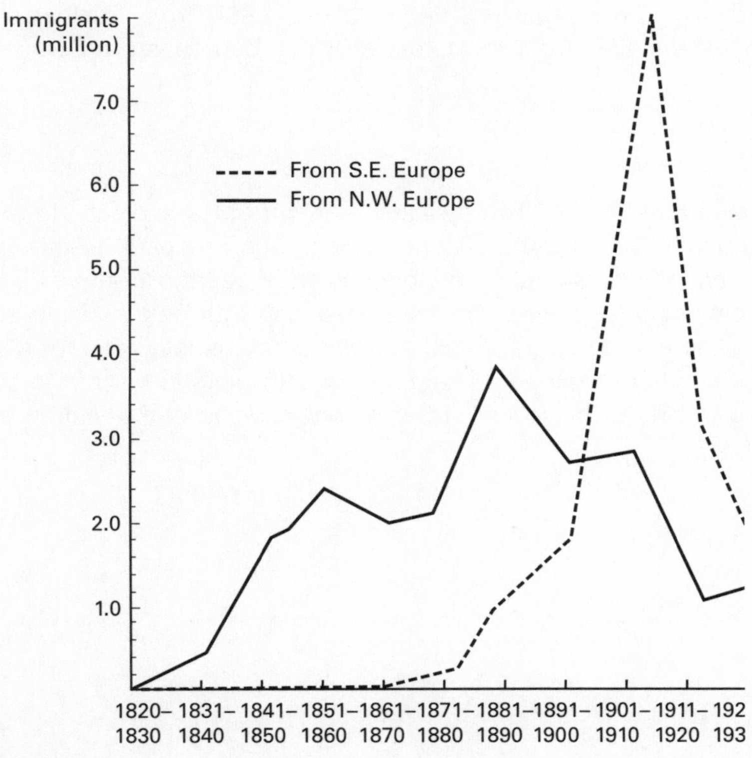

Source: Immigration and Naturalization Service of the U.S. Dept. of Justice

Line graphs are used to track multiple elements of one or more subjects. One element is usually a time factor, over whose span the other element increases, decreases, or remains static. The lines that compose such graphs are connected points that are displayed on the chart through each integral stage. For example, look at the preceding immigration graph.

The average number of immigrants from 1820 to 1830 is represented at one point; the average number of immigrants from 1831 to 1840 is represented at the next. The line that connects these points is used only to ease the visual gradation between the points. It is not meant to give a strictly accurate representation for every year between the two decades. If this were so, the line would hardly be straight, even progression from year to year. The sharp directness of the lines reveals otherwise. The purpose of the graph is to plot the average increases or decreases from point to point. When dealing with more than one subject, a line graph must use either differently colored lines or different types of lines if the graph is black-and-white. In the graph, the dark bold line represents immigration from Northwestern Europe; the broken line represents immigration from Southeastern Europe.

To read a line graph, find the point of change that interests you. For example, if you want to trace immigration from Northwestern Europe from 1861 to 1870, you would find the position of the dark line on that point. Next, trace the position to the vertical information on the chart. In this instance, one would discover that approximately 2 million immigrants arrived from Northwestern Europe in the period of time from 1861 to 1870. If wishing to discover when the number of immigrants reached 4 million you would read across from 4 million on the vertical side of the graph, and see that this number was reached in 1881–1890 from Northwestern Europe, and somewhere over the two decades from 1891 to 1910 from Southeastern Europe.

BAR GRAPHS

Bar graphs are also used to plot two dynamic elements of a subject. However, unlike a line graph, the bar graph usually deals with only one subject. The exception to this is when the graph is three-dimensional, and the bars take on the dimension of depth. However, because we will only be dealing with two-dimensional graphs, we will be working with only a single subject. The other difference between a line and a bar graph is that a bar graph usually calls for a single element to be traced in terms of another, whereas a line graph usually plots either of the two elements with equal interest. For example, in the following bar graph, inflation and deflation are being marked over a span of years.

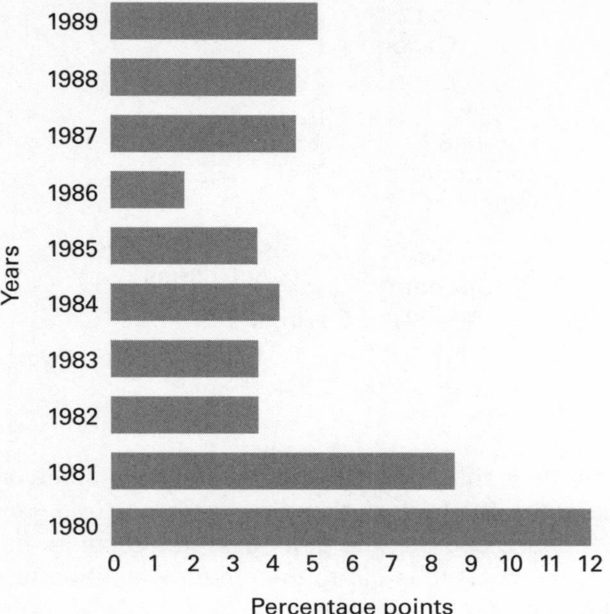

Percentage points are assigned to each year's level of prices, and that percentage decreases (deflation) from 1980 to 1981, and from 1981 to 1982. The price level is static from 1982 to 1983. The price level then increases (inflation) from 1983 to 1984. Therefore, it is obvious that the bar graph is read strictly in terms of the changes exhibited over a period of time or against some other element. Conversely, a line graph is used to plot two dynamic elements of equal interest to the reader (e.g., either number of immigrants or the particular decade in question).

To read a bar graph, simply begin with the element at the base of a bar and trace the bar to its full length. Once reaching its length, cross-reference the other element of information that matches the length of the bar.

PIE CHARTS

Pie charts differ greatly from line or bar graphs. Pie charts are used to help a reader visualize percentages of information with many elements to the subject. An entire "pie" represents 100 percent of a given quantity of information. The pie is then sliced into measurements that correspond to their respective shares of the 100 percent. For example, in the pie chart that follows, Myrna's rent occupies a slice greater than any other in the pie, because no other element equals or exceeds 25 percent of Myrna's monthly budget.

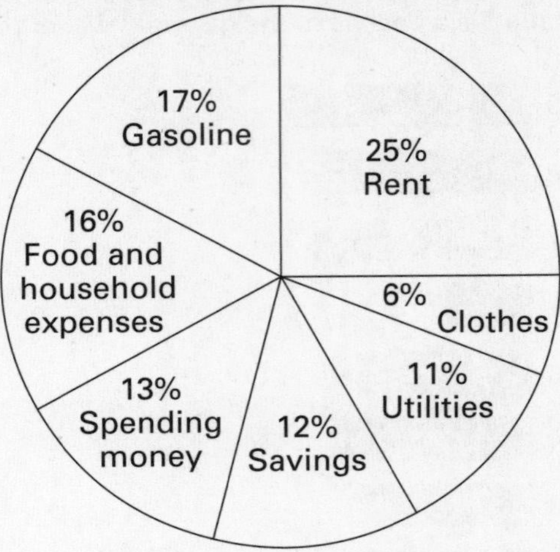

Another aspect of pie charts is that the smaller percentage elements are moved consecutively to the larger elements. Therefore, the largest element in the chart will necessarily be adjacent to the smallest element in the chart, and the line that separates them is the beginning or endpoint of the chart. From this point the chart fans out to the other elements of the chart, going from the smallest percentages to the largest.

To read a pie chart, choose the element of the subject that interests you and compare its size to those of the other elements. In cases where the elements are similar in size, do not assume that they are equal. The exact percentage of the element will be listed within that slice of the chart. For example, Myrna's utilities, savings, and spending money are all similar in size, but it is clear when reading the chart that each possesses a different value.

READING TABLES

Tables are useful because they relate to large bodies of information within a confined area. To read a table, cross-reference the column headings that run horizontally across the top of the table with the row headings that run vertically down the left side of the table. Scanning the table for the overall information within is usually done by reading line by line, as if reading regular text, while referring to the appropriate headings of the table to interpret the information listed. Note that some tables possess horizontal subheadings, which further ease the separation of different areas of information.

Effects of Common Drugs				
Drug	**Psychological Dependence**	**Physical Dependence**	**Physical Withdrawal Effects**	**Development of Tolerance**
Depressants				
Alcohol	Mild to very strong	Very strong	Severe/ dangerous	Minimal
Barbiturates	Develops slowly	Develops slowly	Death possible	Minimal
Narcotics				
Opiates (heroin, morphine)	Very strong; develops rapidly	Rapid/ increases with dosage	Frightening symptoms but not dangerous	Very high; Goes down quickly after withdrawal (Danger if user returns to original dose)
Stimulants				
Amphetamines	Strong	Not in formal sense, but body seeks "rush"	Mild	Extremely high
Cocaine	Very strong	None	None (can cause heart spasms and instant death even if healthy)	None
Crack	Strong	Strong	Mild	High
Psychedelics				
LSD	Unpredictable	None	None	Extremely high
Marijuana	Mild to strong	Some, in high doses	None	None (Some to high doses)

To use the preceding table, one should simply choose a particular drug, and then find the appropriate information needed about that drug through the headings listed at the top of the table. For example, the physical withdrawal effects of amphetamines, a stimulant drug, are mild in effect.

INDEXES

Some questions will ask you to interpret indexes. In order to do so, you should know some of the basic index terms:

- An **entry** is the principal subdivision of an index, consisting of a heading and a locator. Example: In an index, an entry may be "Shakespeare, William, 10, 19, 38." Shakespeare is the entry heading, and the page numbers are the locators. The entry is also called the **first-level heading**. Entries are usually alphabetized.

- A **subentry** is a subheading under a main entry. A subentry represents some aspect of the main heading and gives page numbers. Example: A subentry under the main entry "Shakespeare" might be "life and times," followed by the page numbers for that subject. A subentry is also called a **second-level entry**. Subentries are usually organized alphabetically, although they may also be organized chronologically or by order of appearance in the book. Here is an example of alphabetical organization:

  Shakespeare, William, 10, 19, 38
  and dark lady, 75
  life and times, 45–83
  sonnets, 74–77

  A subentry may (rarely) be broken down into further aspects, or **sub-subheadings**.

- A **complete entry** consists of the principal heading and page numbers, all subheadings and page numbers, and all cross-references.

- A **subject,** or **topical, index** lists only the topics mentioned or discussed in a book.

- A **name index** lists only the proper names (e.g., Shakespeare) mentioned or discussed in a book.

- A **general index** includes subjects (topics) *and* proper names, and perhaps other matters.

- **Cross-references** are guides from one entry to another. Cross-references are usually prefaced with *see* or *see also*. Example: An index entry may give page numbers for Native American references and then guide the reader to *see also* Tribes or *see* Indians.

Indexes with subheadings may be arranged with either run-in style or indented style. **Run-in style** means that subheadings are separated from the main entry and other subheadings by punctuation alone. **Indented style** means that subheadings are separated from the main entry, and from each other, by indentation. For example, the complete Shakespeare entry that appears in indented style above would look like this in run-in style:

> Shakespeare, William, 10, 19, 38: and dark lady, 75; life and times, 45–83; sonnets, 74–77.

HELPFUL HINTS

You should approach any graphic information you encounter as a key to a larger body of information in abbreviated form. Be sure to use the visual aids of the graphics (e.g., the size of slices on pie charts) as aids only; do not ignore the written information listed on the graph, table, et cetera.

Note especially the title and headings so that you know exactly what it is at which you are looking. Also, be aware of the source of the information, where applicable. Know what each element of the graphic information represents; this will help you compare how drastic or subtle any changes are, and over what span of time they take place. Be sure you realize what the actual numbers represent, whether it is dollars, so many thousands of people, millions of shares, and so forth. Finally, note the way in which the graphic information relates to the text it seeks to illustrate; know in what ways the graphic information supports the arguments of the author of the given passage.

Chapter

2

Writing

MULTIPLE-CHOICE ITEMS

The writing portion of the WEST–B multiple-choice section asks you to use skills in the areas of grammar and composition. The objectives for this section of the test are to recognize correct and incorrect grammar and usage and to recognize good and bad features of various kinds of writing.

You will be asked to read a passage and answer questions about the words or punctuation included in that passage. You may also be asked to fill in a blank with a sentence or phrase that makes the passage more effective. This portion of the test is entirely multiple choice. When taking the test, you should skip ahead to read the questions about the particular passage first. This will give you an idea of what to look for and focus on as you are reading. It is also important that you understand the passage as a whole and comprehend its overall intention, meaning, or main idea.

This review was developed to prepare you for the writing section of the WEST–B. You will be guided through a step-by-step approach to attacking reading passages and questions. Also included are tips to help you quickly and accurately answer the questions. By studying this review, you will greatly increase your chances of achieving a good score on the writing section of the WEST–B.

To do well on this portion of the test, you will have to be proficient in the following objectives:

0007 Understand the role of audience and purpose in written communication.

The following are examples of content that may be covered under this objective.

- Assess the appropriateness of a written selection for a specific purpose or audience (e.g., a business letter, a communication to parents/guardians/caregivers).
- Determine the likely effect on an audience of a writer's choice of a particular word or words (e.g., to evoke sympathy, to raise questions about an opposing point of view).
- Recognize persuasive techniques used by a writer in a passage.

0008 Understand idea development, fluency, and organization within writing.

The following are examples of content that may be covered under this objective.

- Identify organizational methods used by the writer of a selection.
- Distinguish between effective and ineffective thesis statements.
- Recognize unnecessary shifts in point of view (e.g., shifts from first to third person) or distracting details that impair development of the main idea within a written selection.
- Recognize the appropriate use of transitional words and phrases to convey text structure.
- Recognize examples of focused, concise, and well-developed writing.

0009 Recognize writing that effectively communicates intended messages.

The following are examples of content that may be covered under this objective.

- Distinguish between effective and ineffective development of ideas within a paragraph.
- Understand the use of paragraphing to reinforce text structure.
- Determine whether supporting details in a written selection are essential or nonessential.

0010 Apply revision strategies to written works.

The following are examples of content that may be covered under this objective.

- Apply revision strategies affecting voice, syntax, transitions, organization, clarity, coherence, and point of view in a written selection.
- Make revisions that improve the fluency and focus of a written selection or that improve cohesion and the effective sequence of ideas.
- Improve the clarity and effectiveness of a written selection through changes in word choice.
- Eliminate or replace unnecessary or imprecise words and phrases.

- Insert appropriate transitional words or phrases (e.g., however, as a result) into a passage to convey the structure of the text and to help readers understand the sequence of a writer's ideas.
- Recognize wordiness, redundancy, and ineffective repetition in sentences and paragraphs.

0011 Recognize the use of standard writing conventions.

The following are examples of content that may be covered under this objective.

- Recognize the use of standard writing conventions (e.g., grammar) that enhance or impair meaning and clarity.
- Understand the standard use of verbs (e.g., subject-verb agreement, verb tense, consistency of tense), nouns (e.g., plural and possessive forms), pronouns (e.g., pronoun-antecedent agreement, standard pronoun cases, use of possessive pronouns, standard use of relative and demonstrative pronouns), and modifiers (e.g., adverbs, adjectives, prepositional phrases).
- Recognize instances in which incorrect or extraneous punctuation has been used or necessary punctuation has been omitted.
- Identify standard initial capitalization and standard capitalization with proper words and titles.
- Recognize the standard spellings of words.
- Identify sentence fragments and run-on sentences.

To help you master these skills, we present examples of the types of questions you will encounter and explanations of how to answer them. A drill section is also provided for further practice. Even if you are sure you will perform well on this section, be sure to complete the drills, as they will help sharpen your skills.

The Reading Passages

The reading passages in this section are designed for several different audiences. The readings will present you with very diverse subjects. Although you will not be expected to have prior knowledge of the information presented in the passages, you will be expected to know the fundamental writing techniques needed to convey the passage's message to its intended audience. Only your ability to write standard English for a specific audience will be tested. For example, you may get a passage like this one, written for a high-school history textbook:

> [1]After the Civil War, raw cotton regained its traditional role as America's largest export good. [2]From 1803 to 1937, the Civil War and two other years excluded, unprocessed cotton was America's largest merchandise export. [3]The United States was also an important exporter of grain and mineral products. [4]What most characterized the growth of American exports in the late nineteenth century, ________, was the rise of manufactured goods exports: refined petroleum, machinery, and other manufactured goods. [5]Most of these goods were mass-produced

products made by methods that were not used abroad, such as sewing machines, harvesters, and, later, automobiles). [6]Exports, increased rapidly, as American goods became highly competitive in world markets.

[7]Exports rose even faster than imports, with the consequence that exports always exceeded imports until 1971. [8]When the balance of trade remained consistently positive, Americans gradually recognized that a high tariff policy was no longer necessary or even desirable. [9]In 1913, with traditionally low-tariff Democrats in control of Congress, the Underwood Tariff lowered duties substantially. [10]International commerce expanded faster in the late nineteenth and early twentieth centuries than did worldwide output, with the gold standard aiding in this growth.

The Questions

Each passage will be followed by a number of questions. Some questions may ask you to find mistakes in standard English usage; others may ask you to supply appropriate words or phrases in blanks. You will commonly encounter questions that will ask you to:

- Identify the incorrect use of words.
- Identify the incorrect use of punctuation.
- Determine which sentence best makes the transition from one thought to another.
- Determine which word or phrase would be best for a specific audience.
- Determine the type of organization the author of the passage is using.

For example, questions for the passage above might be like these:

1. Which of the following parts does not use standard punctuation?

   A. sentence 2

   B. sentence 6

   C. sentence 8

   D. sentence 9

2. Which of the following words used in the blank in sentence 4 would make a good transition from the previous sentence?

   A. consequently

   B. moreover

   C. nevertheless

   D. however

(Note that superscripted numbers in the passage are referred to in the answers as "sentence X.")

Sentence Structure

Parallelism

Sentences should use the same kind of grammatical construction for all items in a series—those usually joined by a coordinating conjunction (*and, but, or,* and *nor*). "No smoking, eating, or drinking" is parallel; "No smoking, food, or drinking" is not, because *food* is not a verb form. Making elements parallel also requires knowledge of parallel correlative pairs—that is, the use of appropriate pairs together: *neither* and *nor, either* and *or, both* with *and, whether* with *or,* and *not only* with *but also.*

Parallel structure is used to express matching ideas. It refers to the grammatical balance of a series of any of the following:

Phrases. The squirrel ran *along the fence, up the tree,* and *into his hole* with a mouthful of acorns.

Adjectives. The job market is flooded with *very talented, highly motivated,* and *well-educated* young people.

Nouns. You will need a *notebook, pencil,* and *dictionary* for the test.

Clauses. The children were told to decide *which toy they would keep* and *which toy they would give away.*

Verbs. The farmer *plowed, planted,* and *harvested* his corn in record time.

Verbals. *Reading, writing,* and *calculating* are fundamental skills we should all possess.

Correlative Conjunctions. *Either* you will do your homework *or* you will fail. ***Note:*** Correlative conjunctions must be used as pairs and not mixed with other conjunctions, such as *neither* with *or* or *not only* with *also*.

Near-parallelisms. Sometimes a string of seemingly parallel thoughts are not in fact parallel. Consider this sentence: "I *have quit* my job, *enrolled* in school, and *am looking* for a reliable babysitter." In this sentence the writer has already *quit* and *enrolled* but is still looking for a babysitter; therefore she cannot include all three in a parallel structure. A good revision of this sentence is, "I have quit my job and enrolled in school, and I am looking for a babysitter."

Misplaced and Dangling Modifiers

Many people, probably including at least some parents of your students, consider misplaced and dangling modifiers to be a sure sign of ignorance about the English language. Although this belief on their part may be unfair, teachers need to be aware that it is firmly held. As the name suggests, a misplaced modifier is one that is in the wrong place in the sentence. Misplaced modifiers come in all forms—words, phrases, and clauses. Sentences containing misplaced modifiers are often very comical: *Mom made me eat the spinach instead of my brother.* Misplaced modifiers, like the one in this sentence, are usually too far away from the word or words they modify. This sentence should read *Mom made me, instead of my brother, eat the spinach.*

Such modifiers as *only, nearly,* and *almost* should be placed next to the word they modify and not in front of some other word, especially a verb, that they are not intended to modify. For example, *I only sang for one reason* is wrong if the writer means to say that there was *only one* reason for singing.

A modifier is misplaced if it appears to modify the wrong part of the sentence or if the reader cannot be certain what part of the sentence the writer intended it to modify. To correct a misplaced modifier, move the modifier next to the word it describes.

UNREVISED: She served hamburgers to the men on paper plates.

REVISED: She served hamburgers on paper plates to the men.

A **squinting modifier** is one that may refer to either a preceding or a following word, leaving the reader uncertain about what it is intended to modify. Correct a squinting modifier by moving it next to the word it is intended to modify.

UNREVISED: Snipers who fired on the soldiers often escaped capture.

REVISED: Snipers who often fired on the soldiers escaped capture. OR Snipers who fired on the soldiers escaped capture often.

A **dangling modifier** is a modifier or verb in search of a subject: the modifying phrase (usually a participle phrase—an *-ing* word group or an *-ed* or an *-en* word group—or an infinitive phrase—a *to + verb* word group) has nothing to modify. It is figuratively *dangling* at the beginning or the end of a sentence. The sentences often look and sound correct at first glance: *To be a student government officer, your grades must be above average.* However, the verbal modifier has nothing to describe. You are supposed *to be a student government officer*; *your grades* cannot become an officer.

To correct a dangling modifier, reword the sentence by either (1) changing the modifying phrase to a clause with a subject, or (2) changing the subject of the sentence to the word that should be modified. Here are some other examples of correct revision of dangling modifiers:

UNREVISED: Shortly after leaving home, the accident occurred.

REVISED: Shortly after we left home, the accident occurred.

UNREVISED: To get up on time, a great effort was needed.

REVISED: To get up on time, I made a great effort.

Sentence Fragments

A fragment is an incomplete construction that either (1) lacks a subject or a verb or (2) is preceded by a subordinating conjunction (e.g., *because, which, when, although*). A complete construction, such as a sentence or an independent clause, expresses a complete thought.

UNREVISED: Traffic was stalled for ten miles on the freeway. Because repairs were being made on potholes. (The second "sentence" is a dependent, or subordinate, clause.)

REVISED: Traffic was stalled for ten miles on the freeway because repairs were being made on potholes.

UNREVISED: It was a funny story. One that I had never heard before. (The second "sentence" has no verb for its subject, "One.")

REVISED: It was a funny story, one that I had never heard.

Run-On/Fused Sentences

A run-on, or fused, sentence is not necessarily a long sentence or a sentence that the reader considers too long; in fact, a run-on might consist of two short sentences: *Dry ice does not melt it evaporates.* A run-on results when the writer fuses, or runs together, two separate sentences without any correct mark of punctuation separating them.

UNREVISED: Knowing how to use a dictionary is no problem each dictionary has a section in the front of the book that tells you how.

REVISED: Knowing how to use a dictionary is no problem. Each dictionary has a section in the front of the book that tells you how.

The most common type of run-on sentence is characterized by a comma splice—the incorrect use of only a comma to separate what are really two separate sentences. There are three quick ways to fix a comma splice: (1) replace the comma with a period and start a new sentence; (2) replace the comma with a semicolon; and (3) add a coordinating conjunction, such as *and* or *but,* after the comma.

UNREVISED: Bob bought dress shoes, a suit, and a nice shirt, he needed them for his sister's wedding.

REVISED: Bob bought dress shoes, a suit, and a nice shirt. He needed them for his sister's wedding.

UNREVISED: One common error in writing is incorrect spelling, the other is the occasional use of faulty diction.

REVISED: One common error in writing is incorrect spelling; the other is the occasional use of faulty diction.

UNREVISED: We have never won the track championship, we have won the cross-country title.

REVISED: We have never won the track championship, but we have won the cross-country title.

If one of the complete thoughts is subordinate to the other, you may also use a subordinate conjunction to connect the two:

UNREVISED: Neal won the award, he had the highest score.

REVISED: Neal won the award because he had the highest score.

Subordination, Coordination, and Predication

Suppose that you wanted to combine the information in these two sentences to create one statement: *I studied a foreign language. I found English quite easy.* How you decide to combine this information should be determined by the relationship you'd like to show between the two facts. *I studied a foreign language, and I found English quite easy* adds little or nothing to the original meaning. The **coordination** of the two ideas (connecting them with the coordinating conjunction *and*) is therefore ineffective. Using **subordination** instead (connecting the sentences with a subordinating conjunction) clearly shows the relationship between the expressed ideas:

> *After I studied a foreign language, I found English quite easy.*
>
> OR
>
> *Because I studied a foreign language, I found English quite easy.*

When using any conjunction—coordinating or subordinating—be sure that the sentence parts you are joining are in agreement:

> UNREVISED: She loved him dearly but not his dog.
>
> REVISED: She loved him dearly, but she did not love his dog.
>
> OR
>
> She loved him, but not his dog, dearly.

Another common mistake is to forget that each member of the pair must be followed by the same kind of construction.

> UNREVISED: She complimented her friends both for their bravery and thanked them for their kindness.
>
> REVISED: She both complimented her friends for their bravery and thanked them for their kindness.

While refers to time and should not be used as a substitute for *though, and,* or *but.*

> UNREVISED: While I'm usually interested in Fellini movies, I'd rather not go tonight.
>
> REVISED: Although I'm usually interested in Fellini movies, I'd rather not go tonight.

Where refers to a place and should not be used as a substitute for *that.*

UNREVISED: We read in the paper where they are making strides in DNA research.

REVISED: We read in the paper that they are making great strides in DNA research.

After words such as *reason* and *explanation,* use *that,* not *because.*

UNREVISED: His explanation for his tardiness was because his alarm did not go off.

REVISED: His explanation for his tardiness was that his alarm did not go off.

Punctuation and Capitalization

Commas

Commas should be placed according to standard rules of punctuation for purpose, clarity, and effect. On the test, you will be given choices that require your knowledge of such rules. The proper use of commas is explained in the following rules and examples.

In **a series**:

When more than one adjective describes a noun, use a comma to separate and emphasize each adjective. The comma takes the place of the word **and** in the series.

the long, dark passageway

another confusing, sleepless night

an elaborate, complex, brilliant plan

Some adjective-noun combinations are thought of as one word. In these cases, the adjective in front of the adjective-noun combination needs no comma. (If you inserted **and** between the adjective-noun combination, it would not make sense.)

a stately oak tree

a superior elementary school

The comma is also used to separate words, phrases, and whole ideas (clauses); it still takes the place of **and** when used this way.

a lovely lady, an elegant dress, and many admirers

She lowered the shade, closed the curtain, turned off the light, and went to bed.

One question that exists about the use of commas in a series is whether one should be used before the final item. It is standard usage to do so, although newspapers and many magazines do not use the final comma. Occasionally, the omission of the comma can be confusing.

With a **long introductory phrase:**

Usually if a phrase of more than five or six words or if a dependent clause precedes the subject at the beginning of a sentence, a comma is used to set it off:

After last night's fiasco at the disco, she couldn't bear the thought of looking at him again.

Whenever I try to talk about politics, my wife leaves the room.

If an introductory phrase includes a verb form that is being used as another part of speech (a **verbal**), it must be followed by a comma:

UNREVISED: When eating Mary never looked up from her plate.

REVISED: When eating, Mary never looked up from her plate.

UNREVISED: Having decided to leave Mary James wrote her a long email.

REVISED: Having decided to leave Mary, James wrote her a long email.

To separate sentences with **two main ideas:**

To understand this use of the comma, you need to be able to recognize compound sentences. When a sentence contains more than two subjects and verbs (clauses), and the two clauses are joined by a coordinating conjunction (**and, but, or, nor, for, yet**), use a comma before the conjunction to show that another independent clause is coming.

I thought I knew the poem by heart, but he showed me some lines I had forgotten.

He is supposed to leave tomorrow, but he is not ready to go.

Jim knows you are disappointed, and he has known it for a long time.

If the two parts of the sentence are short and closely related, it is not necessary to use a comma.

He threw the ball and the dog ran after it.

Be careful not to confuse a sentence that has a compound verb and a single subject with a compound sentence. If the subject is the same for both verbs, there is no need for a comma.

UNREVISED: Charles sent some flowers, and wrote a long note explaining why he had not been able to attend.

REVISED: Charles sent some flowers and wrote a long note explaining why he had not been able to attend.

UNREVISED: Last Thursday we went to the concert with Julia, and afterwards dined at an old Italian restaurant.

REVISED: Last Thursday we went to the concert with Julia and afterwards dined at an old Italian restaurant.

In general, words and phrases that stop the flow of the sentence or are unnecessary for the main idea are set off by commas.

Abbreviations after names

Martha Harris, Ph.D., will be the speaker tonight.

Interjections (An exclamation without added grammatical connection)

Oh, I'm so glad to see you!

Hey, let us out of here!

Direct address

Roy, won't you open the door for the dog?

Hey, lady, watch out for that car!

Tag questions

Jerry looks like his father, doesn't he?

Geographical names and addresses

The concert will be held in Chicago, Illinois, on August 12. [***Note:*** Punctuation must always follow a state name when that name follows a city—except in postal addresses, as illustrated in the next item.]

The letter was addressed to Mrs. Marion Heartwell, 1881 Pine Lane, Palo Alto, California 95824.

Transitional words and phrases

On the other hand, I hope he gets better.

I've always found, however, that the climate is better in the mountains.

Parenthetical words and phrases

In fact, I planted corn last summer.

The Mannes affair was, to put it mildly, a surprise.

With **nonrestrictive elements:**

Parts of a sentence that modify other parts are sometimes essential to the meaning of the sentence and sometimes not. When a modifying word or phrase is not vital to the meaning of the sentence, it is set off by commas. Because it does not restrict the meaning of the words it modifies, it is called **nonrestrictive**. Modifiers that are essential to the meaning of the sentence are **restrictive**; they are not set off by commas.

ESSENTIAL: The girl *who wrote the story* is my sister.

NONESSENTIAL: My sister, *the girl who wrote the story,* has always loved to write.

ESSENTIAL: The man who is wearing the red sweater is the best-dressed person in the class.

NONESSENTIAL: Jorge, who is wearing the red sweater, is the best-dressed person in the class.

To set off **direct quotations:**

Most direct quotes or quoted materials are set off from the rest of the sentence by commas.

"Please read your part more loudly," the director insisted.

"I won't know what to do," said Michael, "if you ever leave me alone."

Who was it who said, "Do not ask for whom the bell tolls; it tolls for thee"?

Note: In American English, commas always go inside the closing quotation mark, even if the comma is not part of the material being quoted.

To set off **contrasting elements.**

Her intelligence, not her beauty, got her the job.

It was a reasonable, though not appealing, idea.

In **dates:**

In the month-day-year form, commas follow the day and year.

She will arrive April 6, 2006, on the *Queen Elizabeth*.

If only the month and year are given, no commas are necessary.

The minister's January 1967 resignation was unexpected.

The day-month-year form requires no punctuation.

The events of 14 April 1865 were unprecedented.

Because a specific date makes a descriptive phrase following it nonessential, that phrase will be nonrestrictive and therefore set off by a comma.

He was married on 7 October 1988, which fell five days after his forty-third birthday.

When a subordinate clause is at the end of a sentence, a comma preceding the clause is optional. However, when a subordinate clause introduces a sentence, a comma should be used after the clause. Here are some common subordinating conjunctions:

after	even though	till
although	if	unless
as	inasmuch as	until
as if	since	when
because	so that	whenever
before	though	while

Semicolons

This review section covers the basic uses of the semicolon: to separate independent clauses not joined by a coordinating conjunction, to separate independent clauses separated by a conjunctive adverb, and to separate items in a series with internal commas.

Use the **semicolon** in the following cases:

To separate independent clauses that are not joined by a coordinating conjunction.

I understand how to use commas; the semicolon I have yet to master.

To separate two independent clauses connected by a conjunctive adverb.

He took great care with his work; therefore, he was very successful.

Usually a comma follows the conjunctive adverb. Note also that a period can be used to separate two sentences joined by a conjunctive adverb. Here are some common conjunctive adverbs:

accordingly	indeed	now
besides	in fact	on the other hand
consequently	moreover	otherwise
finally	nevertheless	perhaps
furthermore	next	still
however	nonetheless	therefore

Then is also used as a conjunctive adverb, but it is not usually followed by a comma.

To combine two independent clauses connected by a coordinating conjunction if either or both of the clauses contain other internal punctuation:

Success in college, some maintain, requires intelligence, industry, and perseverance; *but* others, fewer in number, assert that only geniality is important.

To separate items in a series when each item has internal punctuation. It is important to be consistent; if you use a semicolon between *any* of the items in the series, you must use semicolons to separate *all* of the items in the series.

I bought an old, dilapidated chair; an antique table that was in beautiful condition; and a new, ugly, blue and white rug.

Do *not* use the semicolon in any other cases, especially as a substitute for a comma. Here are some examples of nonstandard semicolon use; all of them should be replaced with a comma:

You should never make such statements; even though they are correct.

My roommate also likes sports; particularly football, basketball, and baseball.

Being of a cynical mind; I should ask for a recount of the ballots.

Note: The semicolon is not a terminal mark of punctuation; therefore, it should not be followed by a capital letter unless the first word in the second clause ordinarily requires capitalization.

Colons

The difference between the colon and the semicolon and between the colon and the period is that the colon is an introductory mark, not a terminal mark. The colon signals the reader that a list, explanation, or restatement of the preceding thought will follow. It is like an arrow, indicating that something is to follow.

Here are some examples of colons used to introduce lists. Note that some lists may have only one item.

> I hate just one course: English.

> Three plays by William Shakespeare will be presented in repertory this summer at Illinois State: *Hamlet*, *Macbeth*, and *Othello*.

> The reasons he cited for his success are as follows: honesty, industry, and a pleasant disposition.

A colon should also be used to separate two independent clauses when the second clause is a restatement or explanation of the first:

> All of my high school teachers said one thing in particular: college would be difficult.

You should also use a colon to introduce a word or word group that is a restatement, explanation, or summary of the first sentence:

> The first week of camping was wonderful: we lived in cabins instead of tents.

In standard English the colon should be used only after statements that are grammatically complete. Do *not*, for example, use a colon after a verb or a preposition.

> UNREVISED: My favorite holidays are: Christmas, New Year's Eve, and Halloween.

> REVISED: My favorite holidays are Christmas, New Year's Eve, and Halloween.

UNREVISED: I enjoy different ethnic dishes, such as those from: Greece, China, Provence, and Italy.

REVISED: I enjoy different ethnic dishes, such as those from Greece, China, Provence, and Italy.

However, the use of a colon to set off a *displayed* list is becoming more common and may now be considered standard.

Apostrophes

Apostrophes are used to make a noun possessive, not plural. Remember the following rules when considering how to show possession:

Add **'s** to singular nouns and indefinite pronouns:

Tiffany's flowers

at the owner's expense

a dog's bark

Add **'s** to singular nouns ending in *s,* unless this distorts the pronunciation:

Delores's paper

the boss's pen

Dr. Yots' class or Dr. Yots's class (depending on pronunciation)

for righteousness' sake

Add **an apostrophe** to plural nouns ending in *s* or *es:*

two cents' worth

three weeks' pay

ladies' night

Add **'s** to plural nouns not ending in *s:*

men's room

children's toys

Add **'s** to the last word in compound words or groups:

brother-in-law's car

someone else's paper

Add **'s** to the last name when indicating joint ownership:

Joe and Edna's home

Ted and Jane's marriage

Add **'s** to both names if you intend to show ownership by each person:

Joe's and Edna's trucks

Ted's and Jane's marriage vows

Possessive pronouns change their forms *without* the addition of an apostrophe:

hers, his, its, yours, theirs

Quotation Marks and Italics

The most common use of double quotation marks (") is to set off quoted words, phrases, and sentences.

"If everybody minded their own business," said Mrs. O'Leary in a huff, "the world would be a much nicer place."

Single quotation marks are used to set off quoted material within a quote.

"Shall I bring 'Rhyme of the Ancient Mariner' along with us?" asked her brother.

"If she said that to me," Katherine insisted, "I would tell her, 'I never intend to speak to you again! Goodbye, Susan!'"

To set off titles of poems, stories, and book chapters, use quotation marks. Book, motion picture, newspaper, and magazine titles are italicized when printed.

The article "Moving South in the Southern Rain," by Jergen Smith, appeared in the *Southern News*.

The assignment is "Childhood Development," which is Chapter 18 of *Abnormal Behavior.*

Remember that commas and periods at the end of quotations are *always* placed inside the quotation marks even if they are not actually part of the quote. Semicolons and colons are always placed outside. Question marks are placed inside or outside, depending on whether the quotation is a question.

UNREVISED: "If my dog could talk", Mary mused, "I'll bet he'd say, 'Take me for a walk right this minute'".

REVISED: "If my dog could talk," Mary mused, "I'll bet he'd say, 'Take me for a walk right this minute.'"

UNREVISED: She called down the stairs, "When are you going"?

REVISED: She called down the stairs, "When are you going?"

UNREVISED: We have to "pull ourselves up by our bootstraps;" we can't just talk about our plans.

REVISED: We have to "pull ourselves up by our bootstraps"; we can't just talk about our plans.

Remember to use only one mark of punctuation at the end of sentence ending with a quotation mark.

UNREVISED: She thought out loud, "Will I ever finish this project in time for that class?".

REVISED: She thought out loud, "Will I ever finish this project in time for that class?"

Capitalization

There are many conventions for beginning words with capital letters; this section will review just a few of the more common ones. In general, capitalize (1) all proper nouns and adjectives, (2) the first word of a sentence, and (3) the first word of a direct quotation. Points (2) and (3) are easy to figure out, but knowing which nouns and adjectives are "proper" is sometimes difficult. Here is a brief list that will help you remember what words to capitalize.

Names of persons, geographical places, and organizations:

> Kelvim Escobar is a pitcher for the Anaheim Angels, who play in the American League.

Titles of books, poems, songs, TV shows, newspapers, and the like:

> The *Washington Post* ran an interesting review of Frost's *Collected Poems*; its opinions about "Mending Wall" were especially interesting.

Geographical regions, but not compass directions:

> Many movies are set in the West.
>
> The Northern Hemisphere is the part of the earth that lies north of the equator.
>
> The cultural division between East and West has persisted throughout modern times.

Titles of persons, if they appear immediately before the person's name:

> President George W. Bush held a press conference last week.
>
> George W. Bush, president of the United States, visited our town twice during his first term.

Political parties and philosophy, but not systems of government or individual adherents to a political philosophy:

> The problems within the Communist Party foreshadowed the difficulties that communism would have in establishing itself.
>
> The Republicans and Democrats often argue about how best to spread democracy to other countries.

Pronouns

Pronoun Case

One of the most embarrassing mistakes you can make in written English is confusing the spelling of common pronouns: *its* and *it's* and *your* and *you're*. The words *its* and *your are* possessive pronouns, meaning "belonging to it" and "belonging to you," respectively. *It's* and *you're* are contractions for *it is* and *you are*.

Watch *your* step; if you don't, you might break *your* neck.

It's not likely that the company will give back *its* windfall profits.

Other commonly asked questions regarding the use of pronouns are about the confusion of nominative case pronouns with objective case pronouns.

Nominative Case	Objective Case
I	me
he	him
she	her
we	us
they	them
who	whom

Use the nominative case (subject of pronouns) in the following:

Subject of a sentence:

We students studied until early morning.

Alan and *I* "burned the midnight oil" too.

Pronouns in apposition to the subject:

Only two students, Alex and *I*, were asked to comment.

Predicate nominative/subject complement:

The cast members nominated for the award were *she* and *I*.

The subject of a subordinate clause:

Robert is the driver *who* reported the accident.

The only pronouns that are acceptable in standard English after prepositions are the objective case pronouns. When deciding between *who* and *whom* in the sentence "We're having difficulty deciding *who* we can trust," try substituting *he* for *who* and *him* for *whom*; then follow these transformation steps:

1. Isolate the *who* or *whom* clause: who we can trust.
2. Invert the natural word order if necessary, to the normal English subject–verb order: we can trust who
3. Read the final form with the *he* or *him* inserted: we can trust ~~who~~ *him*. The correct pronoun is thus *whom*.

Use the objective case (subject of pronouns) for the following:

Direct object of a verb:

Mary invited *us* to her party.

Object of a preposition:

The torn books belonged to *her*.

Just between you and *me*, I'm bored.

Indirect object of a verb:

Soren gave *her* a dozen roses.

Appositive of an object:

The committee selected two delegates, Barbara and *me*.

Object of an infinitive:

The young boy wanted to help *us* paint the fence.

Subject of an infinitive:

The boss told *him* to work late.

Object of a gerund:

Enlisting *him* was surprisingly easy.

When a conjunction connects two pronouns or a pronoun and a noun, one good way to determine the case of a pronoun is to remove the "and" and the noun or other pronoun:

Mom gave ~~Tom and~~ myself a piece of cake.

Mom gave ~~Tom and~~ I a piece of cake.

Mom gave ~~Tom and~~ me a piece of cake.

Removal of the crossed-out words reveals that the correct pronoun should be *me*.

Pronoun-Antecedent Agreement

Some questions might ask you about *pronoun-antecedent agreement*. These kinds of questions test your knowledge of using an appropriate pronoun to agree with its antecedent in number (singular or plural form) and gender (masculine, feminine, or neuter). An *antecedent* is a noun or pronoun to which another noun or pronoun refers.

Here are the two basic rules for pronoun reference-antecedent agreement:

1. Every pronoun must have a conspicuous antecedent.

2. Every pronoun must agree with its antecedent in number, gender, and person.

When an antecedent is one of dual gender—such as *student, singer, person,* or *citizen*—use **his** or **her.** Some careful writers change the antecedent to a plural noun to avoid using the sexist, singular masculine pronoun.

UNREVISED: Everyone hopes that they will win the lottery.

CORRECT BUT AMBIGUOUS: Everyone hopes that he will win the lottery.

CORRECT BUT AWKWARD: Everyone hopes that he or she will win the lottery.

REVISED: Most people hope that they will win the lottery.

Ordinarily, the relative pronoun **who** is used to refer to people, **which** to refer to things and places, **where** to refer to places, and **that** to refer to places or things. The distinction between **that** and **which** is a grammatical distinction (see the section on Word Choice Skills). Many writers prefer to use **that** to refer to collective nouns, even for people: A family that traces its lineage is usually proud of its roots.

Many writers, especially students, are not sure when to use the *reflexive case* pronoun and when to use the *possessive case* pronoun. The rules governing the usage of the reflexive case and the possessive case are simple.

Use the **possessive case**:

Before a noun in a sentence:

My dog has fleas, but *her* dog doesn't.

Before a gerund in a sentence:

Her running helps to relieve stress.

As a noun in a sentence:

Mine was the last test graded that day.

To indicate possession:

Brad thought the book was *his,* but it was someone else's.

Use the **reflexive** case:

As a direct object to rename the subject:

I kicked *myself*.

As an indirect object to rename the subject:

Henry bought *himself* a tie.

As an object of a prepositional phrase:

Tom and Lillie baked the pie for *themselves.*

As a predicate pronoun:

She hasn't been *herself* lately.

Do not use the reflexive in place of the nominative pronoun:

UNREVISED: Both Randy and *myself* plan to go.

REVISED: Both Randy and *I* plan to go.

UNREVISED: *Yourself* will take on the challenges of college.

REVISED: *You* will take on the challenges of college *yourself.*

Watch out for careless use of the pronoun form:

UNREVISED: George *hisself* told me it was true.

REVISED: George *himself* told me it was true.

UNREVISED: They washed the car *theirselves.*

REVISED: They washed the car *themselves.*

Notice that reflexive pronouns are not set off by commas:

UNREVISED: Mary, *herself*, gave him the diploma.

REVISED: Mary *herself* gave him the diploma.

Pronoun Reference

Pronoun reference questions require you to determine whether the antecedent is conspicuously written in the sentence or whether it is remote, implied, ambiguous, or vague, none of which results in clear writing. In the following, make sure that every italicized pronoun has a conspicuous antecedent and that one pronoun substitutes only for another noun or pronoun, not for an idea or a sentence.

Pronoun reference problems occur in the following instances:

1. When a pronoun refers to either of two antecedents.

   UNREVISED: Joanna told Tina that *she* was getting fat.

   REVISED: Joanna told Tina, "I'm getting fat." OR Joanna told Tina, "You're getting fat."

2. When a pronoun refers to a nonexistent antecedent.

   UNREVISED: A strange car followed us closely, and *he* kept blinking his lights at us.

   REVISED: A strange car followed us closely, and its driver kept blinking his lights at us.

3. When **this, that,** and **which** refer to the general idea of the preceding clause or sentence rather than the preceding word.

   UNREVISED: The students could not understand the pronoun reference handout, *which* annoyed them very much.

   REVISED: The students could not understand the pronoun reference handout, *a fact that* annoyed them very much. OR The students were annoyed because they could not understand the pronoun reference handout.

4. When a pronoun refers to an unexpressed but implied noun.

   UNREVISED: My husband wants me to knit a blanket, but I'm not interested in *it*.

   REVISED: My husband wants me to knit a blanket, but I'm not interested in *knitting*.

5. When **it** is used as something other than an expletive to postpone a subject.

   UNREVISED: The football game was canceled because it was bad weather.

   REVISED: The football game was canceled because the weather was bad.

6. When **they** or **it** is used to refer to something or someone indefinitely, and there is no definite antecedent.

   UNREVISED: At the job placement office, *they* told me to stop wearing ripped jeans to my interviews.

   REVISED: At the job placement office, I was told to stop wearing ripped jeans to my interviews.

7. When the pronoun does not agree with its antecedent in number, gender, or person.

   UNREVISED: Any graduate student, if *they* are interested, may tend the lecture.

   REVISED: Any graduate student, if *he or she* is interested, may attend the lecture.

   REVISED: All graduate *students*, if *they* are interested, may tend the lecture.

Verbs

This section covers the principal parts of some irregular verbs, including such troublesome verbs as *lie* and *lay.* The use of regular verbs, such as *look* and *receive*, poses little problem for most writers, because the past and past participle forms end in *-ed*; the irregular forms pose the most serious problems—for example, *seen, written,* and *begun.*

Verb Tenses

Tense sequence indicates a logical time sequence.

Use **present tense:**

In statements of universal truth:

I learned that the sun *is* ninety-million miles from the earth.

In statements about the contents of literature and other published work:

In this book, Sandy *becomes* a nun and *writes* a book about psychology.

Use **past tense:**

In statements or questions about action that happened in the past and is now finished:

I *fell* over the limb and *broke* my arm.

How *did* you break your arm?

In statements concerning writing or publication of a book:

He *wrote* his first book in 1949, and it *was published* in 1956.

Use **present perfect tense:**

For an action that began in the past but continues into the future:

I *have lived* here all my life.

Use **past perfect tense:**

For an earlier action that is mentioned in relation to a later action:

Cindy ate the apple that she *had picked.*

(First she picked it; then she ate it.)

Use **future perfect tense:**

For an action that will have been completed at a specific future time:

You *will have graduated* by the time we next meet.

Use **a present participle:**

For action that occurs at the same time as the verb:

Speeding down the interstate, I saw a cop's flashing lights.

Use **a perfect participle:**

For action that occurred before the main verb:

Having read the directions, I started the test.

Use the **subjunctive mood:**

To express a wish or state a condition contrary to fact:

If it were not raining, we could have a picnic.

In "that" clauses after such verbs as **request, recommend, suggest, ask, require,** and **insist;** and after such expressions as **it is important** and **it is necessary:**

It is necessary that all papers *be* submitted on time.

Subject-Verb Agreement

Agreement is the grammatical correspondence between the subject and the verb of a sentence or clause: *I do; you do; we do; they do; he, she, it does.* One source of confusion for many students is which verb form is singular and which plural, so this section begins by focusing on making that distinction and then tackles the task of identifying the real subject of a sentence. Finally, this section deals with subjects that are commonly construed as singular and those that are construed as plural.

Every English verb has five forms, two of which are the bare form (plural) and the **-s** form (singular). Simply put, singular verb forms end in **-s**; plural forms do not.

Study these rules governing subject-verb agreement:

A verb must agree with its subject, not with any additional phrase in the sentence such as a prepositional or verbal phrase.

Your *copy* of the rules *is* on the desk.

Ms. Craig's *record* of community service and outstanding teaching *qualifies* her for a promotion.

In an inverted sentence beginning with a prepositional phrase, the verb must still agree with its subject.

At the end of the summer *come* the best *sales.* Under the house *are* some old Mason *jars.*

Prepositional phrases beginning with compound prepositions such as **along with, together with, in addition to, and as well as** should be ignored, for they do not affect subject-verb agreement.

Gladys Knight, along with the Pips, *is* riding the midnight train to Georgia.

A verb must agree with its subject, not its subject complement.

Taxes are a problem.

One *problem is* taxes.

His main *source* of pleasure *is* food and women.

Food and women are his main source of pleasure.

When a sentence begins with an expletive such as **there**, **here**, or **it**, the verb agrees with the subject, not the expletive.

Surely there *are* several *alumni* who would be interested in starting a group.

There *are* 50 *students* in my English class.

There *is* a horrifying *study* on child abuse in *Psychology Today*.

Indefinite pronouns such as **each**, **either**, **one**, **everyone**, **everybody**, and **everything** are singular.

Somebody in Detroit *loves* me.

Does either [one] of you have a pencil?

Neither of my brothers *has* a car.

Indefinite pronouns such as **several**, **few**, **both**, and **many** are considered plural.

Both of my sorority sisters *have* decided to live off campus.

Few seek the enlightenment of transcendental meditation.

Indefinite pronouns such as **all**, **some**, **most**, and **none** may be singular or plural, depending on their referents.

Some of the food *is* cold.

Some of the vegetables *are* cold.

I can think of some retorts, but *none seem* appropriate.

None of the children *is* as sweet as Sally.

Fractions such as **one-half** and **one-third** may be singular or plural, depending on the referent.

Half of the mail *has* been delivered.

Half of the letters *have* been read.

Subjects joined by **and** take a plural verb unless the subjects are commonly thought of as one item or unit.

Jim and *Tammy were* televangelists.

Guns and Roses is my favorite group.

In cases when the subjects are joined by **or**, **nor**, **either . . . or**, or **neither . . . nor**, the verb must agree with the subject closer to it.

Either the teacher or the *students are* responsible.

Neither the students nor the *teacher is* responsible.

Relative pronouns—such as **who**, **which**, or **that**—require plural verbs if they refer to plural antecedents. However, when the relative pronoun refers to a singular subject, the pronoun takes a singular verb.

She is one of the best *cheerleaders who have* ever attended our school.

She is the only *cheerleader who has* a broken leg.

Subjects preceded by **every** and **each** are singular.

Every man, woman, and child *was* given a life preserver.

Each undergraduate *is* required to pass a proficiency exam.

A collective noun, such as **audience**, **faculty**, and **jury**, requires a singular verb when the group is regarded as a whole, and a plural when the members of the group are regarded as individuals.

The *jury has* made its decision.

The faculty are preparing their grade rosters.

Subjects preceded by **the number of** or **the percentage of** are singular; subjects preceded by **a number of** or **a percentage of** are plural.

The number of vacationers in Florida *increases* every year.

A number of vacationers *are* young couples.

Certain nouns of Latin and Greek origin have unusual plural forms.

Singular	**Plural**
criterion	criteria
alumnus	alumni
datum	data
medium	media

The *data are* available for inspection.

The only *criterion* for membership *is* a high GPA.

Some nouns, such as *deer*, *shrimp*, and *sheep*, have the same spelling for both their singular and plural forms. In these cases, the meaning of the sentence will determine whether they are singular or plural.

Deer are beautiful animals.

The spotted *deer is* licking the salt block.

Some nouns ending in *-ics*, such as *economics* and *ethics*, take singular verbs when they refer to principles or a field of study; however, when they refer to individual practices, they usually take plural verbs.

Ethics is being taught in the spring.

His unusual business *ethics are* what got him into trouble.

Some nouns that end in **-s** may appear to be plural but are not; examples are *measles* and *news*.

Measles is a very contagious disease.

News of her arrival *was* not welcome.

A verbal noun (infinitive or gerund) serving as a subject is treated as singular, even if the object of the verbal phrase is plural.

Hiding your mistakes *does* not make them go away.

A plural subject followed by a singular appositive requires a plural verb; similarly, a singular subject followed by a plural appositive requires a singular verb.

When the girls throw a party, *they* each bring a *gift.*

The *board,* all ten members, *is* meeting today.

Adjectives and Adverbs

Correct Usage

Be careful and *Drive carefully* are sentences that illustrate the differences that this section discusses: the proper use of an adjective or an adverb, including distinctions between *bad* and *badly* and *good* and *well.*

Adjectives are words that modify nouns or pronouns by defining, describing, limiting, or qualifying those nouns or pronouns.

Adverbs are words that modify verbs, adjectives, or other adverbs and that express such ideas as time, place, manner, cause, and degree. In general, use adjectives as subject complements with linking verbs; use adverbs with action verbs.

The old man's speech was *eloquent.*	ADJECTIVE
Mr. Brown speaks *eloquently.*	ADVERB
Please be *careful.*	ADJECTIVE
Please drive *carefully.*	ADVERB

Good and Well

Good is an adjective; its use as an adverb is colloquial and nonstandard.

NONSTANDARD: He plays *good.*

STANDARD: He plays *well.*

STANDARD: He looks *good* to be an octogenarian.

Well may be either an adverb or an adjective. As an adjective it means "in good health."

He plays *well.*	ADVERB
My mother is not *well.*	ADJECTIVE

Do not confuse *good* and *well* when used with *feel.* If you say "*I feel good,*" you're referring to your general health or mood, whereas "*I feel well*" refers only to your sense of touch.

Bad or Badly

Bad is an adjective used after sense verbs, such as *look, smell, taste, feel,* or *sound,* or after linking verbs (is, am, are, was, were).

UNREVISED: I feel *badly* about the delay.

REVISED: I feel *bad* about the delay.

Badly is an adverb used after all other verbs.

UNREVISED: It doesn't hurt very *bad.*

REVISED: It doesn't hurt very *badly.*

Real or Really

Real is an adjective; its use as an adverb is colloquial and nonstandard. It means "genuine."

NONSTANDARD: He writes *real* well.

STANDARD: This is *real* leather.

Really is an adverb meaning "very."

NONSTANDARD: This is *really* diamond.

STANDARD: Have a *really* nice day.

This is *real* amethyst.	ADJECTIVE
This is *really* difficult.	ADVERB
This is a *real* crisis	ADJECTIVE
This is *really* important.	ADVERB

Faulty Comparisons

This section covers comparisons that use adjectives and adverbs with certain conjunctions, such as *than* and *as,* to indicate a greater or lesser degree of what is specified in the main part of the sentence. Errors occur when the comparison being made is illogical, redundant, or incomplete. Watch for **-er** and **-est** forms of words meaning *more* and *most,* and correlative pairs like *as . . . as.* Other clues are *than* and *other.* Often, sentences containing a faulty comparison sound correct because their problem is not one of grammar but of logic. Read such sentences closely to make sure that like things are being compared, that the comparisons are complete, and that the comparisons are logical.

When comparing two persons or things, use the comparative (**-er**), not the superlative (**-est**), form of an adjective or an adverb. Use the superlative form for comparison of more than two persons or things. Use *any, other,* or *else* when comparing one thing or person with a group of which it, he, or she is a part.

Most one- and two-syllable words form their comparative and superlative forms with **-er** and **-est** suffixes. Adjectives and adverbs of more than two syllables form their comparatives and superlatives with the addition of *more* and *most.*

Word	Comparative	Superlative
good	better	best
old	older	oldest
friendly	friendlier	friendliest
lonely	lonelier	loneliest
talented	more talented	most talented
beautiful	more beautiful	most beautiful

When in doubt, consult a dictionary; most of them give the comparative and superlative forms.

Here are examples of some common types of faulty comparison:

Double comparison

UNREVISED: He is the *most nicest* brother.

REVISED: He is the *nicest* brother.

UNREVISED: She is the *more meaner* of the sisters.

REVISED: She is the *meaner* sister.

Illogical comparison

UNREVISED: The interest at a loan company is higher *than* a bank.

CORRECT: The interest at a loan company is higher *than at* a bank.

Ambiguous comparison

UNREVISED: I like Mary *better than* you. (than you *what*?)

REVISED: I like Mary *better than* I like you. OR I like Mary *better than* you do.

Incomplete comparison

UNREVISED: Skywriting is *more* spectacular.

REVISED: Skywriting is *more* spectacular *than* billboard advertising.

Omission of words **other**, **any**, or **else** when comparing one thing or person with a group of which it, he, or she is a part

UNREVISED: Joan writes better *than any* student in her class.

REVISED: Joan writes better *than any other* student in her class.

Omission of the second *as* in an **as . . . as** construction

> UNREVISED: The University of West Florida is *as large* or larger than the University of North Florida.

> REVISED: The University of West Florida is *as large as* or larger than the University of North Florida.

Word Choice

Usage

Consider this sentence: The high school *principal* resigned for two *principal* reasons. If you think that the second *principal* is the wrong word (that it should be *principle*), think again. This usage is correct. You may be asked about words that are commonly confused and misused, as well as the use of words based on their grammatical appropriateness in a sentence, such as the distinction between *principal* and *principle, fewer* and *less,* and *lie* and *lay.* Here are some commonly confused pairs:

> *principal*—as an adjective, most important; as a noun, the chief authority.

> *principle*—always a noun: a fundamental law. "We hold these principles to be self-evident."

> *affect*—usually a verb, meaning to *influence*; sometimes a noun, with a specific meaning in psychology. "Her performance was adversely affected by the heat."

> *effect*—usually a noun, meaning something that results from something else; occasionally a verb, meaning *to cause to come into being.* "The heat had no effect on his performance." "Her persistence helped to effect the new zoning ordinance."

Connotative and Denotative Meanings

The denotative meaning of a word is its *literal,* dictionary definition: what the word denotes, or "means." The connotative meaning of a word is what the word connotes, or "suggests"; it is a meaning apart from what the word literally means. A writer should choose a word based on the tone and context of the sentence; this ensures that a word bears the appropriate connotation while still conveying some exactness in denotation. For example, a gift might be described as "cheap," but the directness of the word has a negative connotation—something cheap is something of little or no value. The word "inexpensive" has a more positive connotation, although "cheap" is a synonym for "inexpensive." You may very well have to make a decision regarding the appropriateness of words and phrases within the context of a sentence.

Wordiness and Conciseness

Some questions will test your ability to detect redundancies (unnecessary repetitions), circumlocution (failure to get to the point), and padding with loose synonyms. These questions require you to select sentences that use as few words as possible to convey a message clearly, economically, and effectively.

Effective writing is concise. Wordiness, on the other hand, decreases the clarity of expression by cluttering sentences with unnecessary words. Of course, not all short sentences are better than long ones simply because they are brief. As long as a word serves a function, it should remain in the sentence. However, repetition of words, sounds, and phrases should be used only for emphasis or other stylistic reasons. Editing your writing will make a difference in its impact. Notice what revision does here:

> UNREVISED: The medical exam that he gave me was entirely complete.
>
> REVISED: The medical exam he gave me was complete.
>
> UNREVISED: Larry asked his friend John, who was a good, old friend, if he would join him and go along with him to see the foreign film made in Japan.
>
> REVISED: Larry asked his good, old friend John if he would join him in seeing the Japanese film.
>
> UNREVISED: I was absolutely, totally happy with the present that my parents gave to me at 7 AM on the morning of my birthday.
>
> REVISED: I was happy with the present my parents gave me on the morning of my birthday.
>
> UNREVISED: It seems perfectly clear to me that although he went and got permission from the professor, he still should not have played that awful, terrible joke on the dean.
>
> REVISED: It seems clear that, although he got permission from the professor, he should not have played that terrible joke on the dean.

Drill: Editing Skills

DIRECTIONS: Select the sentence that clearly and effectively states the idea and has no structural errors.

(A) South of Richmond, the two roads converge together to form a single highway.

(B) South of Richmond, the two roads converge together to form an interstate highway.

(C) South of Richmond, the two roads converge to form an interstate highway.

(D) South of Richmond, the two roads converge to form a single interstate highway.

The correct answer is (C); *together* is not needed after *converge*, and *single* is not needed to modify *highway*.

(A) Vincent van Gogh and Paul Gauguin were close personal friends and companions who enjoyed each other's company and frequently worked together on their artwork.

(B) Vincent van Gogh and Paul Gauguin were friends who frequently painted together.

(C) Vincent van Gogh was a close personal friend of Paul Gauguin, and the two of them often worked together on their artwork because they enjoyed each other's company.

(D) Vincent van Gogh, a close personal friend of Paul Gauguin, often worked with him on their artwork.

The correct answer is (B). Choices (A) and (C) pad the sentences with loose synonyms that are redundant. Choice (D), although a short sentence, does not convey the meaning as clearly as choice (B).

Transitions and Coherence

On the writing portion of the WEST–B, you will be asked tell whether a particular passage develops its ideas well. You will also be asked to supply missing words, phrases, or sentences that would make a particular passage develop more logically. Let's look at the following passage, which is adapted from a similar passage that appeared in Chapter 1.

Passage

[1]That the area of obscenity and pornography is a difficult one for the Supreme Court is well documented. [2]The Court's numerous attempts to define obscenity have proven unworkable and left the decision to the

subjective preferences of the justices. [3]Perhaps Justice Stewart put it best when, after refusing to define obscenity, he declared, but "I know it when I see it." [4]Does the Court literally have to see it to know it? [5]Specifically, what role does the fact-pattern, including the materials' medium, play in the Court's decision?

[6]Several recent studies employ fact-pattern analysis in modeling the Court's decision making. [7]These studies examine the fact-pattern or case characteristics, often with ideological and attitudinal factors, as a determinant of the decision reached by the Court. [8]In broad terms, these studies owe their theoretical underpinnings to attitude theory. [9]As the name suggests, attitude theory views the Court's attitudes as an explanation of its decisions.

[10]These attitudes, however, do not operate in a vacuum. [11]As Spaeth explains, "the activation of an attitude involves both an object and the situation in which that object is encountered." [12]The objects to which the court directs its attitudes are litigants. [13]The situation—the subject matter of the case—can be defined in broad or narrow terms. [14]One may define the situation as an entire area of the law (e.g., civil liberties issues). [15]On an even broader scale, the situation may be defined as the decision to grant certiorari or whether to defect from a minimum-winning coalition.

[16]Defining the situation with such broad strokes, ________, does not allow one to control for case content. [17]In many specific issue areas, the cases present strikingly similar patterns. [18]In examining the Court's search and seizure decisions, Segal found that a relatively small number of situational and case characteristic variables explain a high proportion of the Court's decisions.

[19]Despite Segal's success, efforts to verify the applicability of fact-pattern analysis in other issue areas and using broad-based factors have been slow in forthcoming. [20]Renewed interest in obscenity and pornography by federal and state governments as a result of lobbying campaigns by fundamentalist groups, the academic community, and other antipornography interest groups pro and con indicate the Court's decisions in this area will get closer examination.

[21]The Court's obscenity and pornography decisions ______ present an opportunity to study the Court's behavior in an area where the Court has granted significant decision-making authority to the states. [22]In *Miller v. California* (1973) the Court announced the importance of local community standards in obscenity determinations. [23]The Court's ________ behavior may suggest how the Court will react in other areas where it has chosen to defer to the states (e.g., abortion).

Questions

1. This passage would be most appropriate in which type of publication?

   A. A popular magazine such as *Time* or *Newsweek*

   B. An editorial about pornography in a newspaper

   C. A chapter on pornography in a sociology textbook

   D. An article in a law journal

2. Which of the following phrases, if inserted in the blank in sentence 16, would best help the reader under the author's progression of ideas.

   A. consequently

   B. however

   C. nevertheless

   D. furthermore

3. In the final paragraph, which words or phrases, if inserted in order in the blanks, help the reader understand the author's logical sequence?

   A. in fact; foolish

   B. will; later

   C. also; subsequent

   D. theoretically; firm

4. Which of the following best describes the method of organization used by the author of this passage?

   A. problem and solution

   B. chronological order

   C. order of importance

   D. comparison and contrast

5. Which of the following sentences, if added between sentences 10 and 11, would be most consistent with the writer's purpose and intended audience?

   A. Situations with which the Court is faced are often quite complex.

   B. Supreme Court justices have been known to read newspapers as well as law journals.

   C. Pornography has been a point of public dispute for many decades now.

   D. If they did operate in a vacuum, predicting a justice's vote on a particular issue from his record before his appointment would be somewhat straightforward.

6. Which word would best replace the underlined words in sentence 20?

   A. deserve

   B. are garnering

   C. will continue to elude

   D. have avoided

Answers

Keep in mind that the first step to answering these types of questions involves applying the Four-Step Approach discussed in Chapter 1. You cannot answer questions about the purpose, audience, or organization of a passage without first having analyzed it through the four-step approach. You will see that, in the practice test in this book and in the actual examination, passages are generally shorter than this passage; this one has been included so that you can review the Four-Step Approach while answering these questions.

The answer to Question 1 is **D**. The quotes from scholars eliminate A and B from consideration, because newspapers and magazines for general readers do not usually quote experts without identifying why they are worthy of being experts. Choice B is further eliminated by the fact that the passage takes no position that the average newspaper reader might act upon. The tone of the passage might conceivably be appropriate to choice C, but the passage focuses on law rather than pornography.

The correct answer to Question 2 is **B**. The previous paragraph ended with a statement about a "broad scale," and the new paragraph begins by saying that looking at the broad scale is inadequate. This sentence, then, must convey that contrast, so choices A and D are immediately eliminated. Choice C conveys the correct general meaning, but the use of *nevertheless* directly before a negative—*does not*—would be confusing to a reader.

The correct answer to Question 3 is **C**. To find this answer, you will first have to notice that the author is switching topics from obscenity to states' rights; therefore, the choice A is eliminated, because *in fact* is a transition that signals an example of what has just been discussed. (In addition, nothing in the passage indicates that the author regards the Court's behavior as "foolish.") Choice B is wrong simply because the word "will" is not accurate: the decisions *already do* present an opportunity for further analysis. Choice D's "theoretically" is plausible, but "firm" is definitely wrong because it does not describe the author's opinion of the Court's 1973 decision, which just announces the importance of local standards rather than making firm law regarding them.

Question 4's answer is **D**. Although a problem and solution are implied in the passage, there is no direct statement of the problem followed by a solution. Chronological order and order of importance are clearly not present here, but the writer does compare and contrast analytical methods and attempts to explicate their strengths and weaknesses.

The best answer to Question 5 is **D**. Choices A and C are far from the point of the paragraph, which concerns how justices reach decisions. The choice of D over B depends on the tone of the two sentences as well as the specific content. The content of the two sentences is similar, although the content of D is somewhat more on message. The tone of choice B, however, is a bit flippant and would undoubtedly be out of place in most articles aimed at law scholars.

The best answer to Question 6 is **A**. Choice D contradicts the facts as presented in the paragraph, and choice C is out of line with the entire passage, which does give close examination to the subject. Choice B is technically correct (although not very informative for a final thought in a paragraph), but the word *garner* would be more at home in a newspaper article ("Duncan Garners Another Award") than in an article like this one.

CONSTRUCTED-RESPONSE ITEMS

The WEST–B contains two writing assignments. The written assignment asks test takers to compose a response, or constructed response, to a given prompt. You will be evaluated on your ability to communicate the written message to a specified audience.

0012 Prepare an organized, developed composition in response to instructions regarding content, purpose, and audience.

The candidate may be asked to respond to persuasive and/or expository writing exercises in which the candidate is asked to do one or more of the following.

- Compose a fluent, focused, and sustained piece of writing on a given topic using language and style appropriate to a specified audience, purpose, and occasion.
- State and maintain a clear main idea and point of view using effective organization to enhance meaning and clarity.
- Take a position on a contemporary social or political issue and defend that position with reasoned arguments and supporting examples.
- Use effective sentence structure.
- Demonstrate the ability to spell, capitalize, and punctuate according to standard writing conventions.

Based on the writing exercise assigned, responses will be evaluated according to the following ***performance characteristics****:*

Focus and appropriateness	The fluency and quality of the discussion, and the sustained attention on a given topic using language and style appropriate to a specified audience, purpose, and occasion
Unity and organization	The effectiveness of the organization, the logical sequence of ideas, and the clarity of the writing used to state and maintain a main idea and point of view

Development and rationale	The relevance, depth, and effectiveness of statements or arguments and examples used to support those statements or defend a position
Usage and sentence structure	The precision in word choice and use of effective sentence structure
Mechanical conventions	The use of spelling, capitalization, and punctuation according to standard writing conventions

A response earning a "4" is a well-organized and developed response that effectively addresses the assigned content, purpose, and audience. In it, the writer addresses the given topic and remains focused on that topic; the discussion includes language and style appropriate for the audience, purpose, and occasion. The response is well organized with a logical sequence of ideas and clear writing. The writer's position is clear and is supported with relevant, convincing information; the reasoning is strong. The writer's word choice is careful and precise, and sentence structures are varied and effective. In addition, the composition generally adheres to standard spelling, capitalization, and punctuation.

A response that earns a "3" contains all the virtues of a "4" response, but it performs them "adequately" rather than "well." Thus, it is an adequately organized and developed composition that addresses the assigned content, purpose, and audience. It addresses the given topic and generally remains focused on that topic; the discussion is coherent and includes language and style generally appropriate for the audience, purpose, and occasion. It is adequately organized with a logical sequence of ideas and generally clear writing. The writer's position is adequately stated and supporting information is adequate; the reasoning is generally sound. Word choice is adequate, and sentence structures are generally effective. The response may include some errors in standard spelling, capitalization, and punctuation.

A response that earns a "2" is less consistently adequate than a "3" response. It is a somewhat organized and developed composition that does not adequately address the assigned content, purpose, and audience, although it does do so to a degree. The writer may address, but lose focus on, the given topic; the discussion may be confused or include some language and style inappropriate for the audience, purpose, and occasion. The organization may be questionable: the ideas may not be developed in a clear sequence, or the writing itself may be unclear. The writer's position is only partially developed, with generally weak supporting information; the reasoning may be simplistic. Word choice is limited and inadequate; sentence structures may be weak or lack variety. The response may include distracting flaws in standard spelling, capitalization, and punctuation.

A "1" is a poorly organized and developed composition that inadequately addresses the assigned content, purpose, and audience. It fails on every one of the points that were discussed on the other scores. You will not write a "1" response if you study this guide.

A response given a U is deemed unscorable. A U score would be given if the essay is not on the given topic, is illegible, too short, or not written in English.

A response given a B is self-explanatory (i.e., a blank sheet that contains no answer).

Sample essays from different scoring levels appear at the end of the Practice Test, accompanied by critical commentary.

Carefully read each assignment before you begin to write. Think about your ideas and what you would like to communicate to the reader. You may wish to make an outline for the topic to help organize your thoughts, but be sure to write the final draft of your response in the test booklet. Your score will be based on what is written in the response booklet. When you have finished writing, be sure to review your work and make any changes you believe would enhance your score.

This review will guide you through a step-by-step process of how to write an essay, from writing strategies to budgeting time during the exam. Even if you feel that you are a good writer, you should still study this review, as it will help you become familiar with essay writing. The strategies included are provided to help you write an essay that is to the point, easily understood, properly structured, well supported, and correct according to the rules of grammar. You will not be expected to write a best-selling book in order to pass this test. Remember, the more you practice the strategies provided in this review, the easier it will be for you to write a good essay.

Strategies for the Essays

To give yourself the best chance of writing a good essay, you should follow these steps.

Before the test, this is your plan:

Step 1: Study the following review to enhance your ability to write an essay. Remember, the sharper your skills, the more likely you are to receive a passing grade on your writing sample.

Step 2: Practice writing an essay. The best way to do this is to complete the Practice Test. Make sure to take this drill under the same types of conditions you will experience when taking the actual exam.

Step 3: Learn and understand the directions, so that you don't waste valuable time reading them on the test day. This will allow you to quickly review them before writing your essay.

Step 4: Develop your essay from the notes you have made. Present your position clearly and logically, making sure to provide adequate examples and/or support. Write your draft on scratch paper.

Step 5: Proofread your essay! Check every word for errors in spelling. Be sure that your sentences are concise and grammatically correct. Make any necessary revisions.

Step 6: Copy the final version of your essay into the response booklet.

Additional Tips

- Be sure that you have not strayed from your topic or introduced points that you have not explained.
- Vary your types of sentences so that your essay flows smoothly and is easy to read.
- Use vocabulary that suits your audience. Make sure not to insult your audience by using simple vocabulary, or by explaining things they already know. Likewise, do not alienate your audience by using complicated jargon, or by assuming that they are already familiar with the subject on which you are writing.

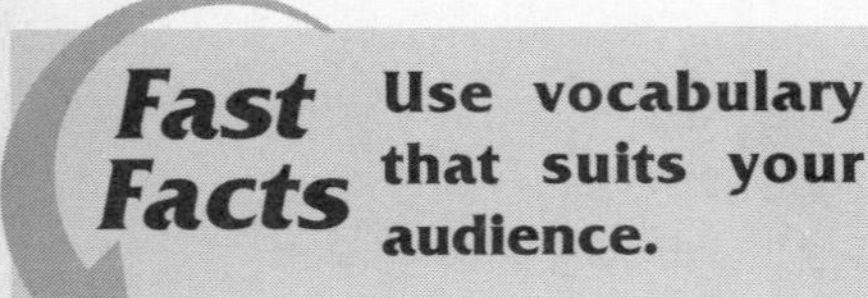

Recognizing Effective Writing

WHY ESSAYS EXIST

People write essays for purposes other than testing. Some of our best thinkers have written essays that we continue to read from generation to generation. Essays offer the reader a logical, coherent, and imaginative written composition showing the nature or consequences of a single controlling idea when considered from the writer's unique point of view. Writers use essays to communicate their opinion or position on a topic to readers who cannot be present during their live conversation. Writers use essays to help readers understand or learn about something that readers should or may want to know or do. Essays always express more or less directly the author's opinion, belief, position, or knowledge (backed by evidence) about the idea or object in question.

ORGANIZATION AND PURPOSEFUL DEVELOPMENT

For this test you will need to recognize and generate the elements of an excellent essay. In essence, you will be taking the principles covered in this review and utilizing them to create your own original essay. With that in mind, read carefully the standards and explanations below to prepare you for what to look for in your own essay response.

ESSAY WRITING

In academic writing, two purposes dominate essays:

1. Persuasion through argumentation using one, some, or all of the logical patterns described here.

2. Informing and educating through analysis and using one, some, or all of the logical patterns described here.

All of an essay's organizational strategies may be used to argue in writing. The author offers reasons and/or evidence so an audience will be inclined to believe the position that the author presents about the idea under discussion. Writers use seven basic strategies to organize information and ideas in essays to help prove their point (thesis). All of these strategies might be useful in arguing for an idea and persuading a reader to see the issue the writer's way. Your job is to use strategies that are appropriate to demonstrate your thesis. For example, you may wish to use comparison and contrast to demonstrate that one thing or idea is better or worse than another.

The following seven steps can be used to prove a thesis.

SEVEN STEPS TO PROVE A THESIS

1. Show how a *process* or procedure does or should work, step by step, in time.

2. *Compare or contrast* two or more things or ideas to show important differences or similarities.

3. *Identify a problem* and then explain how to solve it.

4. *Analyze* into its components, or *classify* by its types or categories, an idea or thing to show how it is put together, how it works, or how it is designed.

5. *Explain* why something happens to produce a particular result or set of results.

6. *Describe* the particular individual characteristics, beauty, and features of a place, person(s), time, or idea.

7. *Define* what a thing is or what an idea means.

Depending upon the purpose of the essay, one pattern tends to dominate the discussion question. (For example, the writer might use *description* and *explanation* to define the varied meanings of "love.")

During this test you will be called upon to exercise control over your writing by using the writing process and by knowing the pitfalls of weak writing and correcting them. Using the steps outlined below, compose your essay in the order suggested and note the elements and qualities to correct during each stage of the process of composing your essay test response. Make any corrections you need during the appropriate stage of the writing process; to correct errors at the wrong stage may waste time and interfere with your producing the best essay response.

COMPOSING YOUR ESSAY: USING THE WRITING PROCESS

Some people (erroneously) think that writers just sit down and churn out a wonderful essay or poem in one sitting in a flash of genius and inspiration. This is not true. Writers use the writing process from start to finish to help them to write a clear document. If you do not reflect on your composition in stages and make changes as you develop it, you will not see all the problems or errors in it. Don't try to write an essay just once and leave the room. Stay and look through it. Reflect upon it using the writing process.

The writing process has five steps: (1) prewriting, or planning time; (2) the rough draft; (3) organizing and revising the ideas (not the words or sentences themselves); (4) polishing, or editing (making sure sentences themselves are sentences, that the words you use are the right words, and that the spelling and punctuation are correct); and (5) proofreading, to make sure no mistakes are left.

Using this process does not mean that you have to write five drafts. Write one draft (stages 1 and 2), leaving space for corrections (e.g., writing on every other line) and then working on the existing draft through the rest of the stages (3 through 5). If time allows, you may want to do the whole process on scrap paper and then copy the finished product onto the allotted test paper. But if you do copy it, make sure you proofread your copy to see whether, while transcribing it, you left anything out or said a word twice or made any other errors.

PREWRITING/PLANNING TIME

Read the essay question and decide on your purpose. Do you want to persuade your reader? Would you rather explain something?

Sample: "Television is bad for people."

Do you agree or disagree with this statement? Decide. Take a stand. Don't be noncommittal. Write down the statement of your position.

Sample: "I agree that television is bad for people."

or

"Television is an excellent learning tool and is good for most people."

This is your thesis.

CONSIDER YOUR AUDIENCE

The writer's responsibility is to write clearly, honestly, and cleanly for the reader's sake. Essays would be pointless without an audience. Why write an essay if no one wants or needs to read it? Why add evidence, organize your ideas, or correct bad grammar? The reason to do any of these things is that someone out there needs to understand what you mean to say. What would the audience need to know in order to believe you or to come over to your position? Imagine someone you know (visualize her or him) listening to you declare your position or opinion and then saying, "Oh yeah? Prove it!"

Fast Facts

The writer's responsibility is to write clearly, honestly, and cleanly for the reader's sake.

In writing your essay, make sure to answer the following questions: What evidence do you need to prove your idea to this skeptic? What would she disagree with you about? What does she share with you as common knowledge? What does she need to be told by you?

CONTROL YOUR POINT OF VIEW

We may write essays from one of three points of view, depending upon the essay's audience. The points of view below are discussed from informal to formal.

1. Subjective/Personal Point of View:
   "I think/believe/feel cars are more trouble than they are worth."

2. Second-Person:
   "If you own a car, you soon find out that it is more trouble than it is worth."

3. Third-Person Point of View (focuses on the idea, not what "I" think of it): "Cars are more trouble than they are worth."

For now, stick with one or another; don't switch your "point of view" in the middle. Any one is acceptable.

CONSIDER YOUR SUPPORT

Next, during prewriting, jot down a few phrases that show ideas and examples that support your point of view. Do this quickly on a separate piece of paper for about five minutes. Don't try to outline; simply list things that you think might be important to discuss. After you have listed several, pick at least three to five things you want or need to discuss, and number them in the order of importance that is relevant to proving your point.

WRITE YOUR ROUGH DRAFT

Spend 10 to 20 minutes writing your rough draft. Looking over your prewriting list, write down what you think is useful to prove your point in the order you think best to convince the reader. Be sure to use real evidence from your life experience or knowledge to support what you say. You do not have to draw evidence from books; your own life is equally appropriate.

For example, don't write, "Cars are more trouble to fix than bicycles," and then fail to show evidence for your idea. Give examples of what you mean: "For example, my father's Buick needs 200 parts to make one brake work, but my bicycle has only four pieces that make up the brakes, and I can replace those myself." Write naturally and quickly. Don't worry too much at this point about paragraphing, spelling, or punctuation—just write down what you think or want to say in the order determined on your list.

TRANSITIONS

To help the reader follow the flow of your ideas and to help unify the essay, use transitions to show the connections among your ideas. You may use transitions at the beginnings of paragraphs, or you may use them to show the connections among ideas within a single paragraph.

Here are some typical transitional words and phrases that you should use when writing your essay.

To link similar ideas, use the words:

again	equally important	in addition	of course
also	for example	in like manner	similarly
and	for instance	likewise	too
another	further	moreover	
besides	furthermore	or	

To link dissimilar or contradictory ideas, use words such as:

although	and yet	as if	but
conversely	even if	however	in spite of
instead	nevertheless	on the contrary	on the other hand
otherwise	provided that	still	yet

To indicate cause, purpose, or result, use:

as	consequently	hence	then
as a result	for	since	therefore
because	for this reason	so	thus

To indicate time or position, use words like:

above	at the present time	first	second
across	before	here	thereafter
afterward	beyond	meanwhile	thereupon
around	eventually	next	
at once	finally	presently	

To indicate an example or summary, use phrases such as:

as a result	in any case	in conclusion	in short
as I have said	in any event	in fact	on the whole
for example	in brief	in other words	to sum up
for instance			

PROVIDING EVIDENCE IN YOUR ESSAY

You may employ any one of the seven steps previously listed to prove any thesis that you maintain is true. You may also call on evidence from one or all of the four following kinds of evidence to support the thesis of your essay. Identify which kind(s) of evidence you can use to prove the points of your essay. In test situations, most essayists use anecdotal evidence or analogy to explain, describe, or prove a thesis. But if you know salient facts or statistics, don't hesitate to call upon them.

1. **Hard data** (facts, statistics, scientific evidence, research)—documented evidence that has been verified to be true.

2. **Anecdotal evidence**—stories from the writer's own experience and knowledge that illustrate a particular point or idea.

3. **Expert opinions**—assertions or conclusions, usually by authorities, about the matter under discussion.

4. **Analogies**—show a resemblance between one phenomenon and another.

ORGANIZING AND REVIEWING THE PARAGRAPHS

Fast Facts

Be sure to supply useful transitions to keep up the flow and maintain the focus of your ideas.

The unit of work for revising is the paragraph. After you have written what you wanted to say based on your prewriting list, spend about twenty minutes revising your draft by looking to see whether you need to indent for paragraphs anywhere. If you do, make a proofreader's mark to indicate to the reader that you think a paragraph should start here. Check to see whether you want to add anything that would make your point of view more convincing. Be sure to supply useful transitions to keep up the flow and maintain the focus of your ideas. If you don't have room on the paper, or if your new paragraph shows up out of order, add that paragraph and indicate with a number or some other mark where you want it to go. Check to make sure that you gave examples or illustrations for your statements. In the examples below, two paragraphs are offered: one without concrete evidence and one with evidence for its idea. Study each. Note the topic sentence (T) and how that sentence is or is not supported with evidence.

PARAGRAPHING WITH NO EVIDENCE

Television is bad for people. Programs on television are often stupid and depict crimes that people later copy. Television takes time away from loved ones, and it often becomes addictive. So, television is bad for people because it is no good.

In this example, the author has not given any concrete evidence for any of the good ideas presented. He just declares them to be so. Any one of the sentences above might make a good opening sentence for a whole paragraph. Take the second sentence, for example:

> *Watching television takes time away from other things.* For example, all those hours people spend sitting in front of the tube, they could be working on building a chair or fixing the roof. (*Second piece of evidence*) Maybe the laundry needs to be done, but because people watch television, they may end up not having time to do it. Then Monday comes around again and they have no socks to wear to work—all because they couldn't stand to miss that episode of "Everybody Loves Raymond." (*Third piece of evidence*) Someone could be writing a letter to a friend in Boston who hasn't been heard from or written to for months. (*Fourth piece of evidence*) Or maybe someone misses the opportunity to take in a beautiful day in the park because she had to see "General Hospital." They'll repeat "General Hospital," but this beautiful day only comes around once.
>
> Watching television definitely keeps people from getting things done.

The primary evidence the author uses here is that of probable illustrations taken from life experience that is largely anecdotal. *Always* supply evidence. Three examples or illustrations of your idea per paragraph is a useful number. Don't go on and on about a single point. You don't have time. In order for a typical test essay to be fully developed, it should have about five paragraphs. They ought to be organized in the following manner:

Introduction: A paragraph that shows your point of view (thesis) about an issue and introduces your position with three general ideas that support your thesis.

Development: Three middle paragraphs that prove your position from different angles, using evidence from real life and knowledge. Each supporting paragraph in the middle should in turn support each of the three ideas you started out with in the introductory or thesis paragraph.

Conclusion: The last paragraph, which sums up your position and adds one final reminder of what the issue was, perhaps points to a solution:

> So, television takes away from the quality of life and is therefore bad for human beings. We should be watching the sun, the sky, the birds, and each other, not the "boob tube."

Write a paragraph using this sentence as your focus: "Television takes valuable time away from our loved ones."

CHECK FOR LOGIC

Make sure that you present your argument in a logical manner. If you have not, you may not have proven your point. Your conclusion must follow from a logical set of premises, such as:

- Either/or—The writer assumes that only two opposing possibilities may be attained: "Either _____, or this _____."
- Oversimplification—The writer simplifies the subject: "The rich only want one thing."
- Begging the question—The writer assumes she has proven something (often counterintuitive) that may need to be proven to the reader: "The death penalty actually increases, rather than deters, violent crime."
- Ignoring the issue—The writer argues against the truth of an issue due to its conclusion: "John is a good boy and, therefore, did not rob the store."
- Arguing against a person, not an idea—The writer argues that somebody's idea has no merit because he is immoral or personally stupid: "Eric will fail out of school because he is not doing well in gym class."
- Non sequitur—The writer leaps to the wrong conclusion: "Jake is from Canada; he must play hockey."
- Drawing the wrong conclusion from a sequence—The author attributes the outcome to the wrong reasons: "Betty married at a young age to an older man and now has three children and is therefore a housewife."

Polishing and Editing Your Essay

If the unit of work for revising is the paragraph, the unit of work for editing is the sentence. Check your paper for mistakes in editing. To help you in this task, use the following checklist.

POLISHING CHECKLIST

- Are all your sentences *really* sentences, or have you written some fragments or run-on sentences?
- Are you using vocabulary correctly?

- Have you used a word that seems colloquial or too informal?
- Did you leave out punctuation anywhere? Did you capitalize, or not capitalize, correctly? Did you check for commas, periods, and quotation marks?

PROOFREADING

In the last three to five minutes, read your paper word for word, first forward and then backward, reading from the end to the beginning. Doing so can help you find errors that you may have missed by having read forward only.

Types of Essays

You may be asked to write either of two basic kinds of essays: expository or persuasive. Each of these has a basic structure that you should follow to some extent. These structures are laid out here in a basic five-paragraph form. You don't have to follow this form exactly, but to the extent that you feel insecure about your writing ability, it is very useful to follow these forms.

The Expository Essay

An expository essay can encompass a variety of subjects. It may tell how to make or do something, or it may explore an idea. Expository writing conveys information to the reader in such a way as to bring about understanding; its subject may be a process or procedure, or perhaps the writer's ideas about a concept. Here are some samples of topics that you may be asked to write about in an expository essay:

- The ideal vacation
- The qualities of a good friend
- How to plan a lesson or create a syllabus (*Note*: Expository essays could be about "how to" do just about anything, but on the WEST–B, you will not be asked how to do something unless you could reasonably be expected to know how to do it—for example, you would not be asked how to bake a cake.)
- Similarities and differences between the younger generation and your own (essays like this are called "comparison-and-contrast essays")
- Characteristics of types of people you have met in school (essays like this are called "classifying essays")

- The reasons that you have decided to become a teacher (essays like this are called "cause-and-effect essays")

The structure of your expository essay will depend somewhat on the topic you are given, but the usual five-paragraph structure is a good starting point.

- Your first paragraph should begin with an attention grabber. For example, the essay about the ideal vacation might start with a sentence or two about something wonderful (or terrible) that you have done on a previous vacation, and the essay about the good friend could start with a very short anecdote about something a friend has done for you. The how-to-plan-a-lesson essay could begin with a humorous story of an unplanned lesson.

- Your first paragraph should end with a thesis statement. Creativity will be rewarded in the opening of the essay, and possibly in the conclusion, but in the thesis statement on a standardized-test essay, it is best to state your thesis as clearly as you can. Because you will be using the five-paragraph structure, try to make your thesis include three major points (for your three body paragraphs). For example, the essay on an ideal friend could include a paragraph on three different friends you've had and the traits of each, or it could focus on three different traits.

    - *This essay will discuss openness and honesty as I have experienced them in my friendships with Amanda, Tom, and Bill.*

    - *The crucial traits of an ideal friend are openness, honesty, and wit, and I shall discuss their value as I have experienced them—or their lack—in my real friendships.*

- Note, from the examples just given, that your thesis will determine the structure of your three body paragraphs. In an expository essay, your body paragraphs are not necessarily carrying an argument, as they are in a persuasive essay. You may arrange the paragraphs in any way that is convenient; just make sure that you include logical transitions between and within the paragraphs. For example, the second thesis statement above would be in an essay that had a paragraph each about openness, honesty, and wit, but you could skip back and forth between friendships in order to illustrate each of the qualities.

- The first part of the conclusion (fifth paragraph) should briefly recap the thesis and body paragraphs. The second part should include a statement that reinforces your position in a meaningful and memorable way. Creativity here will earn you some credit in the grading, but this is probably the least important part of the essay. If you can't think of something clever, don't waste much time trying to do so; the extra time is better spent revising your first four paragraphs.

The Persuasive Essay

The persuasive essay is meant to move its reader to take an action or to form or change an opinion. There are three main reasons it is included on the WEST–B:

- It requires thinking skills such as analysis, synthesis, and evaluation.
- It requires writers to take a stand from among two or more alternatives.
- Persuasive writing is a skill that you will have to both teach and use in your professional life.

Because all the persuasive prompts you will receive on a test (and most persuasive writing situations you will encounter in life) ask you to choose a stand from two or more reasonable alternatives, you will have to demonstrate that you understand why the other alternatives are reasonable. More important, though, you will have to make clear that you believe your stand on the issue is better, and you need to present your supporting evidence in such a way that it might convince a reasonable person who believed an alternative stand was preferable.

Persuasive prompts on the WEST–B will likely ask you to write for a general audience of educated adults, but it might also ask you to write to an audience of parents or to your principal or school board. Here are some samples of topics that you may be asked to write about in a persuasive essay:

- The effects of television on students' grades—good, bad, negligible?
- Is affirmative action appropriate in hiring and promoting teachers?
- Should national elections take place on a weekend day rather than a Tuesday?
- Should states require students to pass standardized tests in order to begin high school?
- Should high-school athletes be subjected to involuntary drug testing?
- Should students and teachers (i.e., not janitors) be responsible for keeping their school clean?

Note that you may not have a particular opinion about some of these matters. Indeed, you may not know much about the topic; the prompt will, however, typically give you enough information to help you write a good five-paragraph essay.

The structure of your persuasive essay will depend somewhat on the topic you are given, but the usual five-paragraph structure is a good starting point.

- Your first paragraph should begin with an attention grabber. One good strategy is to imagine a world in which the point of view you are against has prevailed. For example, if you take a position for affirmative action in hiring and promoting teachers, you might ask your reader to imagine a school system in which many students would go through high school without ever seeing a principal who looks like them. If you take the other side, you might ask the reader to compare two school systems, one of which had teachers who had scored an average of 20 points higher on their certification tests.

- Your first paragraph should end with a thesis statement. Creativity will be rewarded in the opening of the essay, and possibly in the conclusion, but in the thesis statement on a standardized-test essay, it is best to state your thesis as clearly as you can, especially in the persuasive essay. Because you will be using the five-paragraph structure, try to make your thesis include three major points (for your three body paragraphs). In addition, you want your thesis to state your position very clearly. If you include your summary of the other side's arguments in your thesis statement, you should always do so in a subordinate clause. For example, the thesis of the essay on involuntary drug testing might look like this:

    - *Although involuntary drug testing would be a violation of civil rights if participation in athletics were involuntary, such testing would restore integrity to athletic contests, increase student attendance, and help to protect athletes' health.*

    - *Even though participation in athletics is "voluntary," students should not be given an either-or choice between nonparticipation on the one hand and the loss of privacy and the restriction of their civil rights on the other.*

- Note, from the examples just given, that your thesis will determine the structure of your three body paragraphs. In a persuasive essay, your body paragraphs will carry your argument; you will succeed not on the basis of your eloquence in the introductory and concluding paragraphs, but on how well you organize and state facts that support your argument. It is often best to use your best reason in the final body paragraph. For example, the first thesis statement above would introduce an essay that had a paragraph about doubt that currently exists about whether high-school athletes' skill is based on ability or drugs. The next paragraph would be about the good things that would happen if that doubt were resolved. The final paragraph would then switch to your most important point: that performance-enhancing drugs are bad for athletes' health. As an exercise, can you think of a structure for the three body paragraphs of the essay with the second example above as a thesis statement?

- The first part of the conclusion (fifth paragraph) should briefly recap the thesis and body paragraphs (i.e., your argument). The second part should include a statement that reinforces your position in a meaningful and memorable way. Creativity here will earn you some credit in the grading, but this is probably the least important part of the essay. If you can't think of something clever, don't waste much time trying to do so; the extra time is better spent revising your first four paragraphs.

Chapter

Mathematics

3

0013 Understand and apply concepts and principles of numbers and operations.

The following are examples of content that may be covered under this objective.

- Recognize equivalent representations of numbers (e.g., fractions, decimals, percents).
- Apply the principles of integers, fractions, decimals, and percentages.
- Apply understanding of ratios and proportions.
- Demonstrate understanding of the meaning of operations (e.g., addition, subtraction, multiplication, division) and of equality.
- Demonstrate understanding of order of operations.

0014 Understand and apply concepts and procedures of measurement.

The following are examples of content that may be covered under this objective.

- Select an appropriate measurement tool or unit for a specified measurement task.
- Solve problems involving the U.S. or metric systems of measurement.
- Solve problems involving scale (e.g., determine the distance between two locations on a map).
- Demonstrate understanding of the concepts of perimeter, area, and volume.
- Calculate derived measurements (e.g., the average speed of a car given how long it takes to travel a specified distance).

0015 Understand concepts and principles of geometry and solve related problems.

The following are examples of content that may be covered under this objective.

- Demonstrate an understanding of fundamental concepts of geometry (e.g., properties of points, lines, planes, angles).
- Identify types and properties of two- and three-dimensional figures.
- Solve problems involving triangles (e.g., calculate the length of the hypotenuse of a right triangle).
- Analyze figures in terms of symmetry and congruence.
- Describe the locations of points, lines, and objects on coordinate grids.
- Recognize geometric transformations (e.g., slides, flips, turns).

0016 Understand concepts and principles of probability and statistics and solve related problems.

The following are examples of content that may be covered under this objective.

- Calculate the probability of a simple event.
- Identify appropriate ways to collect, organize, and display various data.
- Interpret data displayed in various formats (e.g., tables, graphs, scatterplots).
- Demonstrate an understanding of fundamental statistical concepts, such as mean, median, and mode.
- Make predictions based on given data.

0017 Understand concepts and principles of algebra and solve related problems.

The following are examples of content that may be covered under this objective.

- Recognize and extend arithmetic and geometric patterns and sequences.
- Translate among tabular, symbolic, and graphical representations of relations (e.g., display data from a table as a graph, identify rate of change).
- Identify expressions or equations that represent situations involving variable quantities.
- Simplify expressions and apply formulas.
- Solve linear equations or inequalities involving one variable.
- Demonstrate understanding of the concept of equality.

0018 Apply mathematical reasoning, problem-solving, and communication skills.

The following are examples of content that may be covered under this objective.

- Identify missing or extraneous information in mathematical problems.
- Identify errors in mathematical explanations.
- Use inductive or deductive reasoning to draw conclusions and make predictions.
- Translate among the various ways of communicating mathematical information (e.g., words, equations, graphs, diagrams).
- Express ideas and situations using appropriate mathematical language and notation.

Basic Number Skills

Fractions need to have common denominators before adding. Thus, to add, say, $\frac{1}{2}$ and $\frac{2}{3}$, change both fractions to equivalent fractions. These new equivalent fractions will have the same *value* as $\frac{1}{2}$ and $\frac{2}{3}$ and will have common (same) denominators, but will look different from the original fractions. The lowest common denominator is 6, because both of the original denominators can be changed into 6; $\frac{1}{2}$ can be written as $\frac{3}{6}$, and $\frac{2}{3}$ can be written as $\frac{4}{6}$.

After changing the "appearance" of $\frac{1}{2} + \frac{2}{3}$ to $\frac{3}{6} + \frac{4}{6}$, we can then simply add the numerators together, giving $\frac{7}{6}$, or $1\frac{1}{6}$.

When adding mixed fractions (those made up of a whole number and a fraction), add the fractions first, then—separately—the whole numbers. If the fractions add up to more than 1, add 1 to the whole number sum. For example, if after adding we have 3 and $1\frac{3}{4}$, the final sum is $4\frac{3}{4}$.

The algorithm for subtracting fractions is generally the same as that for adding: Common denominators are required. A problem, however, may be encountered when attempting to subtract mixed fractions such as $3\frac{2}{5}$ and $1\frac{4}{5}$. Note that $\frac{4}{5}$ can't be subtracted from $\frac{2}{5}$ (without involving negative numbers.) The solution is to rename $3\frac{2}{5}$ as $2\frac{7}{5}$. (This is accomplished by "borrowing" 1, or $\frac{5}{5}$, from the 3.) The new problem—still equivalent to the original—is $2\frac{7}{5}$ minus $1\frac{4}{5}$, or $1\frac{3}{5}$.

One approach to multiplying fractions is to multiply the numerators together and the denominators together, then simplify the resulting product. $\frac{2}{3} \times \frac{3}{4}$, for instance, equals $\frac{6}{12}$, or $\frac{1}{2}$. There is no need to use common denominators (as with fraction addition and subtraction.)

If the numbers to be multiplied are mixed fractions, first rewrite them as "improper" fractions, such as $\frac{14}{3}$, then use the procedure described earlier.

To divide fractions, invert the divisor (or the "second" number; the one "doing the dividing") and multiply instead. In the case of $\frac{1}{5}$ divided by $\frac{3}{8}$, change the original problem to the equivalent problem $\frac{1}{5} \times \frac{8}{3}$. Using the algorithm for multiplying fractions, we get $\frac{8}{15}$ as the quotient.

Decimal notation provides a different way of representing fractions whose denominators are powers of 10. $\frac{13}{100}$, for instance, is written as 0.13, $\frac{1}{1000}$ as 0.001, and so forth.

To add or subtract decimal numbers, arrange them vertically, aligning decimal points, then add or subtract as one would whole numbers. (A whole number can be written as a decimal numeral by placing a decimal point to its right, with as many zeros added as needed. Thus, 7 becomes 7.0, or 7.00, etc.) The decimal point then "drops down" directly into the sum or difference; its position is not shifted.

Using the traditional algorithm for multiplying decimal numbers does *not* require aligning decimal points; the numbers to be multiplied can simply be arranged vertically, with right "justification." The numbers can then be multiplied as if they were whole numbers. The number of digits to the right of the decimal point in the product should equal the total number of digits to the right of the two factors. Here is an example:

$$\begin{array}{r} 1.64 \\ \underline{\times\ 0.3} \\ = 0.492 \end{array}$$

One method for dividing decimal numbers is to use the traditional whole number division algorithm, placing the decimal point properly in the answer. The number of digits to the right of the decimal point in the divisor is how far the decimal point in the quotient (the answer) should be moved to the right, with the decimal point in the dividend as our starting position. Here is an example:

$$\begin{array}{r} 4.8 \\ 0.3\overline{)1.44} \end{array}$$

Note that careful placement of digits when writing both the problem and the quotient help insure a correct answer.

The rules for performing operations on integers (whole numbers and their negative counterparts) and on fractions and decimal numbers where at least one is negative are generally the same as the rules for performing operations on non-negative numbers. The trick is to pay attention to the sign (the positive or negative value) of each answer. The rules for multiplication and division when at least one negative number is involved are the same: two positives or two negatives give a positive, whereas "mixing" a positive and a negative gives a negative ($-5 \times 3 = -15$, for instance). When adding or subtracting and at least one negative number is involved, it may be useful to think of the values as money, with "adding" being thought of as "gaining," "subtracting" being thought of as "losing," positive numbers being seen as "credits" and negative numbers, "debts." (Careful: Adding or "gaining" –8 is like *losing* 8.)

Sometimes, mathematical expressions indicate several operations. When simplifying such expressions, there is a universally agreed-upon order for "doing" each operation. First we compute any multiplication or division, left to right. Then, compute any addition or subtraction, also left to right. (If an expression contains any parentheses, all computation within the parentheses must be completed first.) Treat exponential expressions ("powers") as multiplication. Thus, the expression $3 + 7 \times 4 - 2$ equals 29. (Multiply 7 by 4 *before* doing the addition and subtraction.)

Exponential notation is a way to show repeated multiplication more simply. $2 \times 2 \times 2$, for instance, can be shown as 2^3, and is equal to 8. (Note: 2^3 does *not* mean 2×3.)

Scientific notation provides a method for showing any numbers using exponents (although it is most useful for very large and very small numbers.) A number is in scientific notation when it is shown as a number between 1 and 10 times a power of 10. Thus, the number 75,000 in scientific notation is shown as 7.5×10^4.

Other common mathematical notation symbols include the following.

< means "less than"
> means "greater than"
≠ means "not equal to"

Word Problems

The key to converting word problems into mathematical problems is attention to *reasonableness*, with the choice of operations most crucial to success. Often, individual words and phrases translate into numbers and operations symbols, and making sure that the translations are reasonable is important. Consider this word problem:

> Roberto babysat for the Yagers one evening. They paid him $5 just for coming over to their house, plus $7 for every hour of sitting. How much was he paid if he babysat for 4 hours?

"Plus" indicates addition, and "for every hour" suggests multiplication. Thus, the computational work can be set up like this: $5 + (7 \times 4) =$ Roberto's earnings. It would have been unreasonable to use a multiplication symbol in place of the addition sign. He earned $5 *plus* $7 for each of 4 hours.

Each word problem requires an individual approach, but keeping in mind the reasonableness of the computational setup should be helpful. (See more on this topic further in this review, "Solving word problems involving one and two variables.")

Probability and Data Analysis

Probability

Some studies have shown that, out of the hundreds of tornadoes that touch down every year, about 6 out of 10 strike between 2 PM and 8 PM. This fact can be expressed by saying that the ***probability*** that a tornado will touch down between 2 PM and 8 PM is about $\frac{6}{10}$.

Observed data often result from some random phenomenon, which is called a **random experiment**. A random experiment, such as observing whether or not a person with a kidney transplant survives five years, can be repeated over and over. For example, if 72 out of 100 kidney transplant recipients survive five years, then the probability that a kidney transplant patient will survive five years or more could be estimated at around $\frac{72}{100}$ = 0.72. Of course, if another 100 kidney recipients are sampled, the observed survival rate would likely differ, perhaps $\frac{76}{100}$. Such estimates ($\frac{72}{100}$ and $\frac{76}{100}$) vary from sample to sample: They are random.

To model a random experiment, we can list all the possible outcomes. For example, 1, 2, 3, 4, 5, and 6 is the list of all possible results of throwing a die once. Then the **experimental probability of an outcome** of an experiment is the fraction of times (often thought of as the "percentage of the time") the outcome occurs in a series of independent repetitions. For example, if you roll a die eight times and it comes up 1 three times, the experimental probability of the outcome "1" is $\frac{3}{8}$ for that experiment. It would presumably be different for different experiments with the same die, unless the die is not a fair one.

The **theoretical probability of an outcome** is the number that the experimental probability of the outcome approaches as the number of repetitions of the random experiment gets large. The larger the number of repetitions, the closer the experimental probability is likely to be to the theoretical probability. Thus, for practical purposes, when the number of repetitions is very large, we can treat the experimental probability we obtain as the theoretical probability. Usually, we refer to a theoretical probability simply as a **probability**. We often find it by figuring out how many equally likely outcomes there are. For example, we would expect a die to land on "1" about $\frac{1}{6}$ of the time if is thrown, say, 1,000 times. In fact, $\frac{1}{6}$ is the theoretical probability for each of the numbers 1 through 6. Likewise, the theoretical probability that a coin will land up is $\frac{1}{2}$ = .5, because there are two possible outcomes, both equally likely (we think).

Similarly, suppose that there are seven balls in a box, all of the same shape and texture. Four of the balls are red, two are green, and one is blue. What is the probability that the first ball drawn by a blindfolded person will be green? The answer is $\frac{2}{7}$, because any one of the seven balls is likely to be taken, but only two are green.

Figuring the theoretical probability that multiple events will occur is a bit more complicated, but still fairly easy. Here is the general rule:

- If you want to know the probability that event A *or* event B will occur, add the probabilities of A and B.

- If you want to know whether event A *and* event B will *both* occur, multiply the probability of A times the probability of B.

In the seven-ball example, what is the probability that you will draw either a red ball or a green ball on the first draw? The answer is $\frac{4}{7} + \frac{2}{7} = \frac{6}{7}$. What is the probability that you will draw a red ball and a green ball on two successive draws, assuming the first ball drawn is put back into the box? The answer is $\frac{4}{7} \times \frac{2}{7} = \frac{8}{49}$—which, as you can see, is much lower than $\frac{6}{7}$. Remember that this number is the probability that you will draw a red ball followed by a green ball.

If you have trouble understanding this calculation, look at the following list of all 49 possible outcomes of two draws, in which r1–r4 stand for the red balls, g1–g2 for the green, and b1 for the blue:

(r1,g1), (r1,g2), (r1,r1), (r1,r2), (r1,r3), (r1,r4), (r1,b1), (r2,g1), (r2,g2), (r2,r1), (r2,r2), (r2,r3), (r2,r4), (r2,b1), (r3,g1), (r3,g2), (r3,r1), (r3,r2), (r3,r3), (r3,r4), (r3,b1), (r4,g1), (r4,g2), (r4,r1), (r4,r2), (r4,r3), (r4,r4), (r4,b1), (g1,g1), (g1,g2), (g1,r1), (g1,r2), (g1,r3), (g1,r4), (g1,b1), (g2,g1), (g2,g2), (g2,r1), (g2,r2), (g2,r3), (g2,r4), (g2,b1), (b1,g1), (b1,g2), (b1,r1), (b1,r2), (b1,r3), (b1,r4), (b1,b1)

Simply count the pairs that satisfy the conditions; you'll find exactly 8 of the 49 do.

Sometimes you can have a combination of these two types of problems. What if we want to know the probability of drawing a red ball and a green ball, regardless of the order we draw them in? This probability is

$$\left(\frac{4}{7} \times \frac{2}{7}\right) + \left(\frac{2}{7} \times \frac{4}{7}\right) = \frac{8}{49} + \frac{8}{49} = 16/49$$

The first product in parentheses represents the chance of drawing first a red, then a green, ball, and the second represents drawing first a green, then a red, ball. Added together, they give you the probability that the two will be drawn regardless of order. (If necessary, use the list of possible outcomes above to satisfy yourself that exactly 16 of the 49 outcomes meet the requirement.)

What if we do not replace the red ball after drawing it? What then will be our probability of drawing a red and green ball in order? The chance of drawing a red ball on the first try is still $\frac{4}{7}$, but the chance of drawing a green ball on the second draw goes up to $\frac{2}{6}$, because now there are only six balls left. The probability of drawing red followed by green, *without replacement*, is $\frac{4}{7} \times \frac{2}{6} = \frac{4}{21}$, which is somewhat higher than the $\frac{8}{49}$ chance *with replacement*.

Interpret Information from Graphs, Tables, or Charts

Graphs, tables, and charts come in many different forms; most simply represent numerical data in neat visual formats. A bar graph, like the one below, typically shows "how much" for each of many categories (or persons, or time periods, or whatever).

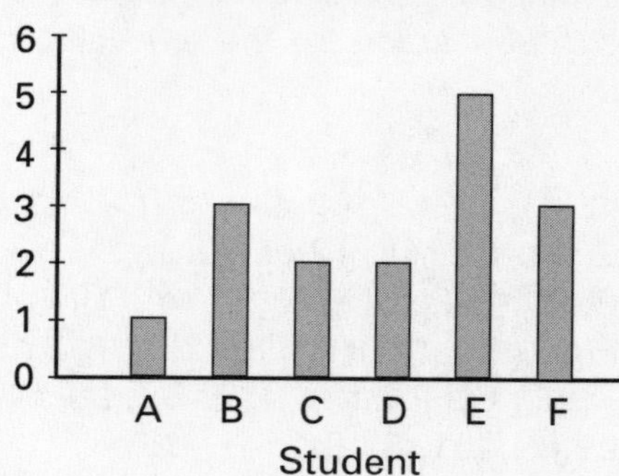

Broken line graphs, like the one below, are reserved for indicating *change over time*. Do not use broken line graphs unless one of the axes (usually the bottom or horizontal axis) indicates time. *Trends* are often revealed by broken line graphs.

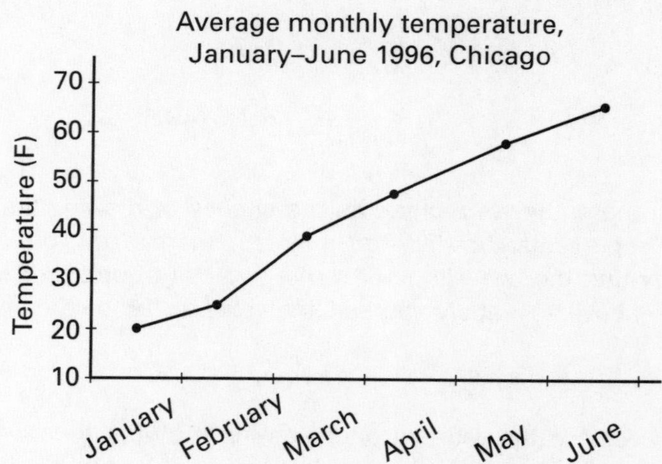

Pie graphs (also known as circle graphs or pie charts) often show how finite quantities are "split up." As with the example below, pie graphs may not necessarily be accompanied by specific numeric values. They are especially good for showing relative amounts or allotments at a glance.

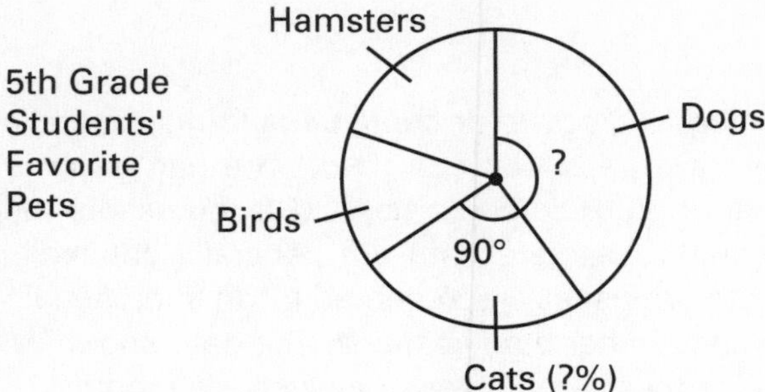

Because pie graphs are circles, the angle formed at the center by the boundaries of each catagory can be determined from the fact that the circle contains 360°. For example, if dogs are the favorite pets of 40% of fifth graders, what is the central angle? (**Answer:** 40% × 360° = .4 × 360° = 144°.) If the central angle of the "Cats" portion of the graph is 90°, what percentage of fifth graders prefer cats? (**Answer:** 90/360 = 1/4 = 25%.)

The graphs of *functions* can be shown on the coordinate plane. Such graphs always indicate a continuous (although not necessarily consistent) "movement" from left to right. Below left is the graph of a function; the graph on the right is *not* a function.

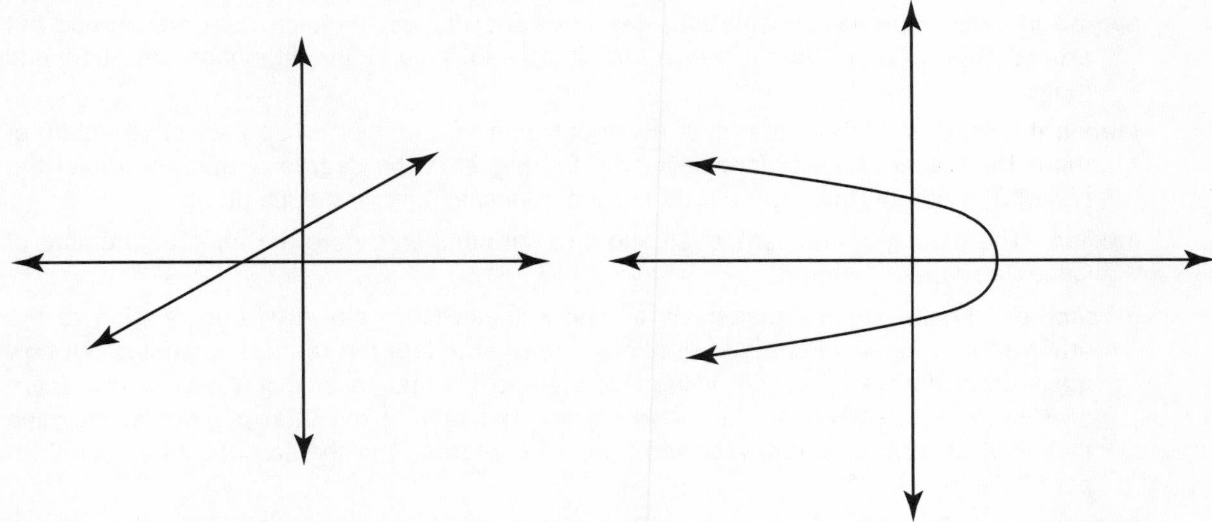

A key to interpretation of graphs, tables, and charts is to pay close attention to labels. Specific axis labels are also important. Don't assume anything about what a graph, table, or chart might be saying without carefully reading all labeled elements.

Statistical Concepts

The term *data* refers to numerical information acquired by counting or measuring. The number of students in a class, their test scores on the WEST–B, and their individual heights are all examples of data.

Data can be represented in *discrete* or *continuous* form, depending on what they represent. If data are discrete, they have gaps between them. The bar graph is a common way to depict discrete data. For example, the bar graph on page 102 represents the number of books read by each of six separate students. Discrete data are generally obtained from counting rather than measuring. Continuous data are usually represented by an unbroken line on a graph, and they are usually obtained by measuring rather than counting. The data shown in the graph at the bottom of 102 are continuous because there are no gaps between the months.

Here is a list of other statistical concepts that you might have to know for the test:

mean The mean is the sum of a set of numbers divided by the quantity of numbers n in the set. It gives the *average value* of a data set.

range The range is the measure of spread (*variation*) that is the difference between the largest value and the smallest value in a set of data.

sample survey This is a survey of a population, usually human, made by taking a sample judged to be representative of the population. Use of a random mechanism for choosing the sample is essential for validity and believability.

spread of data Spread, or **variation**, describes the degree to which data are spread out around their center. Useful measures of spread include the standard deviation and range.

standard deviation This is the most commonly used expression of spread, or variation, of data. The higher the standard deviation, the higher is the degree of spread around the center of the data (that is, the data are more inconsistent with each other).

median The median is the center value in a set of numbers: there are an equal number of values above and below it.

percentiles These are the measures of where a piece of data stands in relation to the other data in its set. Perhaps best known from standardized tests, percentiles tell how many other data are lower in value. For instance, a test taker might have a raw score of 82% (that is, 82% of the answers correct) but rank in the 91st percentile, meaning that 90% of all test takers received lower raw scores. The median occurs at the 50th percentile.

frequency distributions These represent the probability that a statistic of interest will fall in a certain interval; for example, the height of a person chosen at random may follow the *normal distribution*. Following are some samples of kinds of distributions, with location of the means and medians indicated:

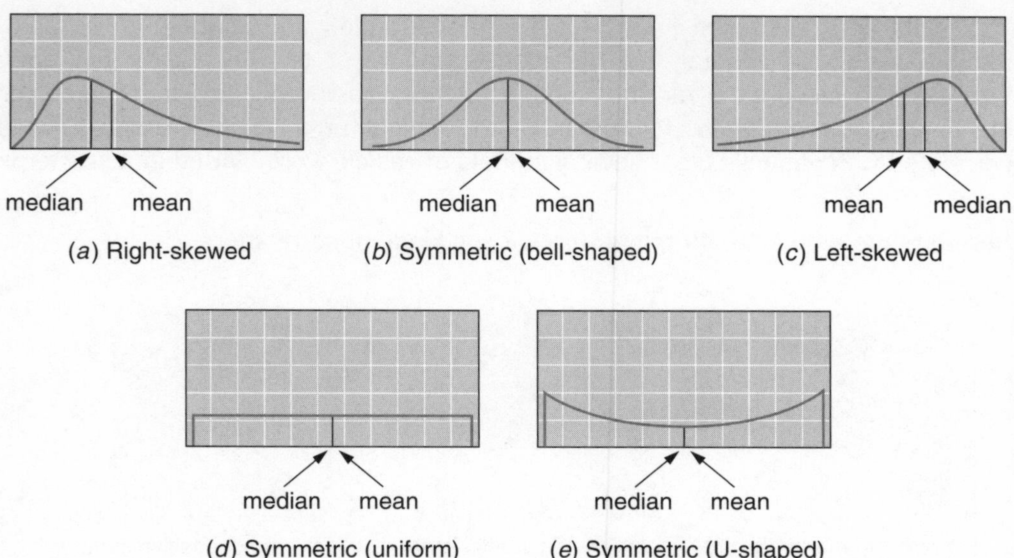

(*a*) Right-skewed (*b*) Symmetric (bell-shaped) (*c*) Left-skewed

(*d*) Symmetric (uniform) (*e*) Symmetric (U-shaped)

Distribution (*b*) in the figure is the famous normal, or bell-shaped, curve on which tests are often said to be graded. Notice that more scores fall in the middle here than on the high or low ends. In the right-skewed distribution, shown in (*a*), more of the scores are low, and in (*c*) more of the scores are high (assuming that all of these graphs represent test scores). The distribution in (*d*) shows that all scores are distributed equally from high to low, and (*e*) shows a distribution in which most scores were either high or low, with very few being average. Notice that in (*a*), the right-skewed distribution, the mean is higher than the median, and in (*c*) the median is higher than the mean.

correlation Correlation is the relationship between two variables. For example, a graph of tar and nicotine in cigarettes might look like this:

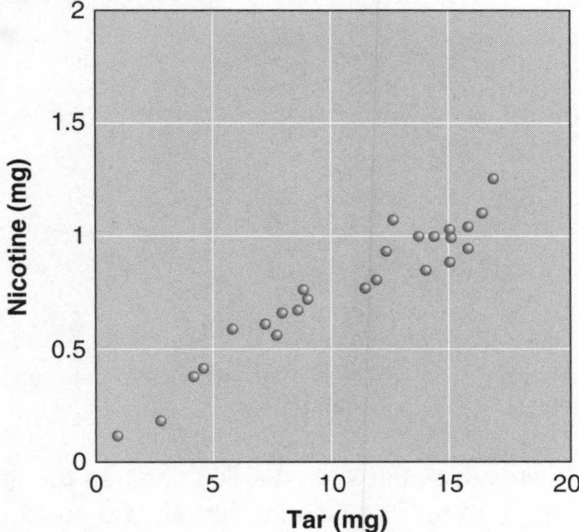

Each dot represents a particular cigarette, and the placement of the dot depends on the amounts of its tar (*x*-axis) and nicotine (*y*-axis). Drawings like this are called *scatterplots*.

You could draw a straight line through this scatterplot, and it would go up and to the right, because, in general, the higher the amount of tar, the higher the amount of nicotine. The amounts of tar and nicotine are thus *positively correlated.* Some variables are *negatively correlated*; for instance, the weight of a vehicle would be negatively correlated with gas mileage if several models of vehicle were plotted in a scatterplot.

Here are some other scatterplots with varying kinds of correlation:

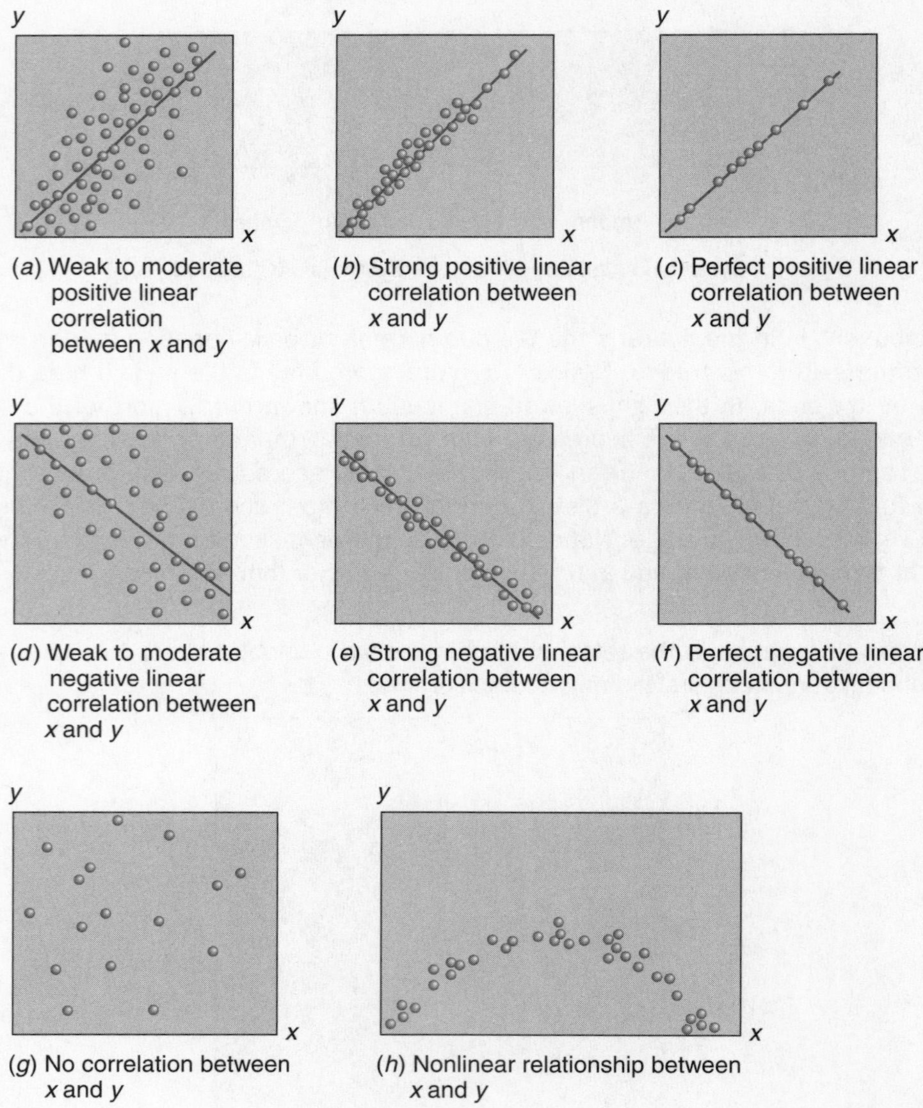

(*a*) Weak to moderate positive linear correlation between *x* and *y*

(*b*) Strong positive linear correlation between *x* and *y*

(*c*) Perfect positive linear correlation between *x* and *y*

(*d*) Weak to moderate negative linear correlation between *x* and *y*

(*e*) Strong negative linear correlation between *x* and *y*

(*f*) Perfect negative linear correlation between *x* and *y*

(*g*) No correlation between *x* and *y*

(*h*) Nonlinear relationship between *x* and *y*

When a correlation is linear or almost linear, you can use the graph to make predictions. For example, in the graph of tar and nicotine above, you could predict with a fair amount of certainty that a cigarette with 10 mg of tar would have between 0.7 and 0.8 mg of nicotine. In scatterplots without a linear correlation [(*g*) and (*h*) above], it's much harder to predict what *y* would be given *x*; in fact, in graph (*g*) it's nearly impossible.

Algebraic Graphing, Equations, and Operations

Two-Dimensional Graphing

The coordinate plane is useful for graphing individual ordered pairs and relationships. The coordinate plane is divided into four quadrants by an *x*-axis (horizontal) and a *y*-axis (vertical). The upper right quadrant is quadrant I, and the others (moving counterclockwise from quadrant I) are II, III, and IV.

Ordered pairs indicate the locations of points on the plane. For instance, (–3, 4) describes a point that's three units *left* from the center of the plane (the "origin") and four units *up*, as shown below.

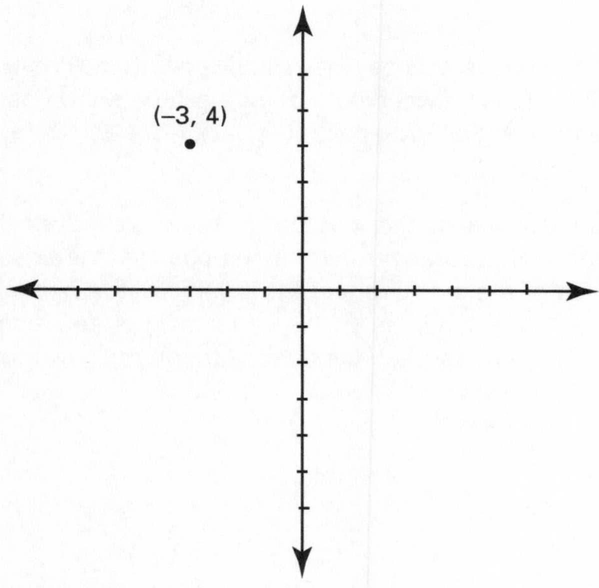

Sets of data can be paired to form many ordered pairs, which in turn can be graphed on the coordinate plane. Consider the following sets of data, which have been paired:

x	*y*
3	5
4	6
5	7
6	8

Considering each pairing individually, the following ordered pairs are produced: (3, 5), (4, 6), (5, 7), (6, 8). *Plotting* each pair on the coordinate plane produces the following graph:

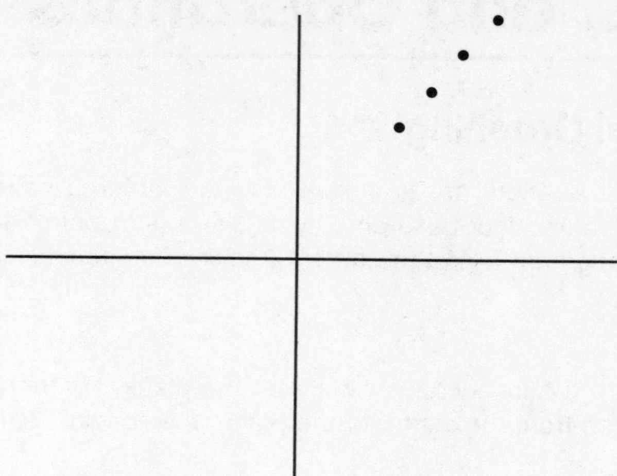

If the sets represent continuous change, the resulting graph may be a line (straight or curved in various ways). Often, relationships between sets of data can be shown as two variable equations or inequalities. Consider the following ordered pairs: (–4, –2), (–2, –1), (0, 0), (2, 1), (4, 2).

Note that the first value in each (the x value) is twice as big as the second (the y value). Assuming that the ordered pairs represent continuous change, the equation $x = 2y$ can be used to describe the relationship of the x values and the y values. It is helpful to think of the equation as stating that "x is always twice as big as y." We can show the equation on the coordinate plane by graphing at least two of the points, then connecting them as shown below.

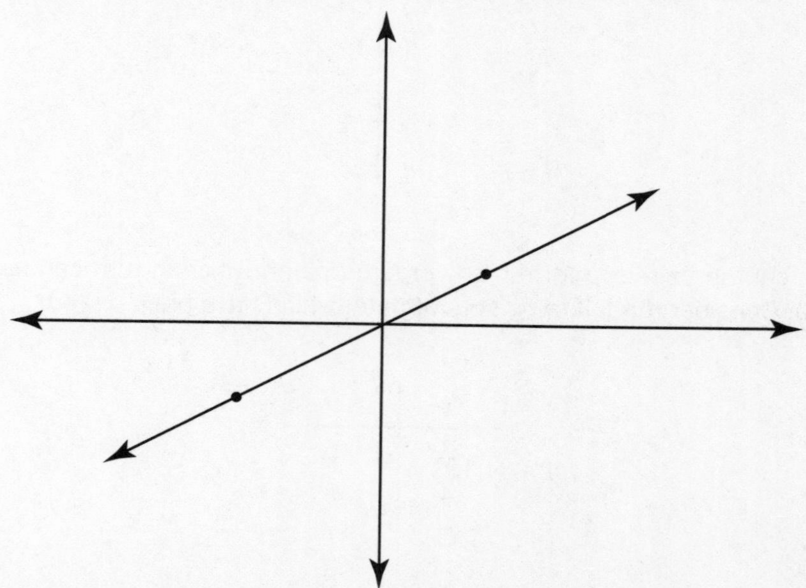

The generic equation $y = mx + b$ is a template for graphs on the plane that are straight lines. That form (sometimes called the "*y*-intercept form" of an equation) is especially useful because it tells two important characteristics of lines at a glance. The coefficient of x in the equation (or m) indicates the steepness, or *slope* of the line on the plane. The larger the absolute value of m, the steeper the slope of the line. (A number's absolute value is its distance from zero, giving no regard to negative signs.) Consider the two equations that follow and their accompanying graphs.

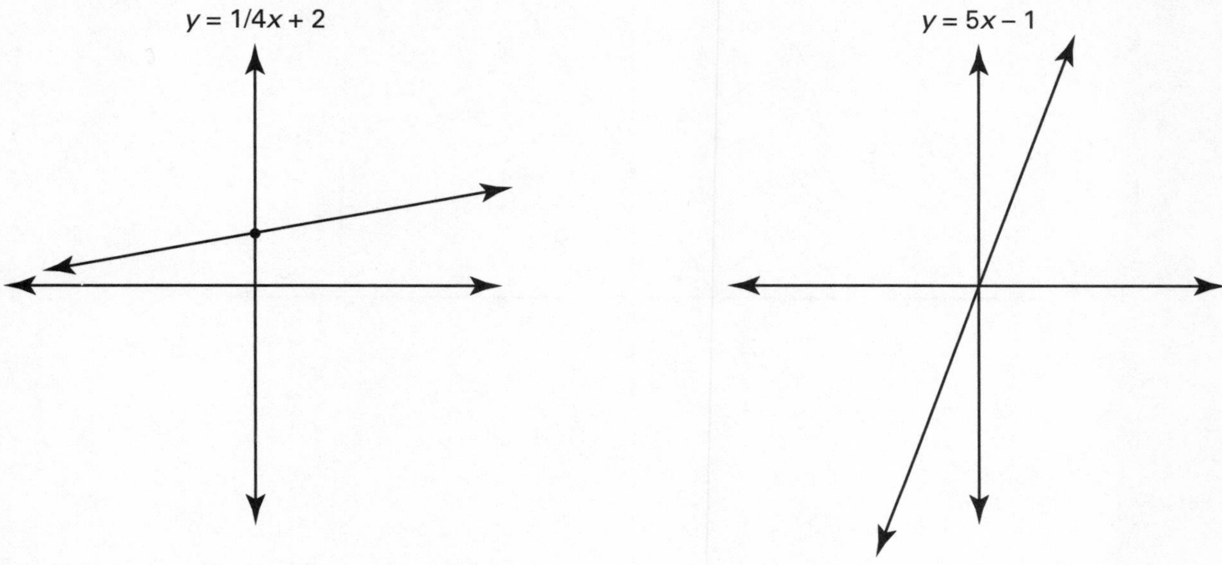

Note that the equation on the left has a small slope ($\frac{1}{4}$), so its graph is nearly horizontal. The other equation has a comparatively large slope (5), so it is steep.

If the coordinates of any two points of a straight line are known, the numerical slope of that line can easily be computed by finding the difference between the points' y values and dividing by the difference of the points' x values. For example, if (2, 5) and (4, 10) are points on a line, the slope of the line is $\frac{5}{2}$[(5 – 10) ÷ (2 – 4)]. Note that slopes are generally shown as fractions or whole numbers, but not as mixed fractions.

The equation of a straight line in the form $y = mx + b$ tells something else about the line at a glance. The b value indicates where the line will cross or *intercept* the y (vertical) axis. Consider the graph of $y = 2x + 3$ that follows.

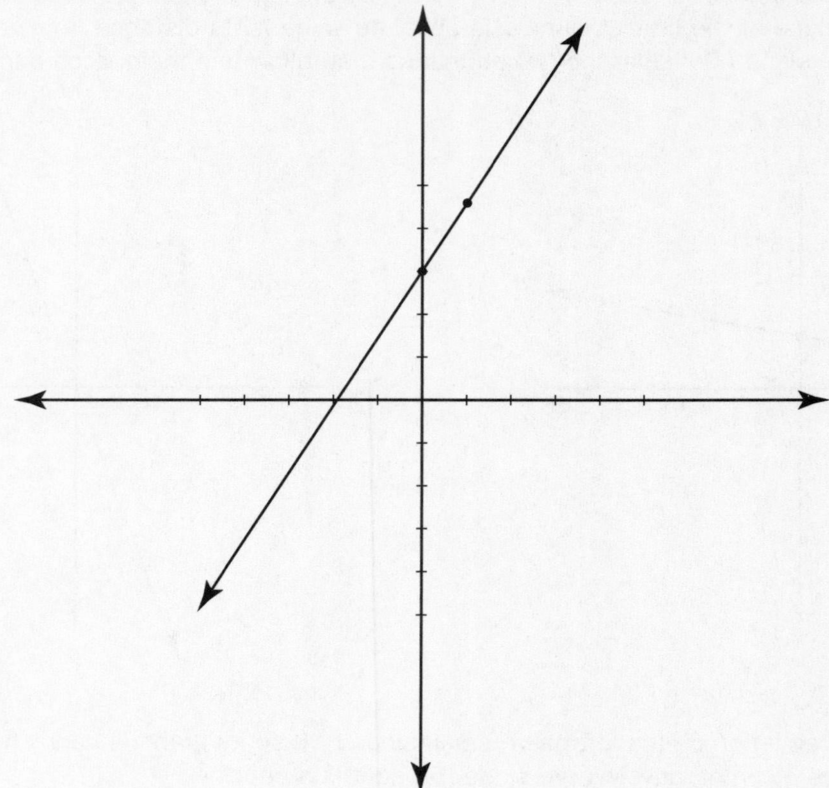

Note that the graph crosses the y-axis at a point that is 3 units above the origin. As long as the equation of a straight line is in the form $y = mx + b$, m gives the slope and b gives the y-intercept. (Note: If $b = 0$, the graph will pass through the origin. In that case, both the equation and the graph are referred to as *direct variations*.)

Other equations may produce curved graphs. For instance, $y = x^2$ produces the following graph, known as a *parabola*.

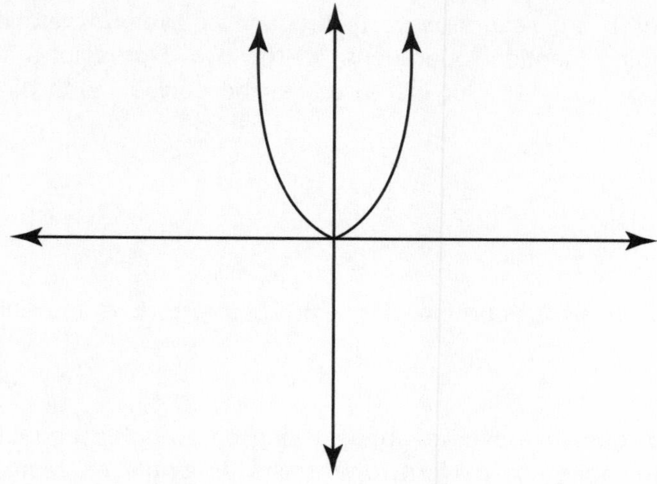

The equation $xy = 4$ is an *inverse variation*; it produces a graph known as a *hyperbola*, as shown below.

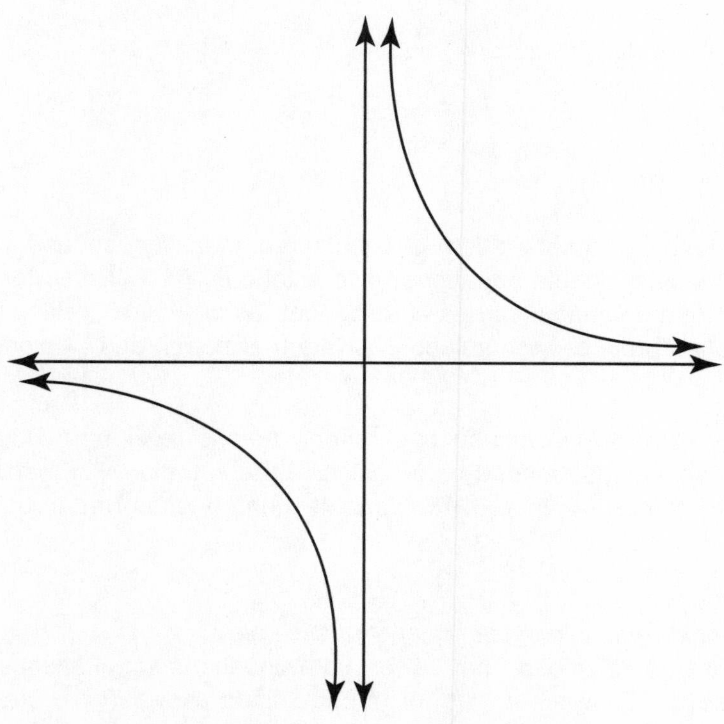

Solving One- and Two-Variable Equations

When attempting to solve one-variable equations, it is helpful to think of the task as that of producing a series of equivalent equations until, in the last equation, the variable has been *isolated* on one side. There are several ways to produce equivalent equations, but chiefly they are produced by performing identical operations on the two expressions making up the sides of equations. The equation $2x = 12$, for instance, can be solved by dividing both sides of the equation by 2, as follows:

$$\frac{2x}{2} = \frac{12}{2}$$

This then gives an equivalent equation of $x = 6$. Therefore, 6 is the solution to the original equation.

There are several caveats to observe when solving one-variable equations in that manner. One is that care must be taken to perform operations on *entire* expressions, and not simply on "parts" of expressions. In the example below, the last equation fails to give a solution to the original equation because, in the second step, only *part* of the expression $2x + 8$ has been divided by 2.

$$2x + 8 = 14$$
$$\frac{2x}{2} + 8 = \frac{14}{2}$$
$$x + 8 = 7$$
$$x = -1$$

Avoid dividing by zero. That operation is considered meaningless and will not provide a solution. Also, not all single-variable equations have solutions. $0x + 3 = 9$, for instance, has no real number solutions. If the variable carries an exponent, as in $x^2 = 16$, taking the square root of each side of the equation produces the solutions. (Note that *both* 4 and –4 work.)

"Solving one variable in terms of a second" simply means rewriting multivariable equations such that the desired variable is isolated on one side of the equation. For instance, the equation $x - 3y = 5$ can be rewritten as $x = 3y + 5$. The variable x has been solved in terms of the second variable y.

Solving a *system* of two-variable linear equations (such as $y = x + 6$ and $2y = 4x$) means finding the ordered pair (or pairs) of numbers that solves both equations simultaneously. Using trial and error, we can see that (6, 12) works in both of the equations above. There are also more formal methods for solving systems of two-variable equations. If we graph each equation on the coordinate plane, the point of intersection (if any) will give the solution to the system. Another method is to literally add or subtract one equation from the other, with the intention of eliminating one variable in the process, enabling us to solve for one variable, then the other. (One or both equations may first require multiplication in order to "line up" variables with opposite coefficients.) In the example that follows, the system of $y = x + 6$ and $2y = 4x$ has been solved using multiplication and addition.

$$y = x + 6$$
$$2y = 4x$$
$$-2y = -2x - 12$$
$$2y = 4x$$
$$0 = 2x - 12$$
$$x = 6$$

If $x = 6$, y must equal 12, so the solution to the system is (6, 12).

Solving Word Problems Involving One and Two Variables

One helpful approach when attempting to solve algebraic word problems is to *translate* the word problem into an equation (or, sometimes, an inequality), then solve the equation. Consider the word problem: "The Acme Taxicab Company charges riders 3 dollars just for getting into the cab, plus 2 dollars for every mile or fraction of a mile driven. What would be the fare for a 10-mile ride?" "Translating into math" we get $x = 3 + (2 \times 10)$. The equation can be read as "the unknown fare (x) is equal to 3 dollars *plus* 2 dollars for each of the 10 miles driven." Solving the equation gives 23 for x, so $23 is the solution to the word problem.

There are several common translations to keep in mind: The word *is* often suggests an equal sign; *of* may suggest multiplication, as does *product*. *Sum* refers to addition; *difference* suggests subtraction; and a *quotient* is obtained after dividing. The key when translating is to make sure that the equation accurately matches the information and relationships given in the word problem.

Understanding Operations with Algebraic Expressions

Only like (or similar) algebraic terms can be added or subtracted to produce simpler expressions. For instance, $3x^2$ and $5x^2$ can be added together to get $8x^2$, because the terms are like terms; they both have a base of x^2. We *cannot* add $8m^3$ and $6m^2$; m^3 and m^2 are unlike bases.

When multiplying exponential terms together, the constant terms are multiplied, but the exponents of terms with the same variable bases are *added* together, which is somewhat counterintuitive. For example, $5w^2$ times $2w^3$ gives $10w^5$ (*not* $10w^6$, as one might guess).

When like algebraic terms are divided, exponents are subtracted. For example,

$$\frac{7w^5}{2w^2}$$

becomes

$$\frac{7w^3}{2}$$

In algebra, we frequently need to multiply two binomials together. (*Binomials* are algebraic expressions of two terms.) The FOIL method is one way to multiply binomials. FOIL stands for "first, outer, inner, last." Multiply the first terms in the parentheses, then the "outermost" terms, followed by the "innermost terms," and finally the last terms, then add the products together. For example, to multiply $(x + 2)$ and $(3x - 1)$, we multiply x by $3x$ (the "firsts"), x by -1 ("outers"), 2 by $3x$ ("inners"), and 2 by -1 ("lasts"). The four products ($3x^2$, $-x$, $6x$ and -2) add up to $3x^2 + 5x - 2$. If the polynomials to be multiplied have more than two terms (*trinomials*, for instance), make sure that *each* term of the first polynomial is multiplied by *each* term of the second.

The opposite of polynomial multiplication is factoring. Factoring a polynomial means rewriting it as the product of factors (often two binomials). The trinomial $x^2 - 4x - 21$, for instance, can be factored into $(x + 3)(x - 7)$. (You can check this by "FOILing" the binomials.)

When attempting to factor polynomials, it is sometimes necessary to first "factor out" any factor that might be common to all terms. The two terms in $3x^2 - 12$, for example, both contain the factor 3. This means that the expression can be rewritten as $3(x^2 - 4)$, and then, $3(x - 2)(x + 2)$.

The task of factoring a polynomial is often aided by first setting up a pair of "empty" parentheses, like this: $2x^2 - 9x - 5 = (\qquad)(\qquad)$. The task is then to fill in the four spaces with values which, when multiplied (FOILed), will "give back" $2x^2 - 9x - 5$.

Factoring is useful when solving some equations, especially if one side of the equation is set equal to zero. Consider $x^2 + 3x - 8 = 2$. It can be rewritten as $x^2 + 3x - 10 = 0$. This allows the left side to be factored into $(x - 2)(x + 5)$, giving equation solutions of 2 and -5.

Geometry and Reasoning

Solving Problems Involving Geometric Figures

The following are formulas for finding the areas of basic polygons (informally defined as closed, coplanar geometric figures with three or more straight sides). Abbreviations used are as follows: A stands for *area*, l stands for *length*, w stands for *width*, h stands for *height*, and b stands for *length of the base*.

Triangle (a three-sided polygon): $A = \frac{b \times h}{2}$. (Note that, as shown in the figure that follows, the height of a triangle is not necessarily the same as the length of any of its sides.)

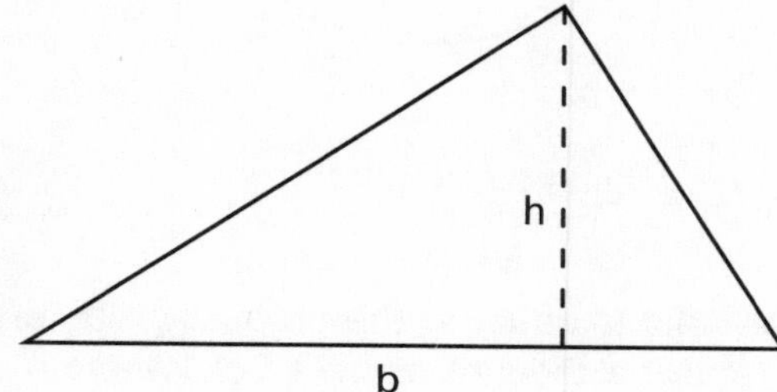

Rectangle (a four-sided polygon with four right angles): $A = l \times w$

Parallelogram (a four-sided polygon with two pairs of parallel sides): $A = l \times w$. (Note that, as with triangles, and as shown in the figure below, the height of a parallelogram is not necessarily the same as the length of its sides.)

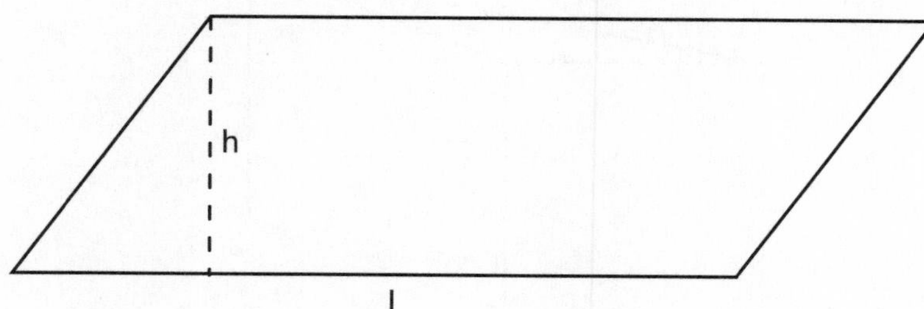

The area of a circle can be found by squaring the length of its radius, then multiplying that product by π. The formula is given as $A = \pi r^2$. (π, or pi, is the ratio of a circle's circumference to its diameter. The value of π is the same for all circles; approximately 3.14159. The approximation 3.14 is adequate for many calculations.) The approximate area of the circle shown below can be found by squaring 6 (giving 36), then multiplying 36 by 3.14, giving an area of about 113 square units.

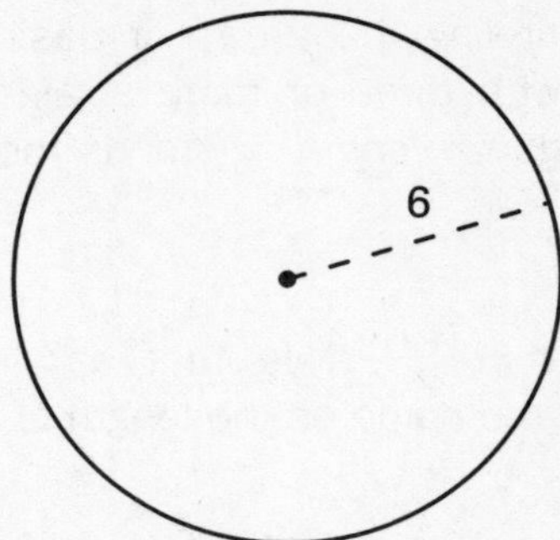

Here are several commonly used volume formulas:

The volume of a rectangular solid is equal to the product of its length, width, and height; $A = l \times w \times h$. (A rectangular solid can be thought of as a box, wherein all intersecting edges form right angles.)

A prism is a polyhedron with two congruent, parallel faces (called bases) and whose lateral (side) faces are parallelograms. The volume of a prism can be found by multiplying the area of the prism's base by its height. The volume of the triangular prism shown hereafter is 60 cubic units. (The area of the triangular base is 10 square units, and the height is 6 units.)

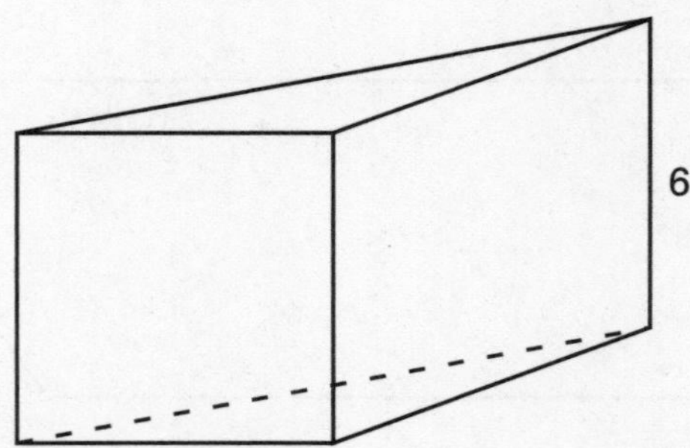

A cylinder is like a prism in that it has parallel faces, but its rounded "side" is smooth. The formula for finding the volume of a cylinder is the same as the formula for finding the volume of a prism: The area of the cylinder's base is multiplied by the height. The volume of the cylinder in the following figure is approximately 628 cubic units. ($5 \times 5 \times \pi \times 8$).

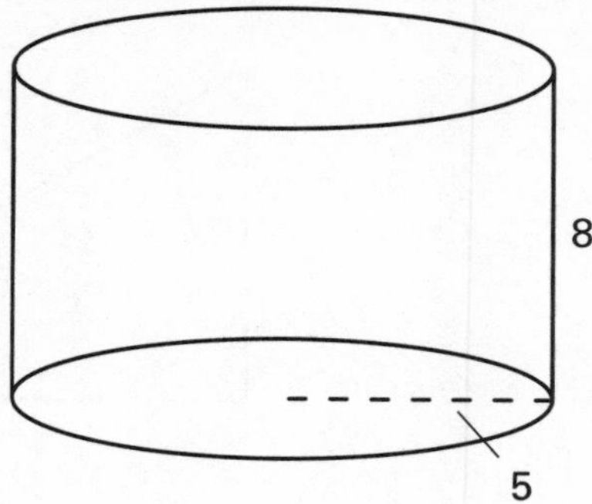

A property of all triangles is that the sum of the measures of the three angles is 180°. If, therefore, the measures of two angles are known, the third can be deduced using addition, then subtraction.

Right triangles (those with a right angle) have several special properties. A chief property is described by the Pythagorean Theorem, which states that in any right triangle with legs (shorter sides) *a* and *b*, and hypotenuse (the longest side) *c*, the sum of the squares of the sides will be equal to the square of the hypotenuse ($a^2 + b^2 = c^2$). Note that in the right triangle shown hereafter, $3^2 + 4^2 = 5^2$.

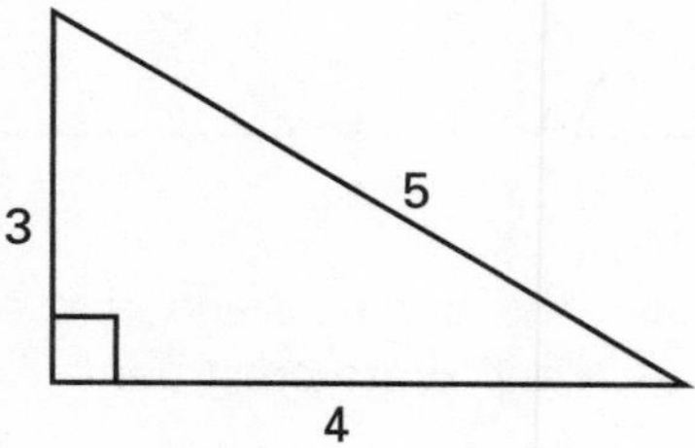

Applying Reasoning Skills

Geometric figures are *similar* if they have the exact same shapes, even if they do not have the same sizes. In transformational geometry, two figures are said to be similar if and only if a similarity transformation maps one figure onto the other. In the figure that follows, triangles A and B are similar.

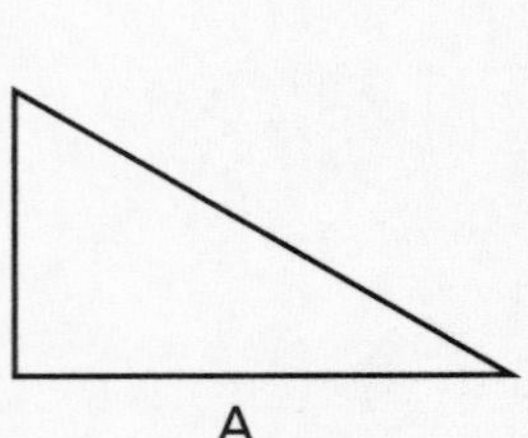
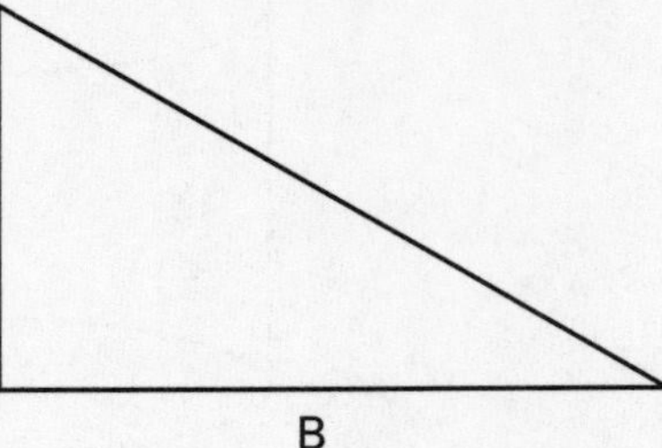

Corresponding angles of similar figures have the same measure, and the lengths of corresponding sides are proportional. In the similar triangles below, $\angle A \cong \angle D$ (meaning "angle *A* is congruent to angle *D*"), $\angle B \cong \angle E$, and $\angle C \cong \angle F$. The corresponding sides of the triangles below are proportional, meaning that:

$$\frac{AB}{DE} = \frac{BC}{EF} = \frac{CA}{FD}$$

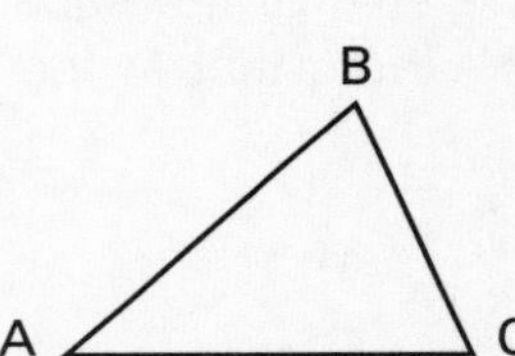
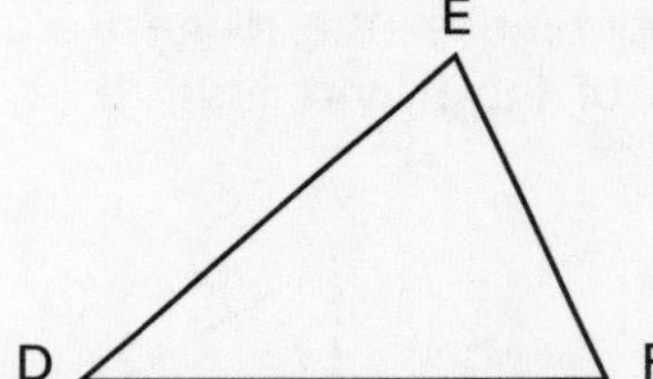

Figures are *congruent* if they have the same shape *and* size. (Congruent figures are also similar.) In the figure below, rectangles A and B are congruent.

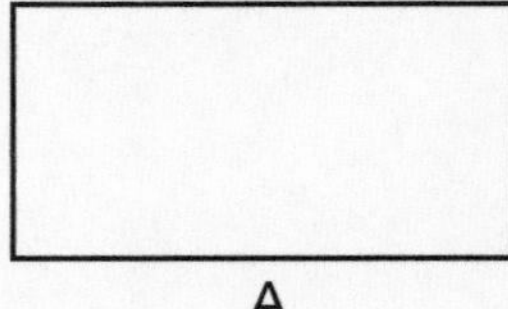
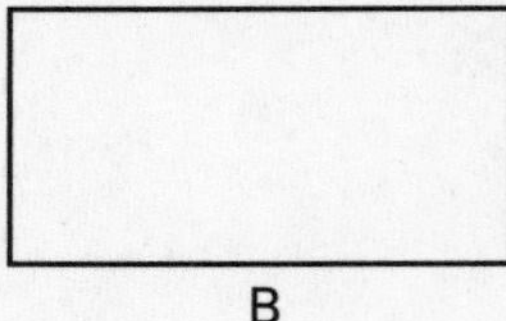

Straight lines within the same plane that have no points in common (that is, they never cross) are parallel lines. Note that the term *parallel* is used to describe the relationship between two coplanar lines that do not intersect. Lines that are not coplanar—although they never cross—are not considered to be parallel. Coplanar lines crossing at right angles (90°) are perpendicular.

When presented with math or logic problems, including geometry problems, *deductive reasoning* may be helpful. Deductive reasoning is reasoning from the general to the specific, and is supported by deductive logic. Here is an example of deductive reasoning:

> All humans who have walked on the moon are males (a general proposition). Neil Armstrong walked on the moon, therefore he is a male (a specific proposition.)

Note that conclusions reached via deductive reasoning are sound only if the original assumptions are actually true.

With *inductive* reasoning, a general rule is inferred from specific observations (which may be limited). Moving from the statement "All fish I have ever seen have fins" (specific but limited observations) to "All fish have fins" (a general proposition) is an example of inductive reasoning. Conclusions arrived at via inductive reasoning are not necessarily true.

An example of how logical reasoning can be used to solve a geometry problem is given hereafter. (In this case *deductive* reasoning is used to find the measure of ∠J.)

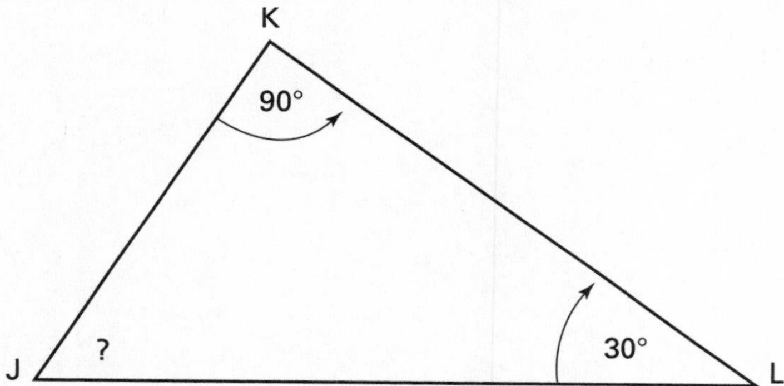

The sum of the measures of the three angles of any triangle is 180° (a general proposition). The sum of the measures of ∠K and ∠L is 120°, therefore the measure of ∠L is 60° (a specific proposition).

WEST–B

Washington Educator Skills Test–Basic

Practice Test

This Basic Skills practice test is also on CD-ROM in our special interactive WEST–B TEST*ware*®. It is highly recommended that you first take this test on computer. You will then have the additional study features and benefits of enforced time conditions and instant scoring. See page x for guidance on how to get the most out of our WEST–B book and software.

General Directions

Time Allotted for the Test: 4½ hours

This practice test contains three subtests: Reading, Mathematics, and Writing. The Reading and Mathematics subtests contain only multiple-choice questions. The Writing Subtest contains multiple-choice questions and two writing prompts, each requiring a written response.

The sections of the answer document correspond to the subtests. Be sure the answers to the subtests are recorded in the corresponding section of the answer document.

Each multiple-choice question has four answer choices. Read each question carefully and choose the ONE best answer. Record your answer on the answer document in the space that corresponds to the question number. Completely fill in the circle having the same letter as the answer you have chosen. *Use only a No. 2 pencil.*

Sample Question:

1. What is the capital of Washington?

   A. Seattle

   B. Spokane

   C. Olympia

   D. Walla Walla

The correct answer to this questions is C. You would indicate that on the answer document as follows:

1. Ⓐ Ⓑ ● Ⓓ

Try to answer all questions. In general, if you have some knowledge about a question, it is better to try to answer it. You will NOT be penalized for guessing.

The Writing subtest contains both multiple-choice questions and two writing prompts. You must respond to BOTH writing prompts. Directions for completing the written responses appear immediately before the writing prompts. You should allow approximately 20 minutes for EACH writing response.

Practice Subtest: Reading

Read the passage below; then answer the five questions that follow.

WATER

The most important source of sediment is earth and rock material carried to the sea by rivers and streams; glaciers and winds may also have transported the same materials. Other sources are volcanic ash and lava, shells and skeletons of organisms, chemical precipitates formed in seawater, and particles from outer space.

Water is a most unusual substance because it exists on the surface of the Earth in its three physical states: ice, water, and water vapor. There are other substances that exist in a solid and liquid or gaseous state at temperatures normally found at the Earth's surface, but there are fewer substances that occur in all three states.

Water is odorless, tasteless, and colorless. It is the only substance known to exist in a natural state as a solid, liquid, or gas on the surface of the Earth. It is a universal solvent. Water does not corrode, rust, burn, or separate into its components easily. It is chemically indestructible. It can corrode almost any metal and erode the most solid rock. A unique property of water is that, when frozen in its solid state, it expands and floats on water. Water has a freezing point of 0°C and a boiling point of 100°C. Water has the capacity to absorb great quantities of heat with relatively little increase in temperature. When *distilled*, water is a poor conductor of electricity but when salt is added, it is a good conductor of electricity.

Sunlight is the source of energy for temperature change, evaporation, and currents for water movement through the atmosphere. Sunlight controls the rate of photosynthesis for all marine plants, which are directly or indirectly the source of food for all marine animals. Migration, breeding, and other behaviors of marine animals are affected by light.

Water, as the ocean or sea, is blue because of the molecular scattering of the sunlight. Blue light, being of short wavelength, is scattered more effectively than light of longer wavelengths. Variations in color may be caused by particles suspended in the water, water depth, cloud cover, temperature, and other variable factors. Heavy concentrations of dissolved materials cause a yellowish hue, while algae will cause the water to look green. Heavy populations of plant and animal materials will cause the water to look brown.

1. Which of the following lists of topics best organizes the information in the selection?

A. I. Water as vapor
II. Water as ice
III. Water as solid

B. I. Properties of seawater
II. Freezing and boiling points of water
III. Photosynthesis
IV. Oceans and seas

C. I. Water as substance
II. Water's corrosion
III. Water and plants
IV. Water and algae coloration

D. I. Water's physical states
II. Properties of water
III. Effects of the sun on water
IV. Reasons for color variation in water

2. According to the passage, what is the most unique property of water?

A. Water is odorless, tasteless, and colorless.

B. Water exists on the surface of the Earth in three physical states.

C. Water is chemically indestructible.

D. Water is a poor conductor of electricity.

3. Which of the following best defines the word *distilled* as it is used in the last sentence of the third paragraph?

A. Free of salt content

B. Free of electrical energy

C. Dehydrated

D. Containing wine

4. The writer's main purpose in this selection is to

A. explain the colors of water.

B. examine the effects of the sun on water.

C. define the properties of water.

D. describe the three physical states of all liquids.

5. The writer of this selection would most likely agree with which of the following statements?
   A. The properties of water are found in most other liquids on this planet.
   B. Water should not be consumed in its most natural state.
   C. Water might be used to serve many different functions.
   D. Water is too unpredictable for most scientists.

Read the passage below; then answer the five questions that follow.

THE BEGINNINGS OF THE SUBMARINE

A submarine was first used as a military weapon during the American Revolutionary War. The *Turtle*, a one-man submersible designed by an American named David Bushnell and hand-operated by a screw propeller, attempted to sink a British warship in New York Harbor. The plan was to attach a charge of gunpowder to the ship's bottom with screws and explode it with a time fuse. After repeated failures to force the screws through the copper sheathing of the hull of the H.M.S. *Eagle*, the submarine gave up and withdrew, exploding its powder a short distance from the *Eagle*. Although the attack was unsuccessful, it caused the British to move their blockading ships from the harbor to the outer bay.

On February 17, 1864, a Confederate craft, a hand-propelled submersible carrying a crew of eight men, sank a Federal corvette that was blockading Charleston Harbor. The hit was accomplished by a torpedo suspended ahead of the Confederate *Hunley* as she rammed the Union frigate *Housatonic*, and is the first recorded instance of a submarine sinking a warship.

The submarine first became a major component in naval warfare during World War I, when Germany demonstrated its full potential. The wholesale sinking of Allied supply ships by the German U-boats almost swung the war in favor of the Central Powers. Then, as now, the submarine's greatest advantage was that it could operate beneath the ocean's surface where detection was difficult. Sinking a submarine was comparatively easy, once it was found—but finding it before it could attack was another matter.

During the closing months of World War I, the Allied Submarine Devices Investigation Committee was formed to obtain from science and technology more effective underwater detection equipment. The committee developed a reasonably accurate device for locating a submerged submarine. This device was a trainable hydrophone, which was attached to the bottom of the ASW ship, and used to detect screw noises and other sounds that came from a submarine. Although the committee disbanded after World War I, the British made improvements on the locating device during the interval between the World Wars, and named it ASDIC after the committee.

American scientists further improved on the device, calling it SONAR, a name derived from letters in the words *so*und *na*vigation *r*anging.

At the end of World War II, the United States improved the snorkel (a device for bringing air to the crew and engines when operating submerged on diesels) and developed the Guppy (short for greater underwater propulsion power), a conversion of the fleet-type submarine of World War II fame. Reducing the surface area, streamlining every protruding object, and enclosing the periscope shears in a streamlined metal fairing changed the superstructure. Performance increased greatly with improved electronic equipment, additional battery capacity, and the addition of the snorkel.

6. The passage implies that one of the most pressing modifications needed for the submarine was to

   A. streamline its shape.

   B. enlarge the submarine for accommodating more torpedoes and men.

   C. reduce the noise caused by the submarine.

   D. add a snorkel.

7. It is inferred that

   A. ASDIC was formed to obtain technology for underwater detection.

   B. ASDIC developed an accurate device for locating submarines.

   C. the hydrophone was attached to the bottom of the ship.

   D. ASDIC was formed to develop technology to defend U.S. shipping.

8. SONAR not only picked up the sound of submarines moving through the water but also

   A. indicated the speed at which the sub was moving.

   B. gave the location of the submarine.

   C. indicated the speed of the torpedo.

   D. placed the submarine within a specified range.

9. According to the passage, the submarine's success was due in part to its ability to

   A. strike and escape undetected.

   B. move more swiftly than other vessels.

   C. submerge to great depths while being hunted.

   D. run silently.

10. From the passage, one can infer that

    A. David Bushnell was indirectly responsible for the sinking of the Federal corvette in Charleston Harbor.

    B. David Bushnell invented the *Turtle*.

    C. the *Turtle* was a one-man submarine.

    D. the *Turtle* sank the USS *Housatonic* on February 18, 1864.

Read the passage below; then answer the five questions that follow.

IMMIGRATION

The influx of immigrants that America had been experiencing slowed during the conflicts with France and England, but the flow increased between 1815 and 1837, when an economic downturn sharply reduced their numbers. Thus, the overall rise in population during these years was due more to incoming foreigners than to a natural, domestically derived increase. Most of the newcomers were from Britain, Germany, and southern Ireland. The Germans usually fared best, since they brought more money and more skills. Discrimination was common in the job market, primarily directed against the Catholics. "Irish Need Not Apply" signs were common. However, the persistent labor shortage prevented the natives from totally excluding the foreign elements. These newcomers huddled in ethnic neighborhoods in the cities, or those who could moved on Westward to try their hand at farming.

In 1790, five percent of the U.S. population lived in cities of 2,500 or more. By 1860, that figure had risen to 25%. This rapid urbanization created an array of problems.

SOURCES OF IMMIGRATION, 1820–1840

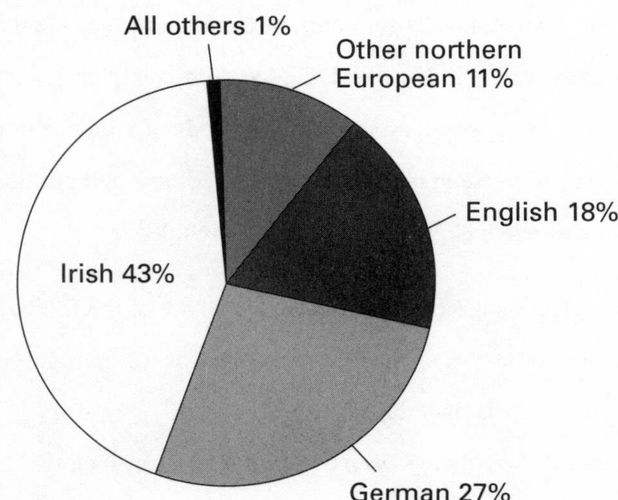

The rapid growth in urban areas was not matched by the growth of services. Clean water, trash removal, housing, and public transportation all lagged behind, and the wealthy got them first. Bad water and poor sanitation produced poor health, and epidemics of typhoid fever, typhus, and cholera were common. Police and fire protection were usually inadequate and the development of professional forces was resisted because of the cost and the potential for political patronage and corruption.

Rapid growth helped to produce a wave of violence in the cities. In New York City in 1834, the Democrats fought the Whigs with such vigor that the state militia had to be called in. New York and Philadelphia witnessed race riots in the mid-1830s, and a New York mob sacked a Catholic convent in 1834. In the 1830s, 115 major incidents of mob violence were recorded. Street crime was common in all major cities.

11. The author's purpose in writing this essay is

    A. to bring to light the poor treatment of immigrants.

    B. to show the violent effects of overpopulation.

    C. to trace the relationship of immigration to the problems of rapid urban growth.

    D. to dissuade an active life in big cities.

12. Which of the following best defines the word *sacked* as it is used in the last paragraph?

    A. robbed

    B. carried

    C. trespassed on

    D. vandalized

13. Which of the following statements best summarizes the main idea of the fourth paragraph?

    A. Racial tensions caused riots in New York City and Philadelphia.

    B. The rapid growth in urban population sowed the seeds of violence in U.S. cities.

    C. Street crimes were far worse in urban areas than race riots and political fights.

    D. The state militia was responsible for curbing urban violence.

14. Ideas presented in the selection are most influenced by which of the following assumptions?

    A. Urban life was more or less controllable before the flow of immigration in 1820.

    B. The British had more skills than the Irish.

    C. Ethnic neighborhoods had always been a part of American society.

    D. France and England often held conflicts.

15. According to the graph, from 1820 to 1840
    A. there were more Irish immigrants than all other nationalities combined.
    B. the combined number of immigrants from England and Germany exceeded those from Ireland.
    C. one percent of American immigrants were from Italy.
    D. there were an equal number of English and German immigrants.

Read the passage below; then answer the three questions that follow.

To receive an "A" on a paper in this class one must write sophisticated prose. The criteria will be based on the complexity of both content and expression. The grade will require a demonstration of obvious familiarity with primary texts, as well as additional readings of the course and secondary materials and research sources. An effective combination of personal opinion and outside sources will also be required. Proficiency in organizational skills, format, rhetoric, grammar, syntax, and sentence structure is a must. An additional requirement is a thoroughly proofread essay resulting in no distracting mechanical errors with the possible exception of occasional arguable usage.

16. To receive an "A" grade in the above class, the student must
    A. turn in a proofread paper with no punctuation errors and demonstrate an understanding of the reading material.
    B. write an effective paper without mistakes and with an abundance of secondary source materials.
    C. turn in a thoughtful paper with no corrections as well as demonstrate a proficiency of organizational skills, such as format, rhetoric, and grammar.
    D. write an intelligent paper without regard for grammar, syntax, or rhetorical strategies, with the possible exception of occasional arguable usage.

17. What does the author mean by "sophisticated prose"?
    A. A readable text that does not make sense.
    B. A readable text made up of knowledgeable or thoughtful language.
    C. A readable text consisting of pompous or ostentatious language.
    D. A readable text made up of poetic metaphor.

18. When the author of the passage refers to the "primary texts," he means
    A. the reference materials, such as the dictionary, encyclopedia, thesaurus, etc.
    B. the primary note pages, works cited page, or preliminary rough draft page.
    C. the source or principal text in the assignment.
    D. the first text written about a certain subject.

Read the passage below; then answer the four questions that follow.

Language not only expresses an individual's ideology, it also sets perimeters while it persuades and influences the discourse in the community that hears and interprets its meaning. Therefore, the language of failure should not be present in the learning environment (i.e., the classroom) because it will have a prohibitive impact on the students' desire to learn as well as a negative influence on the students' self-esteem. The *Oxford English Dictionary* defines *failure* as a fault, a shortcoming, a lack of success, a person who turns out unsuccessfully, becoming insolvent, etc. We as educators might well ask ourselves if this is the sort of doctrine that we want to permeate our classrooms. Perhaps our own University axiom, *mens agitat molem* (the mind can move mountains), will help us discover if, indeed, the concepts of failure are really the types of influences we wish to introduce to impressionable new students. Is the mind capable of moving a mountain when it is already convinced it cannot? One must remain aware that individuals acquire knowledge at independent rates of speed. Certainly no one would suggest that one infant "failed" the art of learning to walk because she acquired the skill two months behind her infant counterpart. Would anyone suggest that infant number one *failed* walking? Of course not. What would a mentor project to either toddler were he to suggest that a slower acquisition of walking skills implied failure? Yet we as educators feel the need to suggest student A failed due to the slower procurement of abstract concepts then student B. It is absolutely essential to shift the learning focus from failure to success.

19. Which of the following statements best conveys the meaning of the passage?

    A. Learning is something that happens at different speeds and is, therefore, natural.

    B. Instructors need to be sensitive to students' individual needs.

    C. Instructors need to shift the educational focus from failure to success in learning environments.

    D. Failure is a potential hazard in the classroom and should be avoided at all costs.

20. As stated in the context of the passage, what does University axiom mean?

    A. University Latin

    B. University motto

    C. University rhetoric

    D. University sophomore

21. According to the passage, what will have a negative effect on student self-esteem?

    A. The rhetoric of diction

    B. The slower procurement of abstract concepts

    C. The learning focus from failure to success

    D. The language of failure

22. According to the passage, what does language do besides aid individual expression?

    A. It establishes individual thought and tells of individual philosophies.

    B. It paints visual images and articulates individual declaration.

    C. It suggests individual axioms and community philosophy.

    D. It persuades and influences the discourse in the community that hears and interprets its meaning.

Read the passage below; then answer the three questions that follow.

Life in seventeenth-century England was tempestuous indeed. It was a time when religious and secular confrontations resulted in new social abstractions, paradoxes, and ironies. The poet-pastor Robert Herrick (1591–1674) illustrates the ability of lyric poetry to serve not only as an adornment of the era, but as social communiqué, as well. Herrick's Mayday celebration poem "Corinna's Going A-Maying" serves as both an argument against conservative religious dogma and as a response to specific Puritan manifestos. Herrick incorporates abundant Greco-Roman tropes into "Corinna" in order to construct a stylized response to Puritanism based upon traditional structure, symmetry, and thematic representation.

23. The author's attitude toward the subject is one of

    A. lethargy.

    B. apathy.

    C. objectivity.

    D. intensity.

24. The passage fundamentally suggests that

    A. Puritanism is based upon a traditional structure, symmetry, and thematic representation.

    B. lyric poetry has the ability to serve not only as an adornment of an era, but also as social communiqué.

    C. life in seventeenth-century England was tempestuous indeed.

    D. the seventeenth century was a time of religious and secular confrontations, resulting in new social abstractions, paradoxes, and ironies.

25. As used in the passage, the word trope means

A. a group of people, animals, etc., such as a herd, a flock, a band, and so on.

B. a style of writing in the Greek or Roman language.

C. a desire to travel to Greece or Rome.

D. the use of a word in a figurative sense; a figure of speech; figurative language.

Read the passage below; then answer the four questions that follow.

A Critic can be equivalent to "a person who pronounces judgment; especially a *Censurer.*" Since the late sixteenth century, the title of Critic has embodied implied meanings such as "professionalism" and "a person *skilled* in textual criticism." Thereby, the title insinuates a distinction of hierarchy among laborers, craftsmen, and the "working class" in general. "Censure" has etymological connotations that date back to the late Middle Ages, "critical recension or revision (along with) expression(s) of disapproval, to give opinion, assess critically, find fault, reprove, blame, pronounce sentence," and "condemnatory (especially ecclesiastical) judgement, opinion, correction," which all furthermore suggest a rather antagonistic posture in relationship to the Humanities. The position of critics is tenuous, as they can serve both as censure or social analyst and commentator. Subsequently, the word is loaded with negative innuendoes, but also innuendoes that denote authority, repression, and judicial propriety. In essence, the Critic who chooses to take the point-of-view of the Censure, sits on the mountaintop, not for a better view of literature, but to establish a false sense of superiority over it in relationship to the Author (as well as the reader for that matter).

26. The passage suggests that

A. critics are good for the social order.

B. the position of critic is tenuous as they can serve both as censure or social analyst and commentator.

C. critics attempt to establish a false sense of superiority over the author and the reader as well.

D. humanitarians do not make good critics as they are too emotional and not callous or impartial enough.

27. The passage indicates that the art of criticism

A. is a modern phenomenon.

B. dates back to the Middle Ages.

C. is a thought-provoking entity.

D. began at around the same time as the Civil War.

28. Which of the following would make the best title for the passage you just read?

    A. Critical Analysis Ruins Literature for the Rest of Us

    B. Critics Assume a False Superiority Thereby Rendering Critical Judgment Null and Void

    C. The Implications and Connotations of the Critic as Author

    D. Criticism is Synonymous with Censorship

29. What does the term etymological mean as it is used in the passage?

    A. The history of the Middle Ages

    B. The history of a word

    C. The history of critical analysis

    D. The history of literature

Read the passage below; then answer the five questions that follow.

Frederick Douglass was born Frederick Augustus Washington Bailey in 1818 to a white father and a slave mother. Frederick was raised by his grandmother on a Maryland plantation until he was eight. It was then that he was sent to Baltimore by his owner to be a servant to the Auld family. Mrs. Auld recognized Frederick's intellectual acumen and defied the law of the state by teaching him to read and write. When Mr. Auld warned that education would make the boy unfit for slavery, Frederick sought to continue his education in the streets. When his master died, Frederick, who was only sixteen years of age, was returned to the plantation to work in the fields. Later, he was hired out to work in the shipyards in Baltimore as a ship caulker. He plotted an escape but was discovered before he could get away. It took five years before he made his way to New York City and then to New Bedford, Massachusetts, eluding slave hunters by changing his name to Douglass.

At an 1841 anti-slavery meeting in Massachusetts, Douglass was invited to give a talk about his experiences under slavery. His impromptu speech was so powerful and so eloquent that it thrust him into a career as an agent for the Massachusetts Anti-Slavery Society. Douglass wrote his autobiography in 1845, primarily to counter those who doubted his authenticity as a former slave. This work became a classic in American literature and a primary source about slavery from the point of view of a slave. Douglass went on a two-year speaking tour abroad to avoid recapture by his former owner and to win new friends for the abolition movement.

He returned with funds to purchase his freedom and to start his own anti-slavery newspaper. He became a consultant to Abraham Lincoln and throughout Reconstruction fought doggedly for full civil rights for freedmen; he also supported the women's rights movement.

30. According to the passage, Douglass's writing of his autobiography was motivated by
    A. the desire to make money for the anti-slavery movement.
    B. his desire to become a publisher.
    C. his interest in authenticating his life as a slave.
    D. his desire to educate people about the horrors of slavery.

31. The central idea of the passage is that Douglass
    A. was instrumental in changing the laws regarding the education of slaves.
    B. was one of the most eminent human rights leaders of the nineteenth century.
    C. was a personal friend and confidant to a president.
    D. wrote a classic in American literature.

32. According to the author of this passage, Mrs. Auld taught Douglass to read because
    A. Douglass wanted to go to school like the other children.
    B. she recognized his natural ability.
    C. she wanted to comply with the laws of the state.
    D. he needed to be able to read so that he might work in the home.

33. The title that best expresses the ideas of this passage is
    A. The History of the Anti-Slavery Movement in America.
    B. The Outlaw Frederick Douglass.
    C. Reading: A Window to the World of Abolition.
    D. Frederick Douglass's Contributions to Freedom.

34. In the context of the passage, *impromptu* is the closest in meaning to
    A. unprepared.
    B. nervous.
    C. angry.
    D. loud.

Read the passage below; then answer the three questions that follow.

The teaching apprentice initiated the discussion in a clear and well-prepared manner. To ____________ the lecture topic, the teaching apprentice utilized overhead transparencies of both lexicon and abstract representation to better ____________ the theories behind various pedagogical concepts. The class culminated whereby students established enthymemes extrapolated from the class discussion. The class maintained integrity and continuity.

35. Which of these grouped words, if inserted ***in order*** into the passage's blank lines, would address the logical sequencing of the narrative?

    A. refute; criticize

    B. conflate; discern

    C. undermine; explain

    D. support; illustrate

36. The definition of the term "pedagogical" as used in the sentence means

    A. academic.

    B. abstract.

    C. meaningless.

    D. obtuse.

37. The passage suggests that the author's classroom experience was

    A. a needless waste of time and energy.

    B. intelligible and pragmatic.

    C. haphazard and disorderly.

    D. too advanced and complicated.

Read the passage below; then answer the three questions that follow.

The early decades of the fifteenth century were a period in our history when English took a "great (linguistic) vowel shift" by redistributing the vowel pronunciation and configuration. Each vowel changed its sound quality, but the distinction between one vowel and the next was maintained. There was a restructuring of the sounds and patterns of communication, as well. One has to conclude that a concurrent stress and exhilaration was occurring within the perimeters of the literate society as well. Musicians, artists, poets, and authors all must have relished the new freedom and experimentation that was now possible with the new-found linguistic shifts.

38. The passage tells about

    A. a shift in vowel pronunciation and configuration.

    B. a fifteenth-century renaissance for musicians, artists, poets, and authors.

    C. a new-found linguistic freedom from conventional sound and linguistic structure.

    D. various vowel stresses and their effect on artistic expression.

39. What is the meaning of the word *linguistic* as used in the passage?

    A. Artistic freedom

    B. Verbal or rhetorical

    C. Social or expressive

    D. Vowel configuration

40. Because "each vowel changed its sound quality,"

    A. there was a restructuring of the sounds and patterns of communication.

    B. language could never be spoken in the same way again.

    C. artists had to develop new means of expression.

    D. communication went through a divergent change of status and culture.

Read the passage below; then answer the four questions that follow.

Lead poisoning is considered by health authorities to be the most common and devastating environmental disease of young children. According to studies, it affects 15% to 20% of urban children and from 50% to 75% of inner-city, poor children. As a result of a legal settlement in July 1991, all California MediCal-eligible children, ages one through five, will now be routinely screened annually for lead poisoning. Experts estimate that more than 50,000 cases will be detected in California because of the newly mandated tests. This will halt at an early stage a disease that leads to learning disabilities and life-threatening disorders.

41. Lead poisoning among young children, if not detected early, can lead to

    A. physical disabilities.

    B. heart disease.

    C. liver disease.

    D. learning disabilities and death.

42. The new mandate to screen all young children for lead poisoning is required of

    A. all young children in California.

    B. all children with learning disabilities.

    C. all MediCal-eligible children, ages one through five, in California.

    D. all minority children in inner cities.

43. The percentages suggest that more cases of lead poisoning are found among

    A. children in rural areas.

    B. inner-city children.

    C. immigrant children.

    D. upper-middle class children.

44. The ultimate goal of the newly mandated tests is to

    A. bring more monies into inner-city medical programs.

    B. bring more health care professionals into California's inner cities.

    C. halt at an early stage a disease that leads to learning disabilities and life-threatening disorders.

    D. screen more test subjects to develop more accurate statistical data.

Read the passage below; then answer the two questions that follow.

America's national bird, the mighty bald eagle, is being threatened by a new menace. Once decimated by hunters and loss of habitat, this newest danger is suspected to be from the intentional poisoning by livestock ranchers. Authorities have found animal carcasses injected with restricted pesticides. These carcasses are suspected to have been placed to attract and kill predators such as the bald eagle in an effort to preserve young grazing animals. It appears that the eagle is being threatened again by the consummate predator, humans.

45. One can conclude from this passage that

    A. the pesticides used are beneficial to the environment.

    B. ranchers believe that killing the eagles will protect their ranches.

    C. ranchers must obtain licenses to use illegal pesticides.

    D. poisoning eagles is good for livestock.

46. The author's attitude is one of

    A. uncaring observation.

    B. concerned interest.

    C. uniformed acceptance.

    D. suspicion.

Read the passage below; then answer the two questions that follow.

The <u>social ostracizing</u> of male hairdressers and ballet dancers, versus the female mechanic or construction worker, presents the case that society classifies individuals by gender. But are these boundaries really changing? That is, what are the implications of a woman in a traditionally male career, who is "surprised" by another female in a traditional male career? What does that say about gender roles?

47. The passage asks the reader to

    A. ostracize various individuals who step outside conventional gender roles.

    B. accept people who take on jobs traditionally occupied by the opposite sex.

    C. classify individuals by gender.

    D. question whether traditional gender boundaries are changing or not.

48. As it is used in the passage, what does social ostracizing mean?

    A. Social acceptance

    B. Social pressure

    C. Social alienation

    D. Social examination

Read the passage below; then answer the two questions that follow.

The paradigm of a universal rational mind implies a form of stagnation, rigidity, or, at the very least, an intellectual elitist form of hierarchy. It suggests that everyone in a discourse community is of an equal mind, or should be. If members of a rhetorical community are not of the same equal mind, then there is an implication that their thinking is skewed by the clutter of culture, politics, and commitment. Additionally, it insinuates a discourse community predicated upon a single universal agenda. Because, after all, rhetoric is argumentation with an agenda.

49. The passage implies that

    A. discourse communities allow for individual thought and freedom of expression.

    B. everyone in a discourse community is of a similar mind, and is, therefore, suspect.

    C. members of a rhetorical community are more liberal than those of a discourse community.

    D. rhetoric is argumentation with an agenda and is, therefore, valuable.

50. What does the term paradigm mean?

    A. Model or standard

    B. Group or community

    C. Language or rhetoric

    D. Social order or intellectual

Read the passage below; then answer the four questions that follow.

The price of cleaning up the environment after oil spills is on the increase. After the massive Alaskan spill that created miles of sludge-covered beach, numerous smaller spills have occurred along the Gulf Coast and off the coast of California. Tides and prevailing winds carried much of this oil to shore in a matter of days. Workers tried to contain the oil with weighted, barrel-shaped plastic tubes stretched along the sand near the water. They hoped to minimize the damage. Generally, the barriers were successful, but there remained many miles of oil-covered sand. Cleanup crews shoveled the oil-covered sand into plastic bags for removal.

Coastal states are responding to the problem in several ways. California is considering the formation of a department of oceans to oversee protection programs and future cleanups. Some states have suggested training the National Guard in cleanup procedures. Other states are calling for the creation of an oil spill trust fund large enough to cover the costs of a major spill. Still other states are demanding federal action and funding. Regardless of the specific programs that may be enacted by the various states or the federal government, continued offshore drilling and the shipping of oil in huge tankers creates a constant threat to the nation's shoreline.

51. According to the passage, where have oil spills occurred?

    A. U. S. Gulf Coast

    B. Alaskan coast

    C. California coast

    D. All of the above.

52. What was the purpose of the barrel-shaped plastic tubes?

    A. To keep sightseers away from the oil

    B. To keep oil-soaked animals off the beach

    C. To force the oil to soak into the sand

    D. To keep the oil from spreading on the beach

53. Which of the following solutions is NOT discussed in the passage?

    A. Create an oil cleanup trust fund

    B. Increase federal funding for cleanups

    C. Reduce oil production

    D. Use the National Guard for cleanups

54. What is the author's opinion of the hazards created by oil spills?

    A. Oil spills must be expected if the present methods of production and shipment continue.

    B. Oil spills are the result of untrained crews.

    C. Oil spills would not be a problem if the government was better prepared to clean up.

    D. Oil spills are the responsibility of foreign oil producers.

Read the passage below; then answer the three questions that follow.

INSTRUCTIONS FOR ABSENTEE VOTING

These instructions describe conditions under which voters may register for or request absentee ballots to vote in the November 5 election.

(1) If you have moved on or prior to October 7, and did not register to vote at your new address, you are not eligible to vote in this election.

(2) If you move after this date, you may vote via absentee ballot or at your polling place, using your previous address as your address of registration for this election.

(3) You must register at your new address to vote in further elections.

(4) The last day to request an absentee ballot is October 29.

(5) You must be a registered voter in the county.

(6) You must sign your request in your own handwriting.

(7) You must make a separate request for each election.

(8) The absentee ballot shall be issued to the requesting voter in person or by mail.

55. A voter will be able to participate in the November 5 election as an absentee if he or she

A. planned to register for the next election.

B. requested an absentee ballot on November 1.

C. voted absentee in the last election.

D. moved as a registered voter on October 13.

56. On October 21, Mr. Applebee requested an absentee ballot for his daughter, a registered voting college student, to enable her participation in the election process. Mr. Applebee will not be successful because of which of the following instructions?

A. 3

B. 2

C. 6

D. 7

57. You can vote in future elections if you

A. register at your new address.

B. registered at your previous address.

C. request a registration form in your own handwriting.

D. moved after October 29.

Read the passage below; then answer the three questions that follow.

Gloves, 59
Goggles, 59
Grinders, portable, 66
Grinding operations, 126–140
  grinding wheels, 126–129
  selecting and using the wheel, 129–140
Grinding wheel selection and use, 129–140
  center punch sharpening, 133
  chisel head grinding, 135
  grinding metal stock, 131–133
  hand sharpening twist drills, 138
  installing the wheel, 130
  screwdriver tip dressing, 133
  sharpening a twist drill by machine, 139
  sharpening a twist drill for drilling brass, 139
  sharpening metal-cutting chisels, 136–138
  thinning the web of a twist drill, 139
  tin snips sharpening, 134
  truing and dressing the wheel, 131
Grinding wheels, 126–129
  markings and composition, 127
  sizes and shapes, 127

58. To which page(s) would one turn for information on how to install a grinding wheel?

A. 126–140

B. 136–138

C. 130

D. 126–129

59. Which of the following best describes the organizational scheme used to index the section dealing with grinding wheel selection and use?

    A. by type of wheel

    B. by physical characteristics

    C. by task

    D. by type of drill

60. On which page(s) would you find information on grinding a rounded edge on metal stock?

    A. 136–138

    B. 131–133

    C. 126–129

    D. 126–140

Practice Subtest: Mathematics

61. Multiply $\frac{3}{4}$ by $\frac{2}{3}$. Show your answer in simplified (reduced) form.

    A. $\frac{5}{7}$

    B. $\frac{5}{12}$

    C. $\frac{1}{2}$

    D. $\frac{6}{12}$

62. Divide 6.2 by 0.05.

    A. 124

    B. 1.24

    C. 12.4

    D. 0.124

63. Perform the indicated operation.

    $(-36) - 11$

    A. 47

    B. 25

    C. –47

    D. –25

64. Simplify: $6 \times 2 + \frac{3}{3}$

    A. 18

    B. 5

    C. 10

    D. 13

65. The number 14 is approximately 22% of which of the following numbers?

A. 64

B. 1.6

C. 308

D. 636

66. Simplify to a single term in scientific notation:

$(2 \times 10^3) \times (6 \times 10^4)$

A. 12×10^7

B. 1.2×10^{12}

C. 1.2×10^8

D. 12×10^{12}

67. Bob gets $6 an hour for babysitting. His sister Keyva gets $7 an hour. One evening Bob babysat for three hours, while Keyva sat for twice that long. How much money did they take in altogether for the evening?

A. $60

B. $54

C. $39

D. $108

68. The daily high temperatures in Frostbite, Minnesota, for one week in January were as follows:

Sunday: –2°F
Monday: 3°F
Tuesday: 0°F
Wednesday: –4°F
Thursday: –5°F
Friday: –1°F
Saturday: 2°F

What was the mean daily high temperature for that week?

A. 7

B. –7

C. –1

D. 1

69. Nelson's Menswear Shop was selling sweaters for $40 at the beginning of the year. In March, the price of the sweaters was raised by 10%. In September, the price was raised by an additional 15%. Ignoring tax, what was the price of the sweaters in September?

    A. $50.00

    B. $65.40

    C. $59.00

    D. $50.60

70. Three pounds of cherries cost $4.65. What would five pounds cost (at the same price per pound)?

    A. $7.75

    B. $7.50

    C. $23.00

    D. $23.25

71. The population of the city of Burnsville increased by approximately 0.2% last year. If the population at the beginning of the year was 1,620, what was the population at the end of the year?

    A. 1632

    B. 1623

    C. 1652

    D. 1640

72. Use the pie chart below to answer the question that follows.

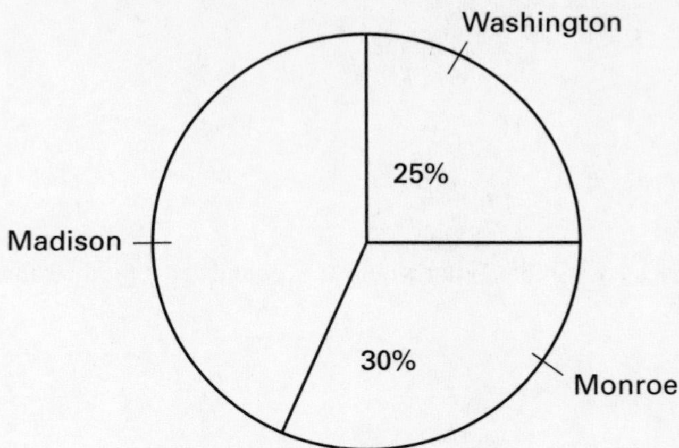

If the total number of people voting was 600, which of the following statements are true?

I. Madison received more votes than Monroe and Washington combined.
II. Madison received 45% of the votes.
III. Monroe received 180 votes.
IV. Madison received 330 votes.

A. I and III only

B. I and IV only

C. II and III only

D. II and IV only

73. Use the graph to answer the question that follows.

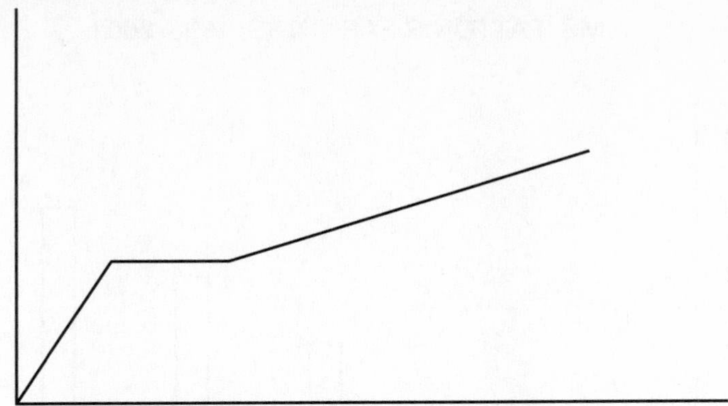

Which of the following scenarios could be represented by the graph above?

A. Mr. Cain mowed grass at a steady rate for a while, then took a short break, and then finished the job at a steady but slower rate.

B. Mr. Cain mowed grass at a steady rate for a while, and then mowed at a steady slower rate, then he took a break.

C. Mr. Cain mowed grass at a variable rate for a while, then took a short break, and then finished the job at a variable rate.

D. Mr. Cain mowed grass at a steady rate for a while, then took a short break, and then finished the job at a steady but faster pace.

74. Use the bar graph that follows to answer the question thereafter.

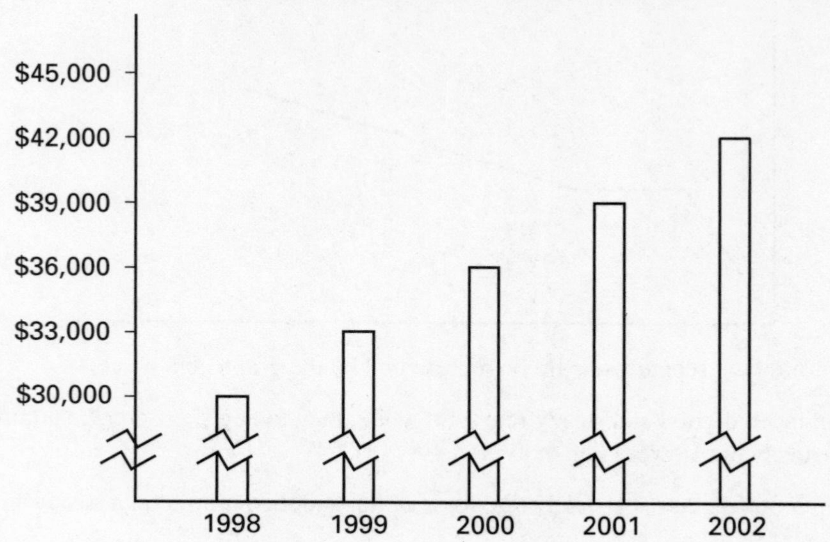

Only one of the statements below is necessarily true. Which one?

A. The range of Ms. Patton's earnings for the years shown is $15,000.

B. Ms. Patton's annual pay increases were consistent over the years shown.

C. Ms. Patton earned $45,000 in 2003.

D. Ms. Patton's average income for the years shown was $38,000.

75. A line passes through points (–6,0) and (0,4) on the coordinate plane. Which of the following statements are true?

I. The slope of the line is negative.
II. The slope of the line is positive.
III. The y-intercept of the line is –6.
IV. The y-intercept of the line is 4.

A. I and III only

B. I and IV only

C. II and III only

D. II and IV only

76. What is the slope of a line passing through points (–2, 6) and (4, –2) on the coordinate plane?

A. $-\frac{3}{4}$

B. $\frac{3}{4}$

C. $-\frac{4}{3}$

D. $\frac{4}{3}$

77. Use the graph to answer the question.

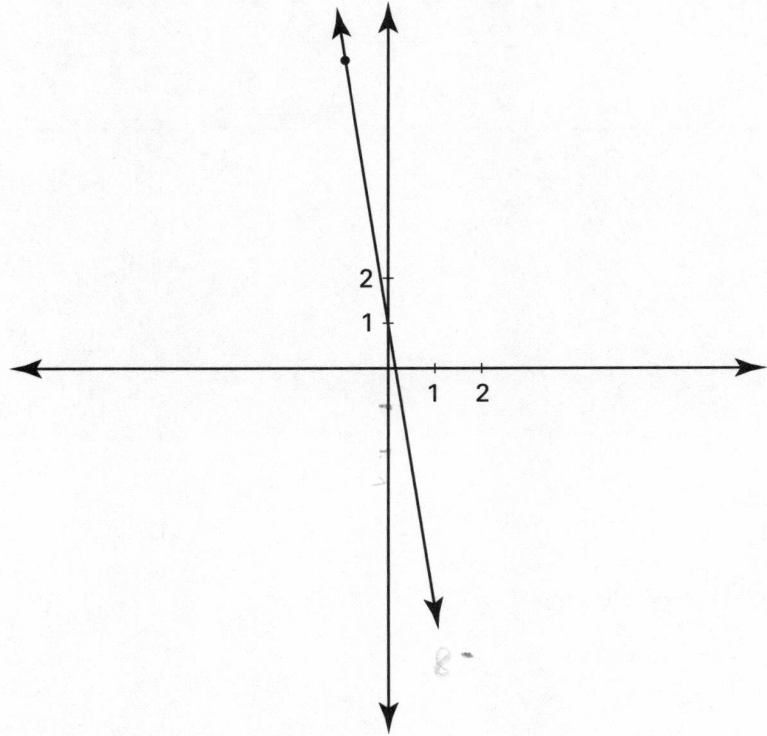

Which equation best describes the graph above?

A. $y = 0x$

B. $y = x + 0$

C. $y = -8x$

D. $y = 8x$

78. Which point represents the y-intercept of the equation $2x = 3y - 12$?

A. (4 ,0)

B. (0, –6)

C. (–6, 0)

D. (0, 4)

79. Use the graph that follows to answer the question.

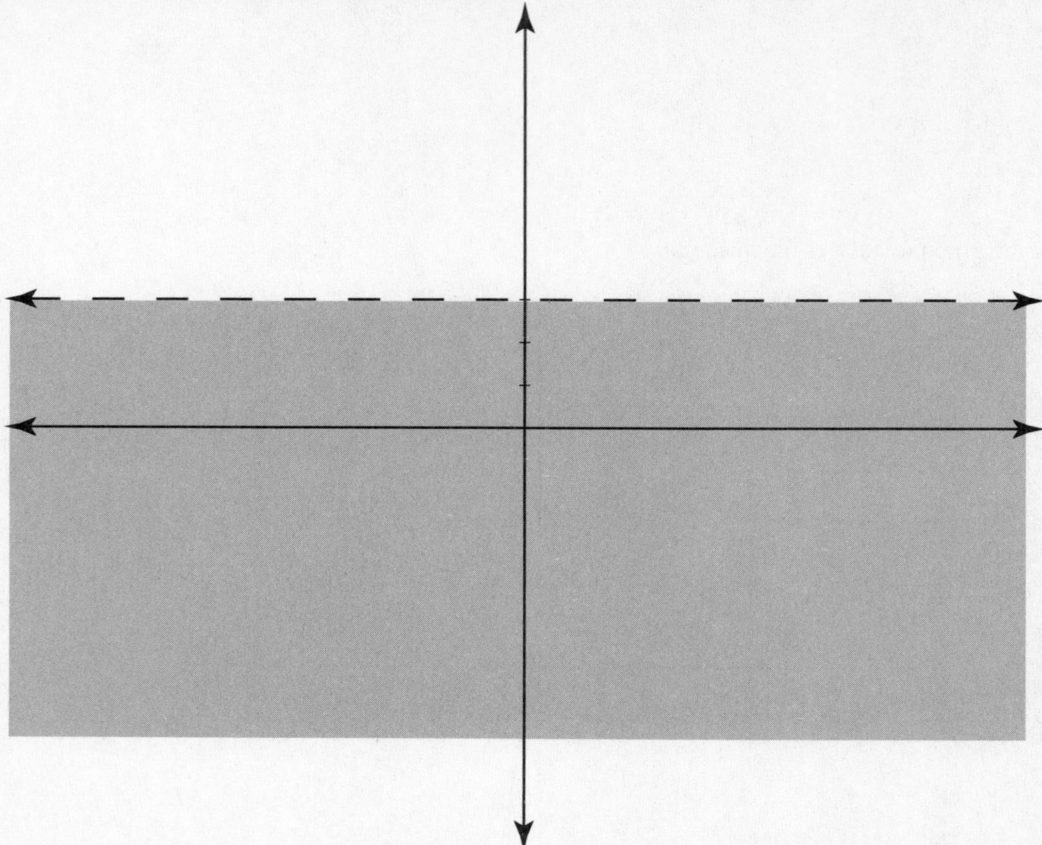

Which inequality describes the graph?

A. $y < 3$

B. $x < 3$

C. $y > 3$

D. $x > 3$

80. Use the figure to answer the question that follows.

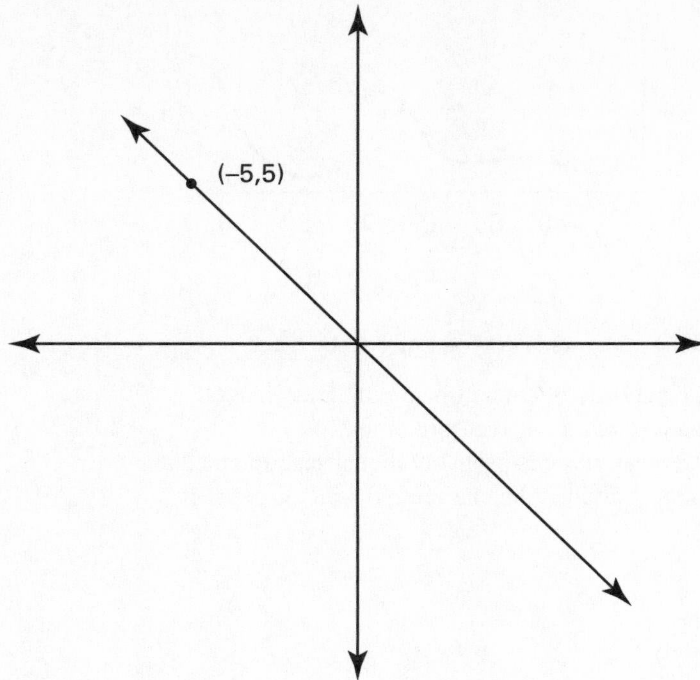

Which of the following statements about the graph of a linear equation (shown) are true?

I. The graph shows an inverse variation.
II. The graph shows a direct variation.
III. The slope of the line is –1.
IV. The slope of the line is 1.

A. I and III only

B. I and IV only

C. II and III only

D. II and IV only

81. The following graph shows the distribution of test scores in Ms. Alvarez's class.

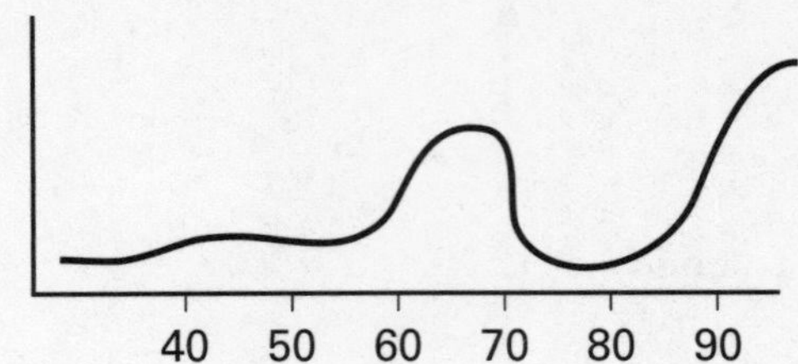

Which of the following statements do you know to be true?

I. The majority of students scored higher than 60.
II. The test was a fair measure of ability.
III. The mean score is probably higher than the median.
IV. The test divided the class into distinct groups.

A. I and II only

B. I and IV only

C. I, III, and IV only

D. IV only

82. What is the solution to this equation?

$\frac{x}{3} - 9 = 15$

A. 18

B. 8

C. 36

D. 72

83. What are the solutions of this equation?

$3x^2 - 11 = 1$

A. 2 and –2

B. 3 and –3

C. 4 and –4

D. 1 and –1

84. Solve for y.

$\frac{y}{3} - \frac{x}{2} = 4$

A. $y = \frac{3x}{2} + 12$

B. $y = \frac{3x}{2} + 12$

C. $y = \frac{3x}{2} - 12$

D. $y = -\frac{3x}{2} - 12$

85. Translate this problem into a one-variable equation, then solve the equation. What is the solution?

"There are ten vehicles parked in a parking lot. Each is either a car with four tires or a motorcycle with two tires. (Do not count any spare tires.) There are 26 wheels in the lot. How many cars are there in the lot?"

A. 8

B. 6

C. 5

D. 3

86. Which equation could be used to solve the following problem?

"Three consecutive odd numbers add up to 117. What are they?"

A. $x + (x + 2) + (x + 4) = 117$

B. $1x + 3x + 5x = 117$

C. $x + x + x = 117$

D. $x + (x + 1) + (x + 3) = 117$

87. Which equation could be used to solve the following problem?

"Here is how the Acme Taxicab Company computes fares for riders: People are charged three dollars for just getting into the cab, then they are charged two dollars more for every mile or fraction of a mile of the ride. What would be the fare for a ride of 10.2 miles?"

A. $3 \times (2 \times 10.2) = y$

B. $3 + (2 + 11) = y$

C. $3 \times (2 + 10.2) = y$

D. $3 + (2 \times 11) = y$

88. Simplify the following expression.

$\frac{2x^2}{3} + 7x + 9 + \frac{x^2}{3} - 12x + 1$

A. $x^2 - 5x + 10$

B. $6x^3 + 10$

C. $6x^2 + 10$

D. $x^4 - 5x + 10$

89. Multiply the following binomials.

$(-2x^2 - 11)(5x^2 + 3)$

A. $-10x^2 - 8$

B. $-10x^2 - 14x - 8$

C. $-10x^4 - 61x^2 - 33$

D. $-10x^2 - 52x - 33$

90. Factor the following expression into two binomials.

$-8x^2 + 22x - 5$

A. $(4x - 1)(-2x + 5)$

B. $(-4x - 1)(-2x - 5)$

C. $(4x + 1)(-2x + 5)$

D. $(4x + 1)(2x + 5)$

91. Fully factor this expression.

$2x^2 - 18$

A. $(2x - 3)(x + 6)$

B. $2(x^2 - 9)$

C. $(2x - 9)(x + 9)$

D. $2(x + 3)(x - 3)$

92. Simplify the following.

$3\sqrt{2} \times 5\sqrt{10}$

A. $30\sqrt{2}$

B. $15\sqrt{12}$

C. $30\sqrt{5}$

D. $15\sqrt{20}$

93. Simplify.

$$\frac{\sqrt{75x^7}}{\sqrt{3x}}$$

A. $25x^5$

B. $5x^5$

C. $5x^3$

D. $25x^4$

94. Use the figure below to answer the question.

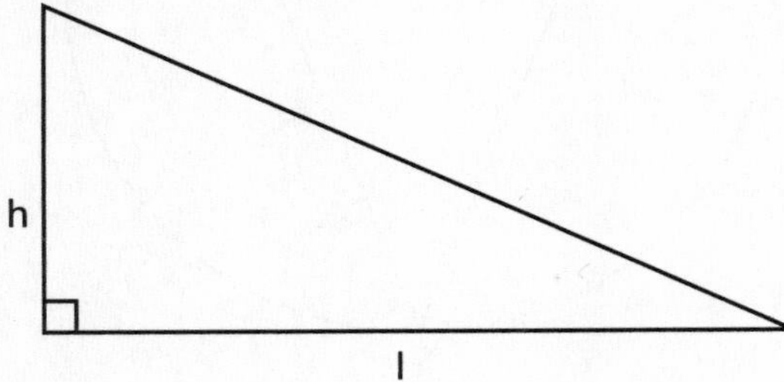

Which formula can be used to find the area of the triangle?

A. $A = \frac{(l \times h)}{2}$

B. $A = \frac{(l + h)}{2}$

C. $A = 2(l + h)$

D. $A = 2(l \times h)$

95. Use the figure below to answer the question.

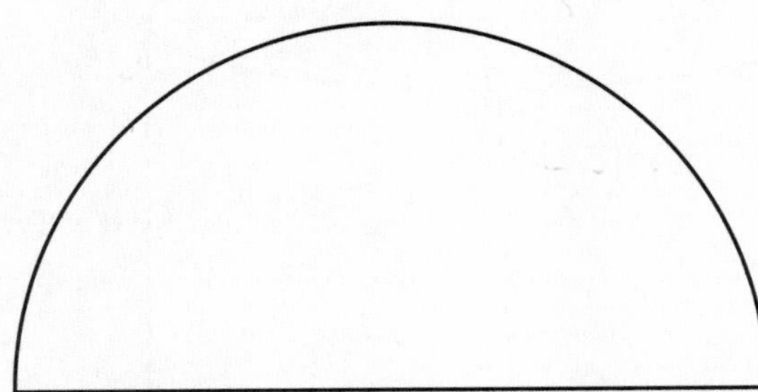

Which formula can be used to find the area of the figure? (Assume the curve is *half* of a circle.)

A. $A = \pi r$

B. $A = 2\pi r^2$

C. $A = \pi r^2$

D. $A = \frac{\pi r^2}{2}$

96. Use the figure below to answer the question that follows. Assume that:
Point C is the center of the circle.
Angles xyz and xcz intercept minor arc xz.
The measure of angle xyz is 40°.

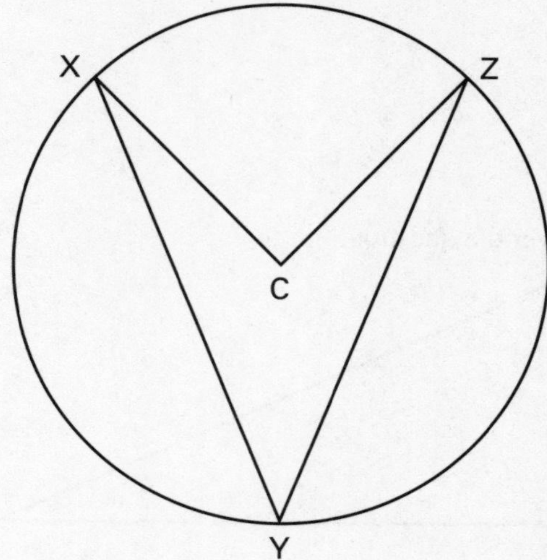

What is the measure of major arc xyz?

A. 140°

B. 280°

C. 160°

D. 320°

97. What is the approximate volume of the following cylinder?

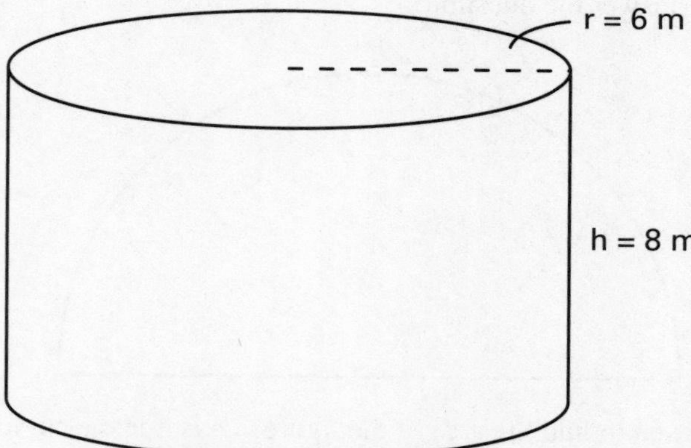

A. 904 cm^3

B. 301 cm^3

C. 151 cm^3

D. 452 cm^3

98. Use the Pythagorean theorem to answer this question: Which answer comes closest to the actual length of side x in the triangle below?

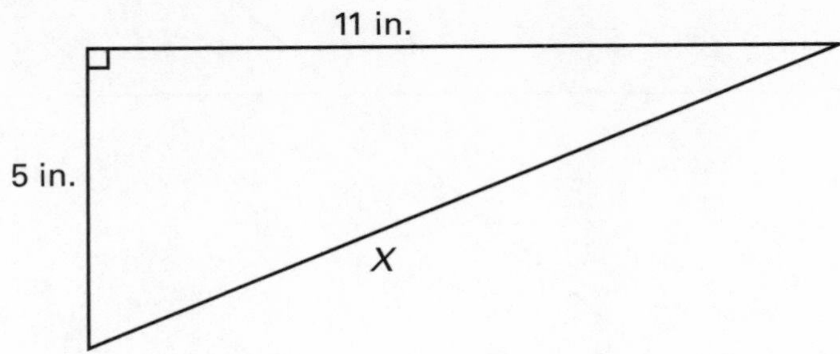

A. 14 in.

B. 12 in.

C. 11 in.

D. 13 in.

99. Use the figures given to answer the question that follows.

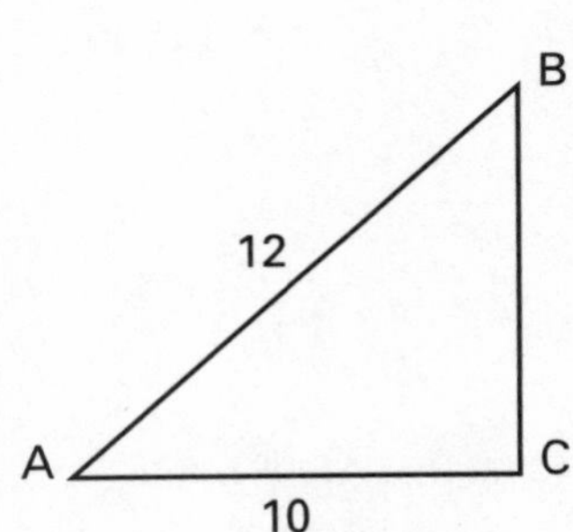

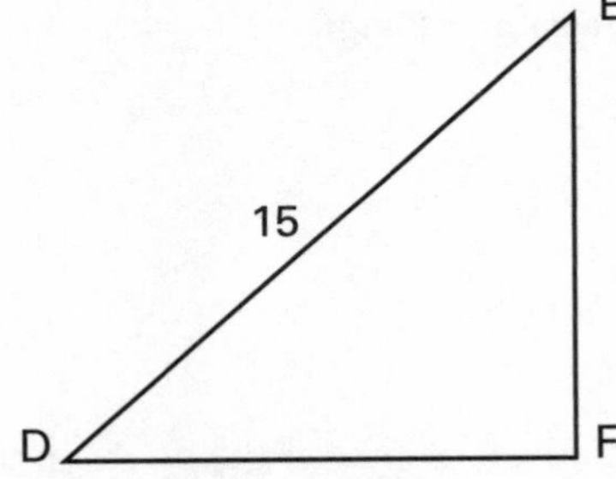

If the two triangles are similar, what is the length of side DF?

A. 12.5 units

B. 13 units

C. 12 units

D. 13.5 units

100. Use the figure given to answer the question that follows.

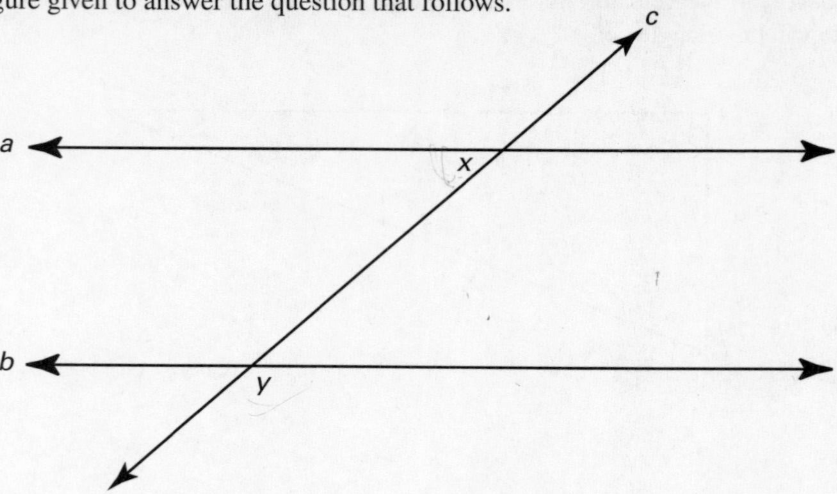

Given:

1. Lines *a* and *b* are parallel,
2. *c* is a line, and
3. the measure of angle *x* is 50°.

What is the measure of angle *y*?

A. 50°

B. 100°

C. 130°

D. 80°

101. Use the figure given to answer the question that follows. Assume that AD is a line.

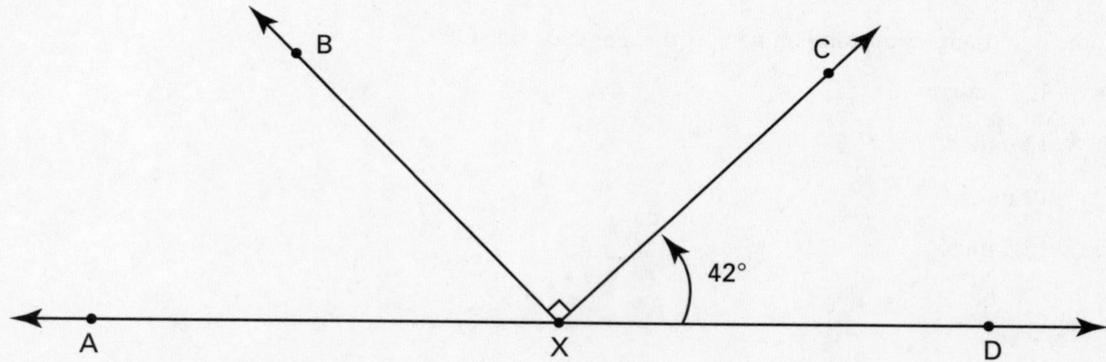

What is the measure of angle AXB?

A. 48°

B. 90°

C. 42°

D. There is not enough information to answer the question.

102. Use the figures to answer the question that follows.

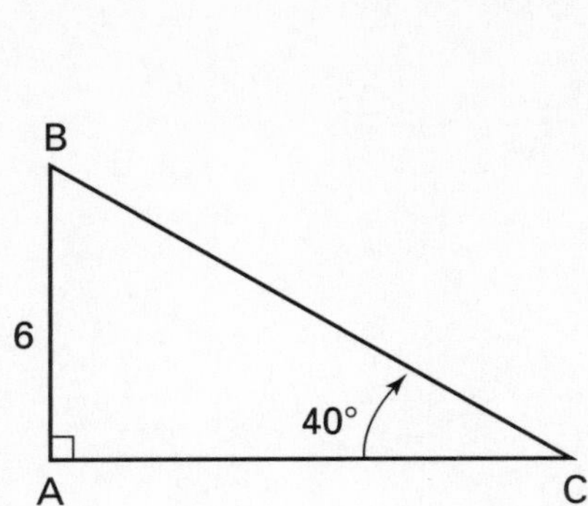

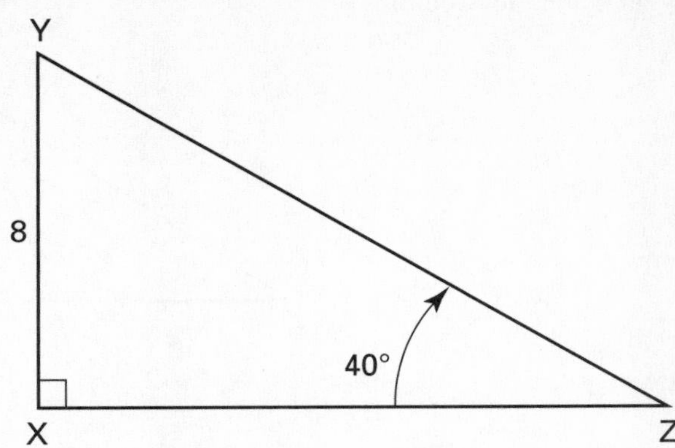

Which of the following statements about the two triangles are true?

I. The triangles are similar.
II. The triangles are congruent.
III. The measures of angles ABC and XYZ are the same.
IV. The lengths of sides BC and YZ are the same.

A. I and III only

B. I and IV only

C. II and III only

D. II and IV only

103. In a foot race, Fred beat Matt, Curt beat Dwayne, both Pat and Matt beat Ivan, Pat beat Curt, and Dwayne beat Fred. If those were the only boys racing, who came in last?

A. Don

B. Matt

C. Curt

D. Ivan

104. Simplify the following expression: $6 + 2(x - 4)$

A. $4x - 16$

B. $2x - 14$

C. $2x - 2$

D. $-24x$

105. Referring to the figure below, if the measure of $\angle C$ is 20° and the measure of $\angle CBD$ is 36°, then what is the measure of $\angle A$?

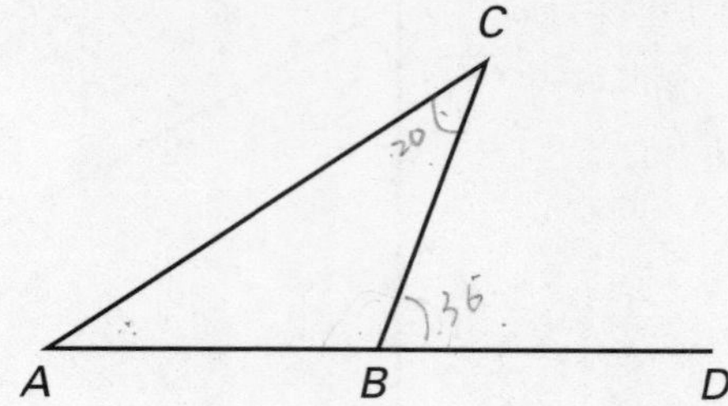

A. 16°

B. 20°

C. 36°

D. 56°

106. If six cans of beans cost $1.50, what is the price of eight cans of beans?

A. $9.60

B. $1.00

C. $1.60

D. $2.00

107. Bonnie's average score on three tests is 71. Her first two test scores are 64 and 87. What is her score on test three?

A. 62

B. 71

C. 74

D. 151

108. In the figure below, what is the perimeter of square ABCD if diagonal AC = 8?

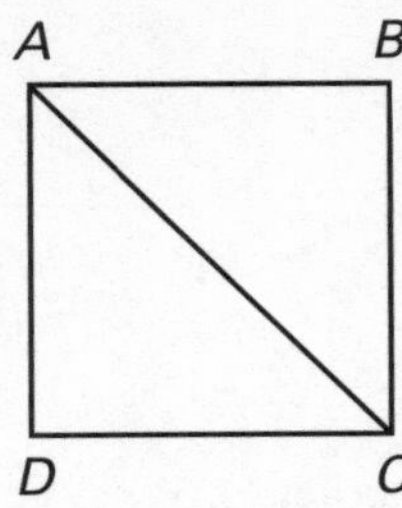

A. 32

B. 64

C. $4\sqrt{2}$

D. $16\sqrt{2}$

109. Three small circles, all the same size, lie inside a large circle as shown above. The diameter *AB* of the large circle passes through the centers of the three small circles. If each of the smaller circles has area 9π, what is the circumference of the large circle?

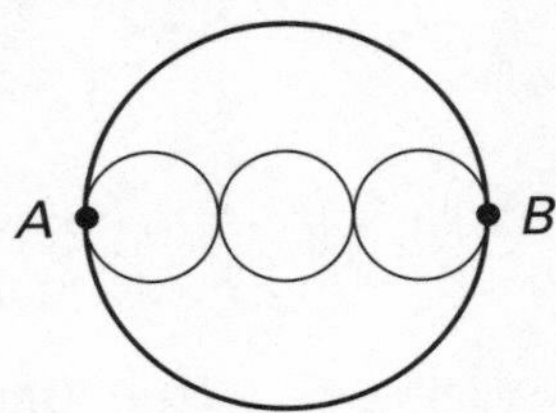

A. 9

B. 18

C. 18π

D. 27π

110. A jar contains 20 balls. These balls are labeled 1 through 20. What is the probability that a ball chosen from the jar has a number on it that is evenly divisible by 4?

A. $\frac{1}{20}$

B. $\frac{1}{5}$

C. $\frac{1}{4}$

D. 5

111. If $2x^2 + 5x - 3 = 0$ and $x > 0$, then what is the value of x?

A. $-\frac{1}{2}$

B. $\frac{1}{2}$

C. 1

D. $\frac{3}{2}$

112. The center of the following circle is the point O. What percentage of the circle is shaded if the measure of arc AB is 65° and the measure of arc CD is 21.4°?

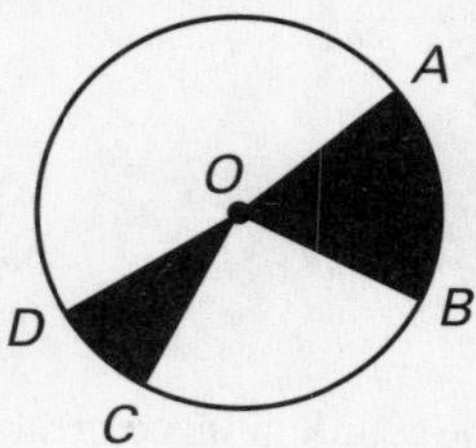

A 86.4%

B 24%

C 43.6%

D. 27.4%

113. According to the chart, in what year was the total sales of Brand X televisions the greatest?

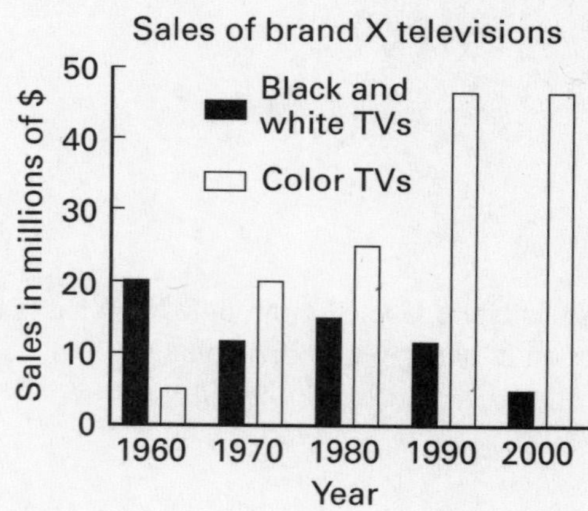

A. 1960

B. 1970

C. 1980

D. 1990

114. Two cards are drawn, without replacement, from a deck of 52 cards. What is the probability that both cards are diamonds?

A. $\frac{1}{17}$

B. $\frac{1}{16}$

C. $\frac{1}{8}$

D. $\frac{1}{5}$

115. Two concentric circles are shown in the figure below. The smaller circle has radius $OA = 4$ and the larger circle has radius $OB = 6$. Find the area of the shaded region.

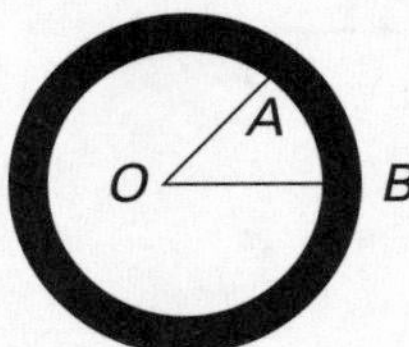

A. 4π

B. 16π

C. 20π

D. 36π

116. Solve the following inequality for x: $8 - 2x \leq 10$

A. $x \leq 1$

B. $x \geq -9$

C. $x \leq -1$

D. $x \geq -1$

117. Working alone, John needs four hours to paint a fence, whereas Linda only needs three hours for this task. If both work together, how many hours will be needed to complete this task?

A. 1

B. $1\frac{5}{7}$

C. 2

D. $2\frac{1}{7}$

118. At the Rest Easy Motel, the cost of a 1-night, 2-night, or 3-night stay is just $100, and the cost for each additional night is $50. If a single dot represents the cumulative bill after each night's stay, which of the following could represent a week-long stay?

A. 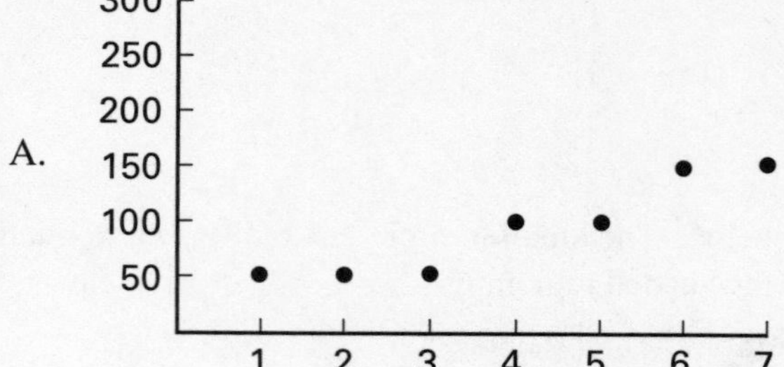

B. 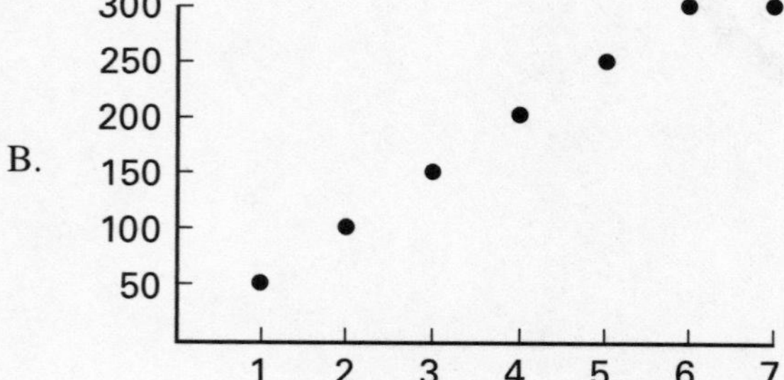

C. 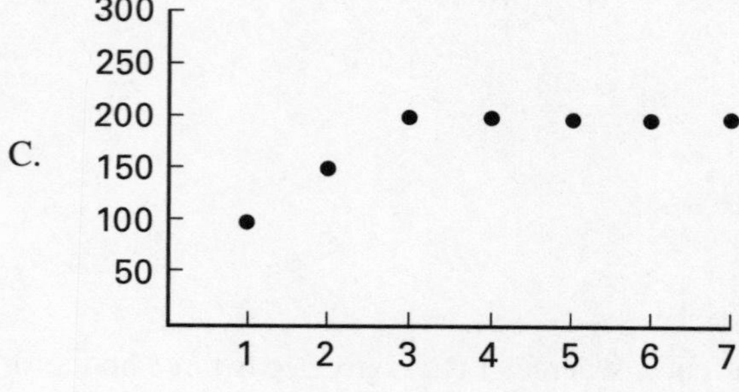

D. 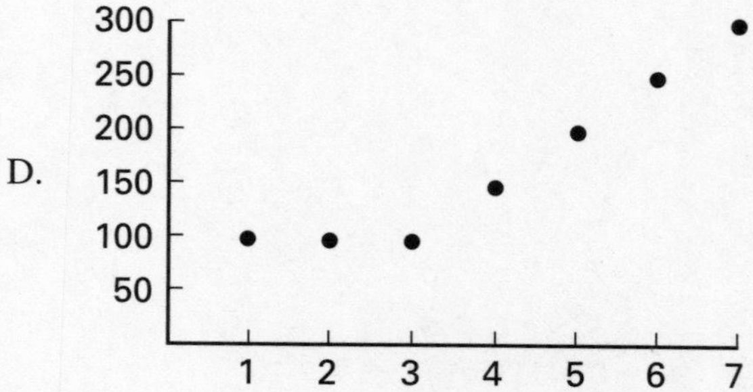

119. Six different cars, identified as *F*, *G*, *H*, *J*, *K*, and *L*, were tested for fuel efficiency and cost. The results are shown below.

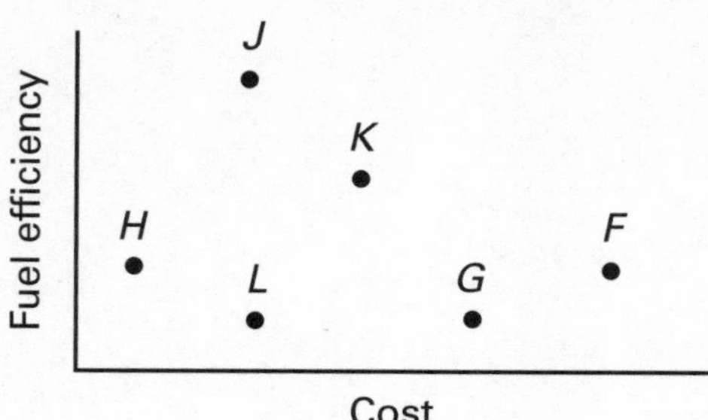

Which car costs the same as *L*, but is more fuel efficient than *L*?

A. *F*

B. *G*

C. *H*

D. *J*

120. In the scatterplot of 30 points shown below, which of the following is a valid conclusion as x increases from zero?

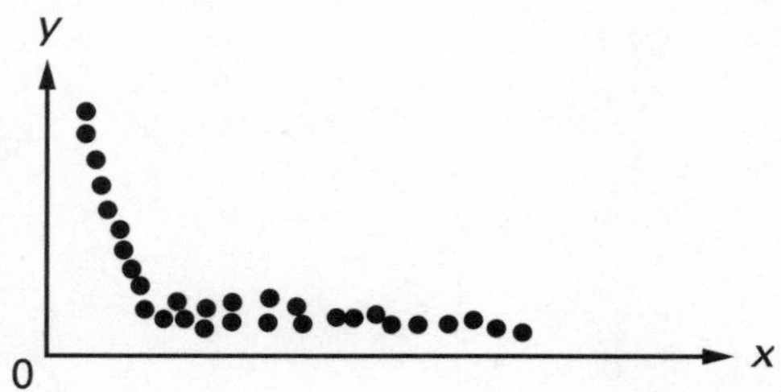

A. y remains constant initially, then increases

B. y increases initially, then remains constant

C. y decreases initially, then increases

D. y decreases initially, then remains constant

Practice Subtest: Writing

Read the passage below, written in the style of a newspaper editorial; then answer the four questions that follow.

[1]The zoning regulations of Westown have long been a thorn in the side of local real estate developers. [2]The authors of those regulations apparently believed that their regulations would be appropriate in perpetuity, because they ____________ to amend. [3]The result is a growing area of blight bounded on the north by Bradley Avenue and on the east by Randolph Street.

[4]This coming Wednesday the Westown's city council has a chance to bring its zoning practices into the twenty-first century. [5]The decisive votes will come from Council members Putman, Beckett, and Reis. [6]The votes of Putman and Beckett in particular will be of interest to their constituents, because the residents of their wards would stand to gain a great deal from rezoning. [7]The proposed changes would bring the Fourth Ward some much-needed commerce in the currently run-down Randolph-MacKenzie area and would help _________ the Fifth Ward's steady population loss. [8]Although each of these self-styled "progressives" have displayed reluctance to vote for anything that would spur development in the recent past, both have strong opposition in the upcoming election and would do well to consider how their votes on this issue will impact the results of that election.

121. Which of the following changes is needed in the passage above?

    A. Sentence 1: Change "have" to "has"

    B. Sentence 4: Change "Westown's" to "Westown"

    C. Sentence 8: Change the comma after "past" to a semicolon

    D. Sentence 8: Change "how" to "that"

122. Which of the following words would be the best to insert into the blank in sentence 7?

    A. alleviate

    B. accelerate

    C. excoriate

    D. exonerate

123. Which of the numbered sentences should be revised to correct an error in verb form?

A. sentence 3

B. sentence 5

C. sentence 6

D. sentence 8

124. Which of the following phrases, inserted into the blank in sentence 2, would make sense and would be free of errors?

A made the regulations very easy

B. ensured that the provisions would be difficult

C. made them almost impossible

D. said the zoning ordinances will be hard

Read the passage below; then answer the five questions that follow.

[1]DeMarco was asked if he had read any of the books that were on display in Mrs. W's classroom. [2]He answered that he had read none of them yet, although he usually keeps one or more in his desk.

[3]Nevertheless, the researcher did see him respond positively to the first classroom reading experience of the year. [4]Mrs. W was reading Louis Sachar's *Sideways Stories from Wayside School* while the children, each of whom had a copy of the book, were silently reading along. [5]Like nearly all of the class, DeMarco was laughing in all the right places. [6]The researcher has since noticed that he grasps and comprehends just about anything well when it is read by a competent reader, whether a teacher or an advanced fellow student.

[7]______________________________ [8]The class writes almost daily in a "Small Moments Journal," in which they are to record, in a few sentences and perhaps a picture, memorable events in their lives. [9]Mrs. W has spent considerable time prompting the students to write down topics, with the result that some students have well over 100 topics listed so far. [10]DeMarco, through the last day he was observed, had seven. [11]He had written only two entries in his journal, both about a visit two years ago to his relatives in Mississippi. [12]Like many of his classmate's accounts of their comings and goings, his writing lacks detail and personality, but most others have written appreciably more. [13]Asked follow-up questions about the events he has written about, his answers were evasive.

125. Which of the following sentences, used in place of the blank labeled sentence 7, would best make a transition to the new paragraph?

A. Another topic of interest was the study was DeMarco's writing ability.

B. Moreover, DeMarco's writing shows no enthusiasm.

C. DeMarco's writing, however, shows no spark at all.

D. Consequently, it is advisable that we look at DeMarco's writing.

126. Which of the numbered parts should be revised to reduce its unnecessary repetition?

A. sentence 3

B. sentence 5

C. sentence 6

D. sentence 8

127. Which of the numbered sentences should be revised to correct an error in sentence structure?

A. sentence 2

B. sentence 9

C. sentence 10

D. sentence 13

128. Which of the following changes is needed in the passage?

A. Sentence 4: Change *Sideways Stories from Wayside School* to "Sideways Stories from Wayside School"

B. Sentence 11: Change "had" to "has"

C. Sentence 11: Change "journal" to "Journal"

D. Sentence 12: Change "classmate's" to "classmates'"

129. Which of the underlined words or phrases in the third paragraph should be replaced by more precise or appropriate words?

A. <u>record</u>

B. <u>considerable</u>

C. <u>comings and goings</u>

D. <u>appreciably</u>

Read the passage below; then answer the five questions that follow.

[1]The Tuskegee Experiment's true nature had to be hidden from the subjects to ensure their cooperation. [2]The sharecroppers' grossly disadvantaged lot in life made them easy to manipulate. [3]Pleased at the prospect of free medical care—almost none of them had ever seen a doctor before—these unsophisticated and trusting men became the dupes in what James Jones, author of the excellent history on the subject, *Bad Blood,* identified as "the longest nontherapeutic experiment on human beings in medical history".

[4]The study was meant to discover how syphilis <u>effected</u> African Americans as opposed to whites—the theory being that whites experienced more neurological complications from syphilis <u>whereas</u> African Americans were more <u>susceptible</u> to cardiovascular damage. [5]____ [6]Although the scientists touted the study as one of great scientific merit, from the <u>outset</u> its actual benefits were hazy. [7]It took almost forty years before someone involved in the study took a hard and honest look at the end results, he reported that "nothing learned will prevent, find, or cure a single case of infectious syphilis or bring us closer to our basic mission of controlling venereal disease in the United States." [8]When the media learns of the experiment in 1972, the CBS news anchor Harry Reasoner called it a project that "used human beings as laboratory animals in a long and inefficient study of how long it takes syphilis to kill someone."

130. Which of the following sentences, used in place of the blank labeled sentence 5, would be most consistent with the writer's purpose and intended audience?

   A. If the theory had been proven, much would have changed in the clinical treatment of syphilis.

   B. How this knowledge would have changed the clinical treatment of syphilis is uncertain.

   C. On the other hand, neurological complications were much more important to the scientists.

   D. We will never know what the racist scientists of the 1920s were thinking when they devised this theory.

131. Which of the underlined words or phrases in the second paragraph should be replaced by more precise or appropriate words?

   A. <u>effected</u>

   B. <u>whereas</u>

   C. <u>susceptible</u>

   D. <u>outset</u>

132. Which of the numbered sentences should be revised to correct a nonstandard use of a comma?

A. sentence 2

B. sentence 3

C. sentence 7

D. sentence 8

133. Which of the following changes is needed in the first paragraph?

A. Sentence 1: Change "experiment's" to "experiments"

B. Sentence 2: Change "Part 3: Change "had" to "has"

C. Sentence 3: Change "easy to manipulate" to "easily manipulated"

D. Sentence 3: Move the period at the end inside the quotation mark

134. Which of the numbered sentences contains nonstandard use of a verb form?

A. sentence 2

B. sentence 3

C. sentence 6

D. sentence 8

Read the passage below; then answer the six questions that follow.

[1]Before the Europeans arrived, animism and spirit worship was the hallmark of Timorese belief in a superior force. [2]The great Hindu, Buddhist, and Islamic kingdoms that dominated South and Southeast Asia had not taken root in Timor. [3]The island's geographic location, which was far from the major ports of Asia, and its subsequent lack of commercial activity, placed it off the beaten track for traders and proselytizers. [4]The exceptions being sandalwood and later slave trade.

[5]All that changed with the arrival of the Europeans. [6]By the late 1500s Dominican friars from Portugal had established a mission on Timor, _____ they made only modest headway in converting the Timorese to Christianity. [7]Although the Portuguese were in Timor for centuries they had little positive influence on Timorese culture until after World War II. [8]For years the local people consistently resisted Portugal's attempts to take control of their island, and some of the Dominican missionaries who were posted there supported them in this effort. [9]It was not until Portugal considered granting East Timor its independence that Catholicism began to be accepted among the people, and _________ it was not until the Indonesian invasion in 1975 that large numbers of Timorese embraced the Catholic faith. [10]Indonesian law requires citizens to have a religious affiliation. [11]The Catholic Church was the only organization that the Indonesian government in Timor allowed relative freedom.

[12]Timorese also found the Church a source of support during the guerrilla war against the Indonesians. [13]Timorese fled to the highlands to escape Indonesian rule, and their families were often relocated in camps far from their villages to prevent them from lending assistance to the guerrillas. [14]The Church saw the abject misery of the people and provided support and comfort. [15]Membership in the Catholic Church grew dramatically from 1975 to 1999 as the Timorese people came to rely on it to protect them and to help them locate missing family members. [16]Today 90% of East Timor's population is Catholic, although many Timorese Catholics include some aspects of animism in their beliefs.

135. Read the following sentence:
"The priests and nuns of the church provided health and education to the Timorese during that chaotic period."
In which of the following locations in the third paragraph should this sentence be placed?

A. Before sentence 13

B. Before sentence 14

C. Before sentence 15

D. Before sentence 16

136. The method of organization for the second and third paragraphs, respectively, is

A. chronological order; problem and solution

B. chronological order; cause and effect

C. order of importance; chronological order

D. comparison and contrast; cause and effect

137. Which of the numbered parts should be revised to correct a nonstandard sentence structure?

A. sentence 2

B. sentence 4

C. sentence 7

D. sentence 8

138. Which of the following changes is needed in the second paragraph?

A. Sentence 7: Insert comma after "centuries"

B. Sentence 8: Change "who" after "missionaries" to "whom"

C. Sentence 9: Change "its" to "their"

D. Sentence 11: Capitalize "government"

139. Which words or phrases would, if inserted *in order* into the blanks in the second paragraph, help the reader understand the logical sequence of the writer's ideas?

A. however; therefore

B. and so; in those circumstances

C. however; even then

D. but; even then

140. Which of the numbered parts should be revised to correct a nonstandard verb form?

A. sentence 1

B. sentence 3

C. sentence 10

D. sentence 16

Read the passage below; then answer the three questions that follow.

[1]The Lincoln Cent was first struck in 1909 to celebrate the 100th Anniversary of the birth of Abraham Lincoln, our 16th President. [2]Designed by Victor D. Brenner, the coin carried the motto "In God We Trust"—the first time it appeared on this denomination coin. [3]It is interesting that the law for the motto was passed during Lincoln's administration as president. [4]Though we might not think so at first glance, the lowly cent is a fitting memorial for the great man whose profile graces this most common coin of the realm, and a tolerable symbol for the nation whose commerce it serves.

[5]The obverse has the profile of Lincoln as he looked during the trying years of the War Between the States. [6]Faced with the immense problems of a divided nation, the prevention of the split between North and South was difficult. [7]"A house divided against itself cannot stand," he warned the nation. [8]With the outbreak of war at Fort Sumter. Lincoln was saddened to see his beloved country caught up in the senseless war in which father fought against son, brother against brother. [9]Throughout America, war captured the attention of people: the woman who saved the lives of the wounded, the soldier waiting to go into battle, the bewildered child trying hard to understand the sound of guns. [10]Lincoln stood on the broad, silent battlefield at Gettysburg in 1863 to dedicate the site as a national cemetery. [11]Gettysburg had been the scene of some of the most bitter fighting of the war and had ended in a Union victory.

[12]In his special address at Gettysburg, he called upon the American people to end the war. [13]His words boomed out over the large audience before him: [14]"It is rather for us [the living] to be here dedicated to the great task remaining before us—[15]that from these honored dead we take increased devotion to that cause for which they gave the last full

measure of devotion; that we here highly resolve that these dead shall not have died in vain; that this nation under God, shall have a new birth of freedom; and that government of the people, by the people and for the people, shall not perish from the earth."

[16]Barely a month before the end of the war, Lincoln took the oath of office a secondly time as President. [17]With the war still raging, his inaugural address took on added meaning: [18] "With malice toward none, with charity for all, with firmness in the right as God gives us to see the right, let us strive on to finish the work we are in, to bind up the nation's wounds, to care for him who shall have borne the battle and for his widow and his orphan, to do all which may achieve and cherish a just and lasting peace among ourselves and with all nations."

141. Which of the following changes is needed in the third paragraph?

A. Sentence 16: Change "end" to "climax."

B. Sentence 16: Change "secondly" to "second."

C. Sentence 17: Change "With" to "Of."

D. Sentence 17: Change "on" to "in."

142. Which of the following changes is needed in the second paragraph?

A. Sentence 5: Change "has" to "had."

B. Sentence 6: Change "the prevention of the split between North and South was difficult" to "Lincoln found it difficult to prevent the split between North and South."

C. Sentence 9: Change "waiting" to "waited."

D. Sentence 10: Change "site" to "sight."

143. Which of the following sentences is a nonstandard sentence?

A. sentence 2

B. sentence 4

C. sentence 8

D. sentence 11

Read the passage below; then answer the three questions that follow.

[1]Dr. Robert Goddard, at one time a physics professor at Clark University, Worcester, Massachusetts, was largely responsible for the sudden interest in rockets back in the twenties. [2]When Dr. Goddard first started his experiments with rockets, no related technical information was available. [3]He started a new science, industry, and field of engineering. [4]Through his scientific experiments, he pointed the way to the development of rockets as we know them today. [5]The Smithsonian Institute agreed to finance his experiments in 1920. [6]From these experiments he wrote a paper titled "A Method of Reaching Extreme Altitudes," in which he outlined a space rocket of the step (multistage) principle, theoretically capable of reaching the moon.

[7]Goddard discovered that with a properly shaped, smooth, tapered nozzle he could increase the ejection velocity eight times with the same weight of fuel. [8]This would not only drive a rocket eight times faster, but 64 times farther, according to his theory. [9]Early in his experiments he found that solid-fuel rockets would not give him the high power or the duration of power needed for a dependable supersonic motor capable of extreme altitudes. [10]Using liquid fuel, he finally launched a successful rocket in 1926.

[11]It attained an altitude of 184 feet and a speed of 60 m.p.h. [12]This seems small as compared to present-day speeds and heights of missile flights, but instead of trying to achieve speed or altitude at this time, Dr. Goddard was trying to develop a dependable rocket motor.

[13]Dr. Goddard later was the first to fire a rocket that reached a speed faster than the speed of sound. [14]He was first to develop a gyroscopic steering thing for rockets. [15]The first to use vanes in the jet stream for rocket stabilization during the initial phase of a rocket flight. [16]And he was first to patent the idea of step rockets. [17]After proving on paper and in actual tests that a rocket can travel in a vacuum, he developed the mathematical theory of rocket propulsion and rocket flight, including basic designs for long-range rockets. [18]All of his information was available to military men before World War II, but evidently its immediate use did not seem applicable. [19]Near the end of World War II we started intense work on rocket-powered guided missiles, using the experiments and developments of Dr. Goddard and the American Rocket Society.

144. Which of the following should be changed to reflect correct punctuation in the first paragraph?

A. Sentence 1: Put commas after "Goddard" and after "Massachusetts."

B. Sentence 2: Remove the comma after "rockets."

C. Sentence 4: Put a comma in after "rockets."

D. Sentence 6: Remove the comma after "principle."

145. Which of the following sentences of the third paragraph is a nonstandard sentence?

A. sentence 14

B. sentence 15

C. sentence 16

D. sentence 17

146. Which of the underlined words in the third paragraph should be replaced by more precise or appropriate words?

A. thing

B. the initial phase

C. actual

D. work

Read the passage below; then answer the three questions that follow.

[1]We've grown accustomed to seeing this working woman hanging from the subway strap during commuting hours. [2]We may refer disparagingly to her tailored suit and little tie, but we no longer visualize her in a house dress with her hair uncombed. [3]The woman who leaves her children to go to work in the morning is no longer a pariah in her community or her family. [4]Her paycheck is more than pin money; it buys essential family staples and often supports the entire family. [5]But she is not the only beneficiary of the increasing presence of women in the workplace.

[6]The situation for men has also changed as a result of women's massive entry into the work force for the better. [7]Men who would once have felt unrelenting pressure to remain with one firm and climb the career ladder are often freed up by a second income to change careers in midlife. [8]They enjoy greatest intimacy and involvement with their children.

[9]The benefits for business are also readily apparent. [10]No senior manager in the country would deny that the huge generation of women who entered management seven or eight years ago has functioned superbly, often outperforming men.

[11]Yet the prevailing message from the media on the subject of women and business is one filled with pessimism. [12]We hear about women leaving their employers in the lurch when they go on maternity leave. [13]Or we hear the flip side, that women are overly committed to their careers and neglectful of their families. [14]And in fact, it is true that problems arising from women's new work force role do exist, side by side with the benefits.

[15]The problems hurt business as well as individuals and their families, affordable quality childcare, for one example, is still a distant dream. [16]Some women are distracted at work, and men who would have felt secure about their children when their wives were home are also anxious and distracted. [17]Distraction also impedes the productivity of some high-achieving women with the birth of their first child and causes some to depart with the birth of their second.

147. Which of the following sentences displays a nonstandard placement of a modifying phrase?

A. sentence 1

B. sentence 3

C. sentence 6

D. sentence 7

148. Which of the following sentences displays a nonstandard use of a comparative form?

A. sentence 4

B. sentence 8

C. sentence 10

D. sentence 13

149. Which of the following sentences is a nonstandard sentence?

A. sentence 14

B. sentence 15

C. sentence 17

D. sentence 18

Read the passage below; then answer the three questions that follow.

[1]In the past 30 years, television has become a very popular pastime for almost everyone. [2]From the time the mother places the baby in her jumpseat in front of the television until the time the senior citizen in the retirement home watches Vanna White turn the letters on "Wheel of Fortune," Americans spend endless hours in front of the "boob tube." [3]How did we get to be this way?

[4]When my mother was a little girl, what did children do to entertain themselves? [5]They played. [6]Their games usually involved social interaction with other children as well as imaginatively creating entertainment for themselves. [7]They also developed hobbies like woodworking and sewing. [8]Today, few children really know how to play with

each other or entertain themselves. [9]Instead, they sit in front of the television, glued to cartoons that are senseless and often violent. [10]Even if they watch educational programs like "Sesame Street," they don't really have to do anything but watch and listen to what the answer to the question is.

[11]Teenagers, also, use television as a way of avoiding doing things that will be helping them mature. [12]How many kids does much homework anymore? [13]Why not? [14]Because they work part-time jobs and come home from work tired and relax in front of the television.

150. Which of the following sentences uses a nonstandard verb form?

A. sentence 4

B. sentence 7

C. sentence 8

D. sentence 12

151. Which of the following sentences in the passage is nonstandard?

A. sentence 2

B. sentence 7

C. sentence 10

D. sentence 14

152. Which of the following changes is needed in the first paragraph?

A. Sentence 1: Change "has become" to "is."

B. Sentence 2: Change "she" to "the mother" or "the baby."

C. Sentence 2: Change "watches" to "watched."

D. Sentence 4: Change "When" to "Being that."

Read the passage below; then answer the two questions that follow.

[1]Actually, the term "Native American" is incorrect. [2]Indians migrated to this continent from other areas, just earlier than Europeans did. [3]The ancestors of the Anasazi—Indians of the four-state area of Colorado, New Mexico, Utah, and Arizona—probably crossed from Asia into Alaska. [4]About 25,000 years ago, while the continental land bridge still existed. [5]This land bridge arched across the Bering Strait in the last Ice Age. [6]About A.D. 500 the ancestors of the Anasazi moved onto the Mesa Verde, a high

plateau in the desert country of Colorado. [7]The Wetherills, five brothers who ranched in the area, are generally given credit for the first exploration of the ruins in the 1870s and 1880s. [8]There were some 50,000 Anasazi thriving in the four-corners area by the 12,000s A.D. [9]At their zenith, 700 to 1300 A.D., the Anasazi had established widespread communities and built thousands of sophisticated structures—cliff dwellings, pueblos, and kivas. [10]They even engaged in trade with Indians in surrounding regions by exporting pottery and other goods.

153. Which of the following is a nonstandard sentence?

   A. sentence 1

   B. sentence 2

   C. sentence 4

   D. sentence 5

154. Which of the following draws attention away from the main idea of the paragraph?

   A. sentence 3

   B. sentence 4

   C. sentence 7

   D. sentence 8

Read the passage below; then answer the three questions that follow.

[1]The dismissal of Dr. Dennis Ruoff is a travesty of justice. [2]It is not a good feeling to know that a tenured professor can be hounded out of his post just because he disagrees with the board of regents. [3]True, his was the only negative vote on the curriculum issue pushed by the university board of regents. [4]However, since when has a dissenting opinion been the catalyst for persecution of faculty members on this campus? [5]________ ________. [6]English professors, especially, have traditionally had the reputation of fighting courageously against blockhead thinking and against lockstep decision making. [7]They have also historically been the school's champions against injustice.

[8]There cannot be an issue closer to the basis of America's founding principles than this one because the foundation of America is based on freedom of speech. [9]The students of this university need to know whose to blame for the loss of Dr. Ruoff. [10]He is a stimulating speaker, an engaging person, and one of the finest teachers. “Where will this issue come to a halt? [12]Will other tenured professors now be even more intimidated and hesitate to express any view not consistent with the general consensus of opinion? [13]Will students receive a quality education from a university that infringes on freedom of speech?

155. Which of the following requires revision for unnecessary repetition?

   A. sentence 3

   B. sentence 6

   C. sentence 8

   D. sentence 12

156. Which of the following, if added between sentences 4 and 6, best supports the writer's purpose and audience?

   A. We should allow teachers to express their own opinions regardless of what we ourselves think.

   B. This university has always prided itself on teachers who are rather maverick in their thinking, to say the least.

   C. Don't you think this is a pitiful way to treat a fine teacher?

   D. One must acknowledge that university professors, as a whole, should support the opinions of fellow faculty members.

157. Which one of the following changes is needed?

   A. Sentence 8: Change "closer" to "closest."

   B. Sentence 9: Change "whose" to "who's."

   C. Sentence 10: Change "finest" to "finer."

   D. Sentence 11: Change "Where" to "When."

Read the passage below; then answer the three questions that follow.

[1]A growing number of businesses are providing day care facilities for the children of their employees. [2]Some companies charge a standard fee, but most provide the day care free or at a nominal cost. [3]These care programs provide services that continue through the early teens of the children. [4]Many companies are trying to decide if they should help with day care at all. [5]In the event parents need to work overtime, centers are even open on weekends, and some companies showing special initiative in building company loyalty of each employee makes arrangements for special field trips to zoos and museums. [6]Is this kind of care really necessary? [7]Should businesses really be in the business of day care?

[8]Experts in the field cite many advantages for this system. [9]Therefore, loyalty to the company is built, so morale climbs. [10]Studies show that when a company helps its employees blend parent and worker roles, absenteeism and tardiness drop. [11]In addition, workers feel the company has taken more of a personal interest in them. [12]Turnover becomes a much less significant factor for managers. [13]Human resource managers also estimate that every $1 spent on these programs returns $2 or more in increased productivity.

158. Which of the following improves the first paragraph?

A. Change the conjunction from "but" to "and" in sentence 2.

B. Delete the phrase "in the event parents need to work overtime" from sentence 5.

C. Delete sentence 4.

D. Change sentence 6 from an interrogative to a declarative sentence, as in "This kind of care is . . ."

159. Which of the following should be substituted for the underlined word in sentence 5?

A. make

B. is making

C. should make

D. making

160. Which of the following improves the sequence of ideas in the second paragraph?

A. Reverse the order of sentences 8 and 9.

B. Place sentence 12 before sentence 9.

C. Delete sentence 13.

D. Place sentence 9 after sentence 11.

Read the passage below; then answer the three questions that follow.

[1]A significant development during the Paleolithic period was the emergence of modern man. [2]During this time, one million years ago to 12,000 B.C.E., man's brain became much larger. [3]There are two suggested reasons for the rapid evolutionary development of man's brain. [4]First, meat eating led to big-game hunting, an activity that necessitated group planning and cooperation; and second, the use of speech to facilitate planning and coordination of group activities. [5]Tool making was once thought to be a major factor in the development of a large brain for man, but it is now known that many animals use tools and even make tools. [6]Otters will balance a rock on their stomachs as an anvil for breaking open mollusks.

[7]There are two other factors which have greatly influenced the emergence of modern man. [8]Also, food supplies increased significantly after the retreat of the great glaciers about 12,000 years ago. [9]It seems that about 100,000 years ago, genetic evolution became less important than cultural evolution as man developed the ability to pass on accumulated knowledge. [10]This increase in food supplies may have contributed to the ability of man to increase his own numbers, thus ensuring the survival of his species.

161. Which of the following would help the focus of the main idea in the first paragraph?

A. Delete sentence 1.

B. Reverse the order of sentence 1 and 2.

C. Add a sentence after sentence 2 describing the measurements and configurations of brains.

D. Delete sentence 6.

162. Which of the following makes the sequence of ideas clearer in the second paragraph?

A. Delete sentence 7.

B. Reverse the order of sentences 7 and 8.

C. Reverse the order of sentences 8 and 9.

D. Delete sentence 10.

163. Which one of the following is needed?

A. Sentence 4: Change "to facilitate" to "facilitated."

B. Sentence 7: Delete "other."

C. Sentence 9: Change "less" to "least."

D. Sentence 10: Change "ensuring" to "ensured."

Read the passage below; then answer the two questions that follow.

1Polar bears, so named because they live near the North Pole, are called "Nanook" by the Eskimo. 2Living along the cold waters and ice floes of the Arctic Ocean, some polar bears spend time along the coastal areas of northern Canada, Alaska, Norway, Siberia, and Greenland, although some bears live on the islands of the Arctic Ocean and never come close to the mainland. 3Most of these areas lie north of the Arctic circle, and about 85% of Greenland is always covered with ice. 4To protect them from the arctic cold and ice, polar bears have water-repellant fur and a pad of dense, stiff fur on the soles of their snowshoe-like feet. 5In addition, the bears have such a thick layer of fat that infrared photos show no detectable heat, except for their breath.

6Polar bears are the largest land-based carnivores. 7However, they are not always easy to see. 8Because their fur is white with a tinge of yellow, they are difficult to spot on ice floes, their favorite hunting ground. 9Polar bears have a small head, a long neck, and a long body, so they make efficient swimmers. 10Polar bears have no natural enemy except man, and since increased human activity in the Arctic region has put pressure on polar bear populations, the Polar Bear Specialist Group was formed to conserve and manage this unique animal. 11An increase in the number of polar bears is due to cooperation between five nations. 12In 1965, there were 8,000 to 10,000 bears reported, but that population is estimated at 25,000 at the present time.

164. Which of the following would help the focus of the main idea in the first paragraph?

A. Delete the phrase "so named" in sentence 1.

B. Change the comma after "Greenland" to a semicolon in sentence 2.

C. Delete sentence 3.

D. Change sentence 5 by placing the phrase "except for their breath" after "In addition."

165. Which of the following changes is needed?

A. Sentence 6: Change "largest" to "larger."

B. Sentence 10: Change "was" to "is."

C. Sentence 11: Change "between" to "among."

D. Sentence 12: Change "but" to "and."

Read the passage below; then answer the question that follows.

[1]Physicians are now emphasizing that health-conscious citizens should pay attention to triglyceride levels in the body. [2]Triglycerides are another form of fat in the bloodstream, and high triglyceride levels are associated with increased risk of heart disease. [3]In considering health risks, people should consider the levels of triglycerides, along with high-density lipoproteins (HDLs)—the "good" cholesterol—and low-density lipoproteins (LDLs)—the "bad" cholesterol. [4]Triglycerides are especially dangerous in high levels in the bloodstream. [5]For most Americans, a normal triglyceride level falls below 200, and the medical community now recommends that anyone with levels above 200 mg/dl should get further testing and attention.

[6]There are several ways high triglycerides can be treated, a mild aerobic exercise, such as swimming, bicycling, or walking, is recommended. [7]Also, alcohol consumption should be restricted, and caloric intake should be reduced. [8]The diet should be adjusted so that no more than 30 percent of calories should come from fat, and no more than 10 percent of calories should come from saturated fats.

166. Which of the following is a nonstandard sentence?

A. Sentence 2

B. Sentence 5

C. Sentence 6

D. Sentence 8

Read the passage below; then answer the two questions that follow.

[1]The Dead Sea Scrolls are considered the archaeological find of the century. [2]The scrolls, about 800 different documents, are written on leather and papyrus. [3]They may be the oldest versions of the Judeo-Christian sacred texts in existence. [4]The manuscripts are believed to have been written between 200 b.c. and a.d. 50 by the Essenes, members of an ascetic Jewish sect. [5]Most of the Old Testament books (except Esther) appear in the scrolls, and some of the scrolls are multiple copies of these books written by different scribes. [6]Other scrolls are books of the Apocrypha, such as Jubilees, Tobit, and the Wisdom of Solomon, as well as hymns, prayers, prophecies, and biblical commentaries.

[7]For nearly 2,000 years this priceless cache of sacred writings lay hidden in the desert of Judah along the Dead Sea. [8]The first find was in 1947 when a Bedouin shepherd boy discovered the scrolls in a rocky cave of Qumran, ten miles from Jerusalem on the edge of the Dead Sea. [9]Shortly after, other manuscripts were uncovered nearby in different caves. [10]The larger group of scrolls was found in 1952.

[11]Four photographic copies of the scrolls were distributed, and these photographic copies were kept under the strict supervision of a group of 40 scholars dedicated to studying the photographs and analyzing the copies. [12]In December 1990, however, the Huntington Library in San Marino, California, began granting access to anyone who wants to view and study the photographs. [13]This move is hailed by those who have felt left out of the elite cadre of 40 scroll scholars.

167. Which of the following changes is needed?

A. Sentence 4: Change "between" to "among."

B. Sentence 7: Change "lay" to "have lain."

C. Sentence 10: Change "larger" to "largest."

D. Sentence 12: Change "who" to "whom."

168. Which of the following requires revision for unnecessary repetition?

A. Sentence 5

B. Sentence 7

C. Sentence 8

D. Sentence 11

Read the passage below; then answer the two questions that follow.

[1]Most banks require that they be responsible for paying hazard insurance premiums and real estate taxes on houses they are financing. [2]The reason is that if the insurance premium or taxes are not paid, the bank's interest in the property may be jeopardized. [3]Therefore, the mortgage servicer sets up a special account called an escrow account to handle these expenses.

[4]A mortgage loan is usually set up so that the homeowner pays to the bank each month an amount that will eventually pay for taxes and insurance when these expenses come due. [5]Each month's house payment, then, is principal and interest plus 1/12 of the estimated total amount due each year for interest and taxes. [6]Because the amount of taxes levied by the county may vary, and because sometimes insurance rates rise, the bank will sometimes collect more then it will actually pay out. [7]The overage is applied toward the next year's payments, so the house payment reflects a lower amount due each month. [8]If the bank has underestimated the taxes and insurance, there will be a shortage in the escrow account, so the house payments will rise in order that the bank may recoup its loss.

169. Which of the following, if added between sentences 4 and 5, is most consistent with the writer's purpose and audience?

   A. This money is put into a special account called a mortgage escrow account.

   B. Some folks resent the fact that the bank hangs on to a part of their money in an interest-free account.

   C. Most mortgage servicers do not set up an escrow account.

   D. How anybody can fail to see that banks are going out of their way to protect clients is beyond me.

170. Which of the following is needed in the second paragraph?

   A. Sentence 4: Change "set" to "sit."

   B. Sentence 6: Change "then" to "than."

   C. Sentence 7: Change "so" to "but."

   D. Sentence 8: Change "rise" to "raise."

Writing Assignments

Topic 1

Read the passage below on studying literature of the past, and then follow the instructions for writing your essay.

Many scholars note the decline of interest in literature written before the twentieth century. A diminishing number of students pursue studies in Classical, Medieval, and even Renaissance literature. Some observers think this trend is acceptable, since the literature of these early periods is not particularly interesting to the general public. Others say that any lessening of study about the past, and especially its artistic expression, is a negative trend.

In this essay, argue whether you feel that the trend of studying modern versus past literature is commendable or contemptible. Reflect on modern culture and the effects of literature upon it. Discuss the advantages and/or disadvantages of a course of study that excludes or minimizes the literature of earlier periods. Finally, draw upon your own exposure to and attitude toward modern and past literatures, respectively.

Topic 2

What specific characteristics do you think a person must possess in order to be an effective teacher? Fully explain each characteristic and show how the absence of each will reduce effectiveness in the classroom.

WEST–B

Washington Educator Skills Test–Basic

Practice Test Answers

Answer Sheets

Reading

1. Ⓐ Ⓑ Ⓒ Ⓓ
2. Ⓐ Ⓑ Ⓒ Ⓓ
3. Ⓐ Ⓑ Ⓒ Ⓓ
4. Ⓐ Ⓑ Ⓒ Ⓓ
5. Ⓐ Ⓑ Ⓒ Ⓓ
6. Ⓐ Ⓑ Ⓒ Ⓓ
7. Ⓐ Ⓑ Ⓒ Ⓓ
8. Ⓐ Ⓑ Ⓒ Ⓓ
9. Ⓐ Ⓑ Ⓒ Ⓓ
10. Ⓐ Ⓑ Ⓒ Ⓓ
11. Ⓐ Ⓑ Ⓒ Ⓓ
12. Ⓐ Ⓑ Ⓒ Ⓓ
13. Ⓐ Ⓑ Ⓒ Ⓓ
14. Ⓐ Ⓑ Ⓒ Ⓓ
15. Ⓐ Ⓑ Ⓒ Ⓓ
16. Ⓐ Ⓑ Ⓒ Ⓓ
17. Ⓐ Ⓑ Ⓒ Ⓓ
18. Ⓐ Ⓑ Ⓒ Ⓓ
19. Ⓐ Ⓑ Ⓒ Ⓓ
20. Ⓐ Ⓑ Ⓒ Ⓓ
21. Ⓐ Ⓑ Ⓒ Ⓓ
22. Ⓐ Ⓑ Ⓒ Ⓓ
23. Ⓐ Ⓑ Ⓒ Ⓓ
24. Ⓐ Ⓑ Ⓒ Ⓓ
25. Ⓐ Ⓑ Ⓒ Ⓓ
26. Ⓐ Ⓑ Ⓒ Ⓓ
27. Ⓐ Ⓑ Ⓒ Ⓓ
28. Ⓐ Ⓑ Ⓒ Ⓓ
29. Ⓐ Ⓑ Ⓒ Ⓓ
30. Ⓐ Ⓑ Ⓒ Ⓓ
31. Ⓐ Ⓑ Ⓒ Ⓓ
32. Ⓐ Ⓑ Ⓒ Ⓓ
33. Ⓐ Ⓑ Ⓒ Ⓓ
34. Ⓐ Ⓑ Ⓒ Ⓓ
35. Ⓐ Ⓑ Ⓒ Ⓓ
36. Ⓐ Ⓑ Ⓒ Ⓓ
37. Ⓐ Ⓑ Ⓒ Ⓓ
38. Ⓐ Ⓑ Ⓒ Ⓓ
39. Ⓐ Ⓑ Ⓒ Ⓓ
40. Ⓐ Ⓑ Ⓒ Ⓓ
41. Ⓐ Ⓑ Ⓒ Ⓓ
42. Ⓐ Ⓑ Ⓒ Ⓓ
43. Ⓐ Ⓑ Ⓒ Ⓓ
44. Ⓐ Ⓑ Ⓒ Ⓓ
45. Ⓐ Ⓑ Ⓒ Ⓓ
46. Ⓐ Ⓑ Ⓒ Ⓓ
47. Ⓐ Ⓑ Ⓒ Ⓓ
48. Ⓐ Ⓑ Ⓒ Ⓓ
49. Ⓐ Ⓑ Ⓒ Ⓓ
50. Ⓐ Ⓑ Ⓒ Ⓓ
51. Ⓐ Ⓑ Ⓒ Ⓓ
52. Ⓐ Ⓑ Ⓒ Ⓓ
53. Ⓐ Ⓑ Ⓒ Ⓓ
54. Ⓐ Ⓑ Ⓒ Ⓓ
55. Ⓐ Ⓑ Ⓒ Ⓓ
56. Ⓐ Ⓑ Ⓒ Ⓓ
57. Ⓐ Ⓑ Ⓒ Ⓓ
58. Ⓐ Ⓑ Ⓒ Ⓓ
59. Ⓐ Ⓑ Ⓒ Ⓓ
60. Ⓐ Ⓑ Ⓒ Ⓓ

Mathematics

61. Ⓐ Ⓑ Ⓒ Ⓓ
62. Ⓐ Ⓑ Ⓒ Ⓓ
63. Ⓐ Ⓑ Ⓒ Ⓓ
64. Ⓐ Ⓑ Ⓒ Ⓓ
65. Ⓐ Ⓑ Ⓒ Ⓓ
66. Ⓐ Ⓑ Ⓒ Ⓓ
67. Ⓐ Ⓑ Ⓒ Ⓓ
68. Ⓐ Ⓑ Ⓒ Ⓓ
69. Ⓐ Ⓑ Ⓒ Ⓓ
70. Ⓐ Ⓑ Ⓒ Ⓓ
71. Ⓐ Ⓑ Ⓒ Ⓓ
72. Ⓐ Ⓑ Ⓒ Ⓓ
73. Ⓐ Ⓑ Ⓒ Ⓓ
74. Ⓐ Ⓑ Ⓒ Ⓓ
75. Ⓐ Ⓑ Ⓒ Ⓓ
76. Ⓐ Ⓑ Ⓒ Ⓓ
77. Ⓐ Ⓑ Ⓒ Ⓓ
78. Ⓐ Ⓑ Ⓒ Ⓓ
79. Ⓐ Ⓑ Ⓒ Ⓓ
80. Ⓐ Ⓑ Ⓒ Ⓓ
81. Ⓐ Ⓑ Ⓒ Ⓓ
82. Ⓐ Ⓑ Ⓒ Ⓓ
83. Ⓐ Ⓑ Ⓒ Ⓓ
84. Ⓐ Ⓑ Ⓒ Ⓓ
85. Ⓐ Ⓑ Ⓒ Ⓓ
86. Ⓐ Ⓑ Ⓒ Ⓓ
87. Ⓐ Ⓑ Ⓒ Ⓓ
88. Ⓐ Ⓑ Ⓒ Ⓓ
89. Ⓐ Ⓑ Ⓒ Ⓓ
90. Ⓐ Ⓑ Ⓒ Ⓓ
91. Ⓐ Ⓑ Ⓒ Ⓓ
92. Ⓐ Ⓑ Ⓒ Ⓓ
93. Ⓐ Ⓑ Ⓒ Ⓓ
94. Ⓐ Ⓑ Ⓒ Ⓓ
95. Ⓐ Ⓑ Ⓒ Ⓓ
96. Ⓐ Ⓑ Ⓒ Ⓓ
97. Ⓐ Ⓑ Ⓒ Ⓓ
98. Ⓐ Ⓑ Ⓒ Ⓓ
99. Ⓐ Ⓑ Ⓒ Ⓓ
100. Ⓐ Ⓑ Ⓒ Ⓓ
101. Ⓐ Ⓑ Ⓒ Ⓓ
102. Ⓐ Ⓑ Ⓒ Ⓓ
103. Ⓐ Ⓑ Ⓒ Ⓓ
104. Ⓐ Ⓑ Ⓒ Ⓓ
105. Ⓐ Ⓑ Ⓒ Ⓓ
106. Ⓐ Ⓑ Ⓒ Ⓓ
107. Ⓐ Ⓑ Ⓒ Ⓓ
108. Ⓐ Ⓑ Ⓒ Ⓓ
109. Ⓐ Ⓑ Ⓒ Ⓓ
110. Ⓐ Ⓑ Ⓒ Ⓓ
111. Ⓐ Ⓑ Ⓒ Ⓓ
112. Ⓐ Ⓑ Ⓒ Ⓓ
113. Ⓐ Ⓑ Ⓒ Ⓓ
114. Ⓐ Ⓑ Ⓒ Ⓓ
115. Ⓐ Ⓑ Ⓒ Ⓓ
116. Ⓐ Ⓑ Ⓒ Ⓓ
117. Ⓐ Ⓑ Ⓒ Ⓓ
118. Ⓐ Ⓑ Ⓒ Ⓓ
119. Ⓐ Ⓑ Ⓒ Ⓓ
120. Ⓐ Ⓑ Ⓒ Ⓓ

Writing

121. Ⓐ Ⓑ Ⓒ Ⓓ
122. Ⓐ Ⓑ Ⓒ Ⓓ
123. Ⓐ Ⓑ Ⓒ Ⓓ
124. Ⓐ Ⓑ Ⓒ Ⓓ
125. Ⓐ Ⓑ Ⓒ Ⓓ
126. Ⓐ Ⓑ Ⓒ Ⓓ
127. Ⓐ Ⓑ Ⓒ Ⓓ
128. Ⓐ Ⓑ Ⓒ Ⓓ
129. Ⓐ Ⓑ Ⓒ Ⓓ
130. Ⓐ Ⓑ Ⓒ Ⓓ
131. Ⓐ Ⓑ Ⓒ Ⓓ
132. Ⓐ Ⓑ Ⓒ Ⓓ
133. Ⓐ Ⓑ Ⓒ Ⓓ
134. Ⓐ Ⓑ Ⓒ Ⓓ
135. Ⓐ Ⓑ Ⓒ Ⓓ
136. Ⓐ Ⓑ Ⓒ Ⓓ
137. Ⓐ Ⓑ Ⓒ Ⓓ
138. Ⓐ Ⓑ Ⓒ Ⓓ
139. Ⓐ Ⓑ Ⓒ Ⓓ
140. Ⓐ Ⓑ Ⓒ Ⓓ
141. Ⓐ Ⓑ Ⓒ Ⓓ
142. Ⓐ Ⓑ Ⓒ Ⓓ
143. Ⓐ Ⓑ Ⓒ Ⓓ
144. Ⓐ Ⓑ Ⓒ Ⓓ
145. Ⓐ Ⓑ Ⓒ Ⓓ
146. Ⓐ Ⓑ Ⓒ Ⓓ
147. Ⓐ Ⓑ Ⓒ Ⓓ
148. Ⓐ Ⓑ Ⓒ Ⓓ
149. Ⓐ Ⓑ Ⓒ Ⓓ
150. Ⓐ Ⓑ Ⓒ Ⓓ
151. Ⓐ Ⓑ Ⓒ Ⓓ
152. Ⓐ Ⓑ Ⓒ Ⓓ
153. Ⓐ Ⓑ Ⓒ Ⓓ
154. Ⓐ Ⓑ Ⓒ Ⓓ
155. Ⓐ Ⓑ Ⓒ Ⓓ
156. Ⓐ Ⓑ Ⓒ Ⓓ
157. Ⓐ Ⓑ Ⓒ Ⓓ
158. Ⓐ Ⓑ Ⓒ Ⓓ
159. Ⓐ Ⓑ Ⓒ Ⓓ
160. Ⓐ Ⓑ Ⓒ Ⓓ
161. Ⓐ Ⓑ Ⓒ Ⓓ
162. Ⓐ Ⓑ Ⓒ Ⓓ
163. Ⓐ Ⓑ Ⓒ Ⓓ
164. Ⓐ Ⓑ Ⓒ Ⓓ
165. Ⓐ Ⓑ Ⓒ Ⓓ
166. Ⓐ Ⓑ Ⓒ Ⓓ
167. Ⓐ Ⓑ Ⓒ Ⓓ
168. Ⓐ Ⓑ Ⓒ Ⓓ
169. Ⓐ Ⓑ Ⓒ Ⓓ
170. Ⓐ Ⓑ Ⓒ Ⓓ

Practice Test Answer Sheets

DIRECTIONS

The directions and Topic 1 are presented in the Practice Test. Read them carefully before you begin to write.

Go on to the next page.

Continue your response here.

Stop. End of Topic 1.

Practice Test Answer Sheets

DIRECTIONS

The directions and Topic 2 are presented in the Practice Test. Read them carefully before you begin to write.

Go on to the next page.

Continue your response here.

Stop. End of Topic 2.

Practice Test Answer Key

Reading

1. (D)
2. (B)
3. (A)
4. (C)
5. (C)
6. (A)
7. (D)
8. (D)
9. (A)
10. (A)
11. (C)
12. (D)
13. (B)
14. (A)
15. (B)
16. (A)
17. (B)
18. (C)
19. (C)
20. (B)
21. (D)
22. (D)
23. (C)
24. (B)
25. (D)
26. (B)
27. (B)
28. (C)
29. (B)
30. (C)
31. (B)
32. (B)
33. (D)
34. (A)
35. (D)
36. (A)
37. (B)
38. (A)
39. (B)
40. (A)
41. (D)
42. (C)
43. (B)
44. (C)
45. (B)
46. (B)
47. (D)
48. (C)
49. (B)
50. (A)
51. (D)
52. (D)
53. (C)
54. (A)
55. (D)
56. (C)
57. (A)
58. (C)
59. (C)
60. (B)

Mathematics

61. (C)
62. (A)
63. (C)
64. (D)
65. (A)
66. (C)
67. (A)
68. (C)
69. (D)
70. (A)
71. (B)
72. (C)
73. (A)
74. (B)
75. (D)
76. (C)
77. (C)
78. (D)
79. (A)
80. (C)
81. (B)
82. (D)
83. (A)
84. (B)
85. (D)
86. (A)
87. (D)
88. (A)
89. (C)
90. (A)
91. (D)
92. (C)
93. (C)
94. (A)
95. (D)
96. (B)
97. (A)
98. (B)
99. (A)
100. (C)
101. (A)
102. (C)
103. (D)
104. (C)
105. (A)
106. (D)
107. (A)
108. (D)
109. (C)
110. (C)
111. (B)
112. (B)
113. (D)
114. (A)
115. (C)
116. (D)
117. (B)
118. (D)
119. (D)
120. (D)

Writing

121. (B)
122. (A)
123. (D)
124. (B)
125. (C)
126. (C)
127. (D)
128. (D)
129. (C)
130. (B)
131. (A)
132. (C)
133. (D)
134. (D)
135. (A)
136. (B)
137. (B)
138. (A)
139. (D)
140. (A)
141. (B)
142. (B)
143. (C)
144. (A)
145. (B)
146. (A)
147. (C)
148. (C)
149. (B)
150. (D)
151. (D)
152. (B)
153. (C)
154. (C)
155. (C)
156. (B)
157. (B)
158. (C)
159. (A)
160. (D)
161. (D)
162. (C)
163. (A)
164. (C)
165. (C)
166. (C)
167. (C)
168. (D)
169. (C)
170. (D)

Detailed Explanations of Answers: Reading

1. **D**

D is correct because its precepts are summations of each of the composition's main paragraphs. Choice A only mentions points made in the second paragraph; B and C only mention scattered points made throughout the passage, each of which does not represent a larger body of information within the passage.

2. **B**

The second paragraph states that this is the reason that water is a most unusual substance. Choices A and C list unusual properties of water, but are not developed in the same manner as the property stated in B. Choice D is not correct under any circumstances.

3. **A**

The sentence contrasts distilled water to that which contains salt, so A is correct. Choices B, C, and D are not implied by the passage.

4. **C**

The writer's didactic summary of water's properties is the only perspective found in the passage. Choices A and B are the subjects of individual paragraphs within the passage, but hardly represent the entire passage itself. An in-depth discussion of the physical states of liquids is not offered within the passage.

5. **C**

The correct choice is C because of the many properties of water ascribed to it in the passage, each of which might serve one practical purpose or another. Choices A and D are contradicted within the passage, while B is not implied at all by the passage.

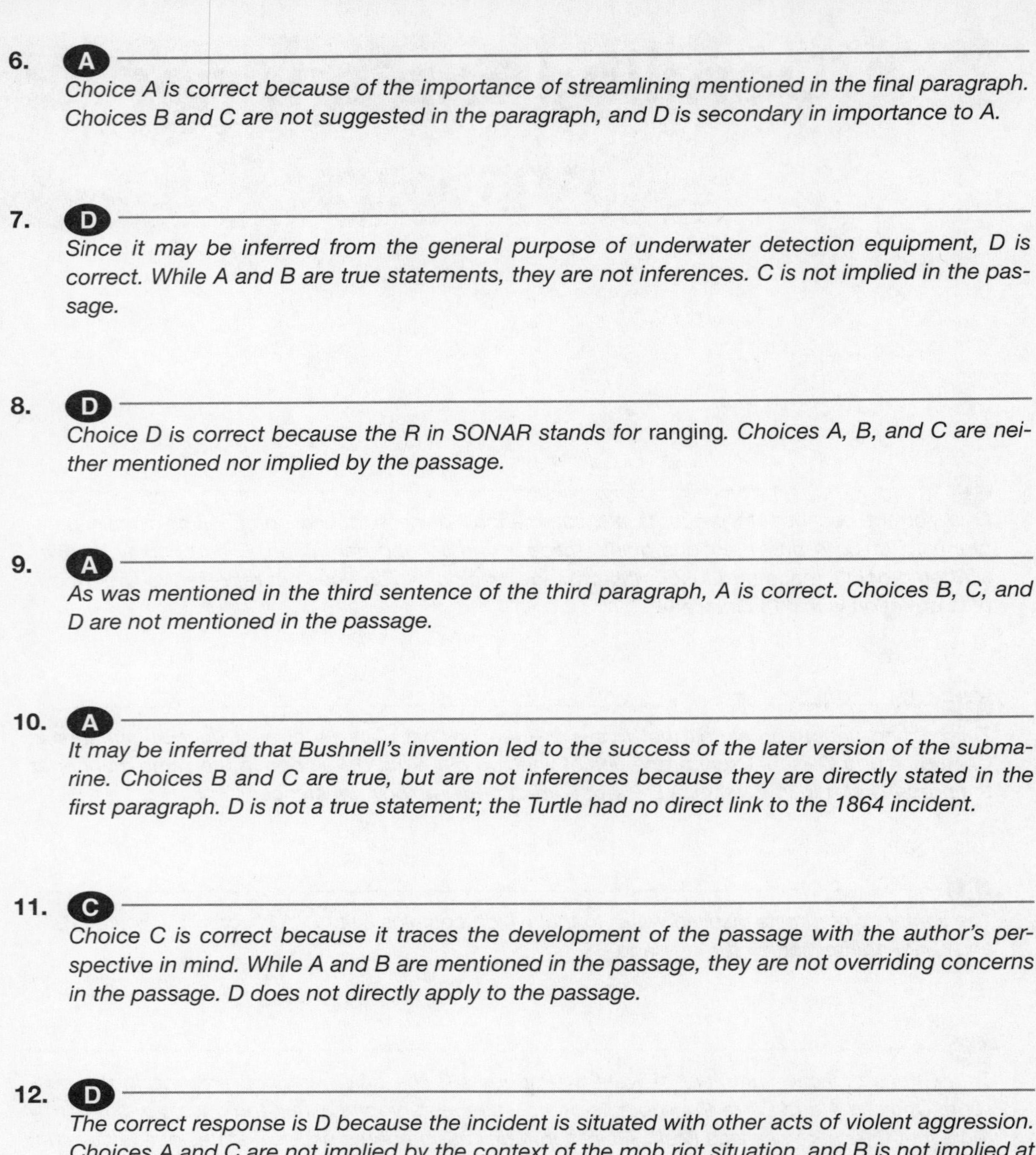

6. **A**

Choice A is correct because of the importance of streamlining mentioned in the final paragraph. Choices B and C are not suggested in the paragraph, and D is secondary in importance to A.

7. **D**

Since it may be inferred from the general purpose of underwater detection equipment, D is correct. While A and B are true statements, they are not inferences. C is not implied in the passage.

8. **D**

Choice D is correct because the R in SONAR stands for ranging. *Choices A, B, and C are neither mentioned nor implied by the passage.*

9. **A**

As was mentioned in the third sentence of the third paragraph, A is correct. Choices B, C, and D are not mentioned in the passage.

10. **A**

It may be inferred that Bushnell's invention led to the success of the later version of the submarine. Choices B and C are true, but are not inferences because they are directly stated in the first paragraph. D is not a true statement; the Turtle had no direct link to the 1864 incident.

11. **C**

Choice C is correct because it traces the development of the passage with the author's perspective in mind. While A and B are mentioned in the passage, they are not overriding concerns in the passage. D does not directly apply to the passage.

12. **D**

The correct response is D because the incident is situated with other acts of violent aggression. Choices A and C are not implied by the context of the mob riot situation, and B is not implied at all by the paragraph.

13. **B**

The correct answer is B because it represents a theme prevalent in the fourth paragraph. Both A and D represent individual strands within the paragraph, but do not express its main idea; C is not mentioned or implied in the paragraph.

14. A

All of the urban difficulties that are mentioned in the passage stem from the rapid growth of immigration. Neither B nor C is implied within the passage. Choice D has no direct bearing on the development of the passage.

15. B

The combined percentages of English and German immigrants equal 45 percent (Irish immigrants represent 43 percent of the graph). Choice A is incorrect because the Irish immigrants represent less than half of the graph. Choice C is incorrect because the graph nowhere implies that the "All Others" section of the graph is restricted to Italian immigrants. D is incorrect because the English and German percentages are unequal.

16. A

The last sentence in these instructions tells the student that the paper must be proofread with no "mechanical" (punctuation) errors. The third sentence states that an understanding of the reading material is required. Answers (B) and (C) contain only a portion of the needed requirements, while (D) is completely inaccurate. Thus, (A) is the correct answer.

17. B

As used in the passage, the term "sophisticated prose" means that the student must write a readable paper using thoughtful language, thereby demonstrating a familiarity with the primary text. Answers (A), (C), and (D) all contain language that suggests the opposite of a readable paper.

18. C

A primary text is the source material, main, or principal text used in an assignment. The remaining answers (A), (B), and (D) refer to either secondary materials or reference sources.

19. C

The passage suggests that education is primarily based on failure as negative reinforcement and that, in order to create a more productive and positive learning environment, the emphasis must shift to success. While answers A and B may be correct, they are not the main idea of the passage. D is simply a statement that is not based upon any factual evidence whatsoever. Therefore, C is the correct answer.

20. B

An axiom in this case is another word for motto. It can also mean an accepted truism or principle, which would also apply here. Answers A, C, and D are erroneous definitions and, therefore B, University motto or principle, is the correct answer.

21. D

The passage states that "the language of failure . . . will have a prohibitive impact on the students' self-esteem," and, thus, D is the correct answer. Answers A, B, and C do not apply in this case.

22. D

The first paragraph of the passage tells the reader that, in addition to personal expression, language also has the power to "persuade and influence." While answers A, B, and C may indeed be attributes of language, they are not focused upon in the passage.

23. C

The author remains objective throughout the passage. That is, he remains impartial and factual. Answer A, "lethargy," means sluggish; B, "apathy," means unconcerned. D, "intensity," means vehement or fierce, and thus does not apply.

24. B

The third sentence suggests that poetry has the ability to serve both as an adornment or embellishment of an era and as a social commentary. The passage fundamentally suggests that poetry is more than just lyrical fluff, it is a means of social analysis, protest, and interpretation. While A, C, and D are components of the passage, they are not the passage's main topic.

25. D

The word trope *means that a word is used in a figurative sense. That is, it conjures images of Greco-Roman representations. Answer A is a troop; B, and C are types of terminology that do not apply.*

26. B

The passage suggests that a critic is a viable political force that serves both as a censure and a social commentator. Answers A, C, and D are subjective answers and are, therefore, inappropriate.

27. **B**

The passage states that the etymology of the word "censure" dates to the Middle Ages, suggesting that it was in use at that time. The passage also states that a critic can also be equivalent to a censurer. It, therefore, could not be A, a modern phenomenon, or D, developed around the time of the Civil War. Answer C is not addressed in the passage, leaving B as the best answer.

28. **C**

The passage addresses both the implications (indications) and the connotations (meaning) associated with the role of the critic as author. Answers B, and D are only alluded to, while A is a supposition. Thus, C is the correct answer.

29. **B**

Etymology is the study of the history and/or origin of a word. This definition renders the remaining answers false.

30. **C**

The passage suggests that Douglass was concerned with raising social consciousness about slavery. His interest in refuting those who doubted his claims was for the sake of authenticity.

31. **B**

Douglass was one of the eminent human rights leaders of the nineteenth century. All the other choices, while true, are irrelevant to the question and are not supported by the text.

32. **B**

The passage states "Mrs. Auld recognized Frederick's intellectual acumen." A synonym for "acumen" is intelligence, insight, or natural ability. The other choices are inaccurate.

33. **D**

Choices A, B, and C are too vague or ill-defined. Thus, choice D is correct.

34. **A**

An "impromptu" speech is one given extemporaneously, or off the cuff.

35. **D**

A teaching assistant would be expected to lay the foundation for her lecture and the present greater detail by way of example, or as the passage puts it, "illustration." Someone in this position, having set this task for herself, would not be prone to refuting her own lecture notes (A), attempting to cause confusion (B), or perhaps least of all, working to subvert the lecture topic she herself had elected to teach (C).

36. **A**

The definition of the term "pedagogical" is A, academic. The answers B, abstract, C, meaningless, and D obtuse are incorrect.

37. **B**

The author's classroom experience was B, intelligible (understandable) and pragmatic (practical or utilitarian). The passage gives credence to this by the author's use of such words as "clear and well prepared." Answers A, and C suggest the opposite of a positive experience, and there is no evidence given that the experience was too advanced or complicated (D).

38. **A**

The passage tells of the "great (linguistic) vowel shift" of the early fifteenth century. While the passage speaks of B, an artistic renaissance; C, new linguistic freedoms; and D, effects on artistic expression, these are all results of the shift and not the shift itself. The shift is what the passage is about. Thus, A is the correct answer.

39. **B**

In this case, linguistic *refers to speaking, talking, verbiage, and/or the act of oration. A, C, and D are not acceptable definitions for the word* linguistic*. Consequently, Choice B, verbal or rhetorical, is the correct answer.*

40. **A**

Answers B, C, and D are generalized answers resulting from the vowel shift. Choice A is a direct result of the shift and is quoted directly from the passage.

Therefore, A is the correct answer.

41. **D**

The passage states that lead poisoning leads to learning disabilities and possibly even death. Choice A is too broad, and B and C are not directly addressed, leaving D as the correct answer.

42. **C**

The passage states that "all California MediCal-eligible children, ages one through five, will now be routinely screened." Answer choices A, children in California, B, children with learning disabilities, and D, minority children, are generalities not stated in the passage. Only Choice C is clearly stated in the passage.

43. **B**

The statistics suggest that inner-city children are at the greatest risk from lead poisoning. The statistics do not support answers A, C, and D, leaving B as the only legitimate answer.

44. **C**

The last sentence of the passage suggests that testing will catch the disease "at an early stage" and prevent serious disorders. Choices A, B, and D do not address this ultimate goal of the testing program. Only Choice C reiterates the program's ultimate purpose.

45. **B**

The ranchers believe that killing the eagles will protect their ranches. This is understood by the implication that "attract[ing] and kill[ing] predators . . . in an effort to preserve young grazing animals" will protect their ranches.

46. **B**

The author's use of words such as "mighty bald eagle" and "threatened by a new menace" supports concern for the topic. For the most part, the author appears objective; thus, Choice B, concerned interest, is the correct answer.

47. **D**

The passage asks the reader to question traditional gender issues. The punctuation at the end of the passage affirms this. A, B, C, and D do not assert questions. Rather, they suggest a declarative action or stance to be taken regarding social gender issues. Only D addresses the passage's questioning of gender roles; therefore, D is the correct answer.

48. **C**

To "ostracize" is to alienate, exile, or banish. A, acceptance, B, pressure, and D, examination, are false definitions and are incorrect.

49. **B**

The passage states that discourse communities are of similar mindsets, thus making them suspect. A, C, and D do not address this issue directly. Only B reiterates the second sentence of the passage; therefore, it is the correct answer.

50. **A**

The definition of the noun paradigm *is that it is a model, criterion, or standard that others follow or by which they are measured. Thus, A, model or standard, is the correct answer.*

51. **D**

Choice D is correct because the passage specifically mentions the California coast, the Alaskan coast, and the U. S. Gulf Coast as sites of oil spills.

52. **D**

Choice D is correct because workers were trying to keep the oil in the water and away from the beach. Choices A and are incorrect because neither sightseers nor animals are discussed in the passage. Choice C is incorrect because the cleanup crews wanted to remove the oil, not let it soak into the sand.

53. **C**

Choice C is correct. This question must be answered using the process of elimination. Cleanup trust funds, increased federal spending, using the National Guard, and creating a department of oceans are all discussed in the passage. Therefore, choices A, B, and D are incorrect. Only choice C names a solution not mentioned in the passage.

54. **A**

Choice A is correct. The last sentence of the passage specifically states that spills are a constant threat if offshore drilling and the shipment of oil in tankers continues. Choice B is incorrect because the passage does not discuss crews or training programs. While the passage does imply that the government should be better prepared to clean up, the author does not state that oil spills would cease to be a problem if the government was better prepared. Therefore, choice C is incorrect. Choice D is incorrect because foreign oil producers are not mentioned.

55. **D**

Answer D fulfills the requirements stated in rules 2 and 4 of the instructions for absentee voting. None of the other choices do.

56. C

Mr. Applebee's daughter must sign the request in her own handwriting, as stated in instruction (6).

57. A

You can vote in future elections only if you are registered at your new address, as explained in instruction (3).

58. C

Choice A, "Grinding operations, 126–140," would be expected to discuss how the grinders are operated, but "grinding wheels" is too general in the context of the question posed. Pages 136–138 (choice B) describe an unrelated function. Choice D, "Grinding wheels, 126–129," is overly broad, particularly when considered alongside choice C, which proves to be the best choice because it specifically uses the phrase "installing the wheel."

59. C

While the extract is surely arranged alphabetically, there is another pattern that emerges—one governed by task. This is clear by the preponderance of task-oriented descriptors (e.g., "grinding," "sharpening," "truing and dressing," etc.). Choice B, "Physical characteristics," addresses a level of detail that does not figure to any appreciable extent in the passage. Thus, choice C is the best answer.

60. B

Choice A is incorrect because finding information on grinding a rounded edge is not relevant to the idea of sharpening a chisel. Choice C, "grinding wheels," gives no particular indication of holding the answer. Choice D, while pointing generally to the answer, proves inferior when juxtaposed with choice B because the latter contains some of the specific language sought in the extract (i.e., "grinding metal stock").

Detailed Explanations of Answers: Mathematics

61. C

The useful, traditional approach to multiplying simple fractions (those between 0 and 1) is to first multiply the numerators together and then to multiply the denominators together to find the product. In this case, $\frac{3}{4} \times \frac{2}{3} = \frac{6}{12}$. *That fraction is then shown in simplest form,* $\frac{1}{2}$.

62. A

The traditional whole number division algorithm (method) is helpful when dividing decimals longhand. The work can be set up like this:

$$0.05\overline{)6.2}$$

Dividing (while temporarily ignoring the zeros and decimal points) gives

$$\begin{array}{r} 124 \\ 0.05\overline{)\,6.2} \\ \underline{50} \\ 12 \\ \underline{10} \\ 20 \end{array}$$

Next, you count the number of digits to the right of the decimal point in the divisor (two). Two, then, is the number of places that you shift the "inside" decimal point to the right, then "up" into the answer:

$$\begin{array}{r} 124 \\ 0.05\overline{)\,6.2} \end{array}$$

Because the answer is a whole number, the decimal point does not have to be shown.

63. **C**

When subtraction involves any negative numbers, a good rule to use is, "Don't subtract the second number. Instead, add its opposite." Using that rule, the original expression,

(–36) – 11

becomes

(–36) + (–11).

To be "in debt" by 36, then to be further *"in debt" by 11, puts one "in debt" by 47, shown as –47.*

64. **D**

When presented with a simplification problem involving several different operations, the universally accepted order of operations *must be used. In this case, working from left-to-right, the multiplication (6 × 2) and the division (3 ÷ 3) must be completed first, giving 12 + 1, or 13.*

65. **A**

One way to arrive at the answer is to set up an incomplete proportion, with one corner being x:

$$\frac{14}{x} = \frac{22}{100}$$

To complete the proportion (and to find the answer), you can cross-multiply 14 and 100, equaling 1400, which you then divide by 22, giving approximately 64.

Estimation works well for this problem too. Think of 22% as nearly *20%, or one-fifth. If 14 is one-fifth of something, you can multiply 14 by 5 to get you near the answer. 14 × 5 = 70, which is close to 64, or answer A.*

66. **C**

Because multiplication is commutative (factors can be multiplied in any order), you multiply the 2 and the 6, giving 12; and 10^3 *and* 10^4*, giving* 10^7*. (Note: To multiply exponential expressions with like bases you* add *the exponents.) This gives* 12×10^7*.*

That expression is not in scientific notation (the first number must be between 0 and 10), so you change the 12 into 1.2, and 10^7 *into* 10^8 *to "compensate."*

67. **A**

*Bob earned $6 an hour for three hours, or $18. Keyva babysat for six hours (*twice as long as *Bob), earning $7 each hour. That's $42. $18 + $42 = $60.*

68. 

To find the average (mean) of a set of values, first add them together. In this case, the negative and the positive integers should be added together separately. Those two sums are –12 and 5. (The zero can be ignored; it does not affect either sum.) Then –12 and 5 should be added together for a sum of –7.

To complete the work, the sum of –7 must be divided by the number of values (7), giving –1.

69. 

The first price increase is for 10%. That's the same as one-tenth, and one-tenth of $40 is $4. Adding $4 to $40 gives $44 as the March price.

The next increase is 15% of $44. Multiplying 44 by 0.15 (0.15 being another way to represent 15%) gives 6.6, which is read as $6.60. You then increase the March price of $44 by $6.60, giving you $50.60.

Note that you cannot arrive at the answer by adding the individual percent increases (10 + 15 = 25) and then multiplying by 40.

70. 

Finding the answer by setting up a proportion works well here:

$$\frac{3}{4.65} = \frac{5}{x}$$

Proportions often are two fractions set equal to each other, with one "corner" being the unknown value, or x. The equation above can be read as "3 is to 4.65 as 5 is to what?"

One way to solve a proportion (that is; to find the value of x), is to cross-multiply the two corners that have known values (in this case 4.65 and 5.) That gives 23.25, which is then divided by the remaining known value (3), giving 7.75.

71. 

The percentage "0.2%" must be seen as "two-tenths of one percent" (and not as "two percent"). Given as a decimal numeral, 0.2% is 0.002. (You move the decimal point two places to the left when converting from a percent to a decimal numeral.)

You then multiply the starting population of 1620 by 0.002, giving 3.24, or approximately 3 people. Adding 3 to 1620 gives 1623.

72. **C**

The chart shows that Madison received less than half of the votes (his slice takes up less than half of the pie), so statement I cannot be true.

Washington and Monroe together received 55% of the votes, and everyone else voted for Madison, so Madison must have received 45% of the votes (all of the candidates' percents must add up to 100%.) Statement II is therefore true.

Monroe received 30% of the 600 votes. 0.30 times 600 is 180, so statement III is true.

Madison received 45% of the vote, and 45% of 600 is 270, so statement IV is false.

73. A

The somewhat steep straight line to the left tells you that Mr. Cain worked at a steady rate for awhile. The completely flat line in the middle tells you he stopped for a while—the line doesn't go up because no grass was cut then. Finally the line continues upward (after his break) less steeply (and therefore more flatly), indicating that he was working at a slower rate.

74. B

Because Ms. Patton's increases were *consistent ($3,000 annually), and because the directions tell you that only one statement is true, answer B must be correct. To be more confident however, you can examine the other statements:*

The range of Ms. Patton's earnings is $12,000 (the jump from $30,000 to $42,000), not $15,000, so answer A cannot be correct.

Although Ms. Patton may have earned $45,000 in 2003, you don't know that, so answer C cannot be correct.

Answer D gives the incorrect earnings average; it was $36,000, not $38,000.

75. D

It is helpful to make a sketch of the line on the coordinate plane. (To do to that you need to know how to plot individual points.)

The line "travels" from the lower left to the upper right, meaning that it has a positive slope. Statement II is therefore true. The y-intercept of a line is the spot at which the line crosses, or intercepts, *the vertical axis. In this case, that's at point (0, 4). (You can simply say that the y-intercept is 4, without mentioning the 0). Statement IV is therefore true as well.*

76. C

There are several methods for finding the slope of a line if two points are known. The most straightforward method is to use the slope formula*:*

$$m = \frac{y_2 - y_1}{x_2 - x_1}$$

This can be read as "the slope of a line (m) *is equal to the difference of the y coordinates of any two points on the line* ($y_2 - y_1$) *divided by the difference of the x coordinates.*

($x_2 - x_1$).

For this problem, you subtract the first y coordinate from the second [(–2) – 6], giving –8. You then do the same for the x coordinates [4 – (–2)], giving 6. Dividing –8 by 6 is the same as showing the fraction $-\frac{8}{6}$ *or, in lowest terms,* $-\frac{4}{3}$.

77. 

There are several ways to determine which equation matches the line. An easy way is to decide first whether the line has a positive or a negative slope. Because the line moves from the upper left to the lower right, you would say it has a negative slope.

In a linear equation of the form y = mx + b *(where* y *is isolated on the left side of the equation), the coefficient of* x *is the slope of the line. The only equation with a negative slope (–8) is response C, so that is the correct answer.*

Another clue that C is correct can be found by considering the apparent slope, or steepness/shallowness of the line. The line in problem 17 is fairly steep, and a slope of –8 (or 8) is considered fairly steep too, suggesting that C is correct.

78. 

The y-intercept *of a linear equation is the point at which its graph passes through, or* intercepts, *the vertical y-axis. One way to determine the y-intercept is by rewriting the equation in* y-intercept form*:*

$y = mx + b$

If a linear equation is in that form, b *tells you where the graph of the line intercepts the y-axis. In this case, you rewrite (or* transform*) the equation following these steps:*

$2x = 3y - 12$

$3y - 12 = 2x$

$3y = 2x + 12$

$y = 2 \div 3\ x + 4$

That final version of the equation is indeed in y-intercept form. The 4 tells you that the graph of the equation intercepts the y-axis at point (0, 4).

79. 

Consider various random points in the shaded area: (5, –2), (–1, 2), (12, 2.5) and (–9, 1). Notice that all points in the shaded area have a y-coordinate value less than 3. *The inequality that states this is the one in A ("*y *is less than 3.")*

80. 

Inverse variations give graphs that are curves. As equations, they take the forms $xy = k$ or $y = \frac{k}{x}$. The graph shown in problem 20 is simpler than that, so statement I is false.

The graphs of direct variations *are straight lines that pass through the point* (0,0) *(the* origin.*) As equations, they take the form $y = mx + 0$, or simply $y = mx$. The line shown in problem 20 is the graph of a direct variation, so statement II is true.*

Because point (–5, 5) is equally distant from both the x- and y-axes, the line "cuts" quadrant II at a 45° angle. Lines that form 45° angles with the x- and y-axes (assuming the same scales on both axes) have slopes of 1 *or* –1. *The line in problem 20 travels from upper left to lower right, meaning that its slope is negative, so statement III is also true.*

81. **B**

Just from looking at the graph, it's clear that most of the space under the curve is past the 60 mark on the x-axis, answer D is eliminated because it doesn't include statement I.

Statement II can't be answered by what the graph shows. It appears possible that certain questions were too hard for many in the class and that there weren't enough questions to differentiate B students from C students, but perhaps the class performed exactly as it should have, given the students' ability and Ms. Alvarez's teaching. The distribution can give a teacher many clues about the test and the students and even herself, but by itself tells us nothing about the fairness of the test. Thus, answer A can be eliminated.

Statement III is also false; in left-skewed distributions such as this one, the median is higher than the mean. This is true because the mean is lowered by the lowest scores while the mean is relatively unaffected by them.

Statement IV is true: one fairly large group has scored in the high 80s and 90s and another discernible group in the low to mid 60s, whereas few students fall outside these two groups. Thus, the answer has to be B.

82. **D**

Using the rules for solving one-variable equations, the original equation is transformed as follows:

$$\frac{x}{3} - 9 = 15$$

Adding 9 to each side of the equation gives

$$\frac{x}{3} = 24$$

Multiplying both sides by 3 gives

$x = 72$.

83. **A**

Again, using the rules for solving one-variable equations produces these transformations:

$3x^2 - 11 = 1$

Adding 11 to each side of the equation gives

$3x^2 = 12$

Dividing both sides by 3 gives

$x^2 = 4$

You next find the square roots of 4; 2 and –2.

The solutions can be checked by substituting them (one at a time) into the original equation to see if they work. In this case, both 2 and –2 indeed do work.

84. B

Solving for a particular variable in an equation means to isolate that variable on one side of the equation. In this case, use of the rules for transforming equations allows you to change the original equation into the desired one:

$$\frac{y}{3}-\frac{x}{2}=4$$

Adding $\frac{x}{2}$ *to each side gives*

$$\frac{y}{3}=\frac{x}{2}+4$$

Then, multiplying each side by 3 gives

$$y=\frac{3x}{2}+12$$

85. D

One way to solve the problem is by writing a one-variable equation that matches the information given:

$4x + 2(10 - x) = 26$

The "4x" represents four tires for each car. You use x *for the number of cars because at first, you don't know how many cars there are.*

(10 – x) represents the number of motorcycle tires in the lot. (If there are ten vehicles total, and x *of them are cars, you subtract* x *from 10 to get the number of "leftover" motorcycles.) Then 2(10 – x) stands for the number of motorcycle tires in the lot.*

You know that the sum of the values 4x and 2(10 – x) is 26, and that gives you your equation. Using the standard rules for solving a one-variable equation, you find that x (the number of cars in the lot) equals 3.

Another approach to the problem when given multiple answer choices is to try substituting each answer for the unknown variable in the problem to see which one makes sense.

86. A

You know that the correct equation must show three consecutive odd numbers being added to give 117. Odd numbers (just like even numbers) are each two apart. *Only the three values given in answer A are each two apart.*

Because the numbers being sought are odd, one might be tempted to choose answer D. However, the second value in answer D (x + 1) is not *two numbers apart from the first value (x); it's different by only* one.

87. D

All riders must pay at least three dollars, so 3 will be added to something else in the correct equation. Only answers B and D meet that requirement. The additional fare of two dollars "for every mile or fraction of a mile" tells you that you will need to multiply *the number of miles driven (you use 11 because of the extra fraction of a mile) by 2, leading you to answer D.*

88. **A**

The key to simplifying expressions such as these is to combine only like terms. Like terms are those with identical bases. $4x^2$ and $\frac{3}{5x^2}$, for instance, have like bases. So do $9x$ and $\frac{1}{5x}$. Real numbers without attached variables are their own like terms: 4, –21, 0.12, and $\frac{5}{8}$ are all like terms.

In the aforementioned expression, $\frac{2x^2}{3}$ and $\frac{x^2}{3}$ are like terms; their sum is $\frac{3x^2}{3}$, or $1x^2$, or just x^2; $-12x$ and $7x$ are like terms; they add up to $-5x$; 9 and 1 are also like terms, with a sum of 10.

Those three terms; x^2, $-5x$, and 10, are then separated by addition symbols to give the simplified version of the original expression.

89. **C**

Each term of each binomial must be multiplied by both terms in the other binomial. That means that four products are generated:

$(-2x^2) \times (5x^2)$ gives $-10x^4$ (and right here you see that answer C is correct).

$(-2x^2) \times (3) = -6x^2$

$(-11) \times (5x^2) = -55x^2$

$(-11) \times (3) = -33$

The two middle terms are like terms, and can be combined into $-61x^2$. The three terms (which cannot be further combined) give you the answer of $-10x^4 - 61x^2 - 33$.

90. **A**

One approach to factoring the expression is to start with a set of two empty parentheses written as follows: (__ + __) (__ + __). The task is to then fill in the four blanks with values that "multiply back" to the original expression. Educated trial and error works well here. Here's a good place to start: You know that the two blanks at the end of the parentheses must be 1 and 5, because 5 is a prime number; no other whole numbers multiply by anything to give you 5.

A bit more experimentation shows that only $(4x - 1) \times (-2x + 5)$ "multiplies back" to $-8x^2 + 22x - 5$. (Be sure to pay attention to whether values are positive or negative.)

91. **D**

Before attempting to factor the expression into two binomials, you must look for any factors common to both terms. Both $2x^2$ and (–18) are divisible by 2, so you can "factor out" the 2, giving $2(x^2 - 9)$.

$(x^2 - 9)$ should be recognized as the difference of two perfect squares, and can itself be factored into $(x + 3)(x - 3)$. Placing the "factored out" 2 back into the expression as a coefficient, you get $2(x + 3)(x - 3)$.

92. **C**

Multiplication is commutative, meaning that the factors being multiplied can be in any order. You can, therefore, rearrange the expression in problem 32 to look like this:

$3 \times 5 \times \sqrt{2} \times \sqrt{10}$

which gives

$15\sqrt{20}$

The key to completing the task of simplification is to see that the number 20 contains a perfect square (4). You can rewrite $\sqrt{20}$ *as* $\sqrt{4} \times \sqrt{5}$*, or* $2\sqrt{5}$*.*
Multiplying that 2 by 15 gives a coefficient of 30, times the remaining $\sqrt{5}$*.*

93. **C**

As always when simplifying such expressions, you try to find common factors in the various terms. You see that both 75 and 3 "contain" 3. You can take advantage of this by rewriting the expression this way:

$$\frac{\sqrt{25} \times \sqrt{3} \times \sqrt{x^7}}{\sqrt{3} \times \sqrt{x}}$$

You can further assist the task by rewriting $\sqrt{x^7}$ *as* $\sqrt{x^6} \times \sqrt{x}$*, giving*

$$\frac{5 \times \sqrt{3} \times \sqrt{x^6} \times \sqrt{x}}{\sqrt{3} \times \sqrt{x}}$$

You may then cancel equal terms, leaving you with $5x^3$*.*

94. **A**

The area of any rectangle is equal to the measure of its length times the measure of its width (or to say it differently, the measure of its base times the measure of its height). A right triangle can be seen as half of a rectangle *(sliced diagonally). Answer A represents, in effect, a rectangle's area cut in half (i.e., divided by 2).*

95. **D**

The formula for finding the area of any circle is $A = \pi r^2$ *(about 3.14 times the length of the radius times itself). In this case you need to take half of* πr^2*; hence, answer D.*

96. **B**

Angle xyz is an inscribed angle *(its vertex is on the circle). Angle xcz is a* central angle *(its vertex is at the circle's center). When two such angles intercept (or "cut off") the same arc of the circle, there exists a specific size relationship between the two angles. The measure of the central angle will always be* double the measure of the inscribed angle*. In this case, that means that the measure of angle xcz must be 80°.*

That means that minor arc xz also has measure 80°. Every circle (considered as an arc) has measure 360°. That means that major *arc xyz has measure 280° (360 – 80).*

97. **A**

The formula for finding the volume of a cylinder is:

$V = \pi r^2 h$

This means that the volume is equal to pi (about 3.14) times the measure of the radius squared times the height of the cylinder. In this case, that's

$3.14 \times 6^2 \times 8$

or

$3.14 \times 36 \times 8$

or about 904. (Note that the final answer is given in cubic centimeters.)

98. **B**

You can use the Pythagorean theorem to compute the length of any side of any right triangle, as long as you know the lengths of the other two sides. Here is the theorem:

For any right triangle with side lengths of a, b *and* c, *and where* a *is the length of the hypotenuse (the longest side, and the one opposite the right angle),* $a^2 = b^2 + c^2$.

Substituting the real values for a *and* b *from problem 38, you get*

$a^2 = 11^2 + 5^2$

or

$a^2 = 146$

To complete the work, you take the (positive) square root of 146, which is slightly over 12 (12 × 12 = 144).

99. **A**

If two triangles are similar, that means that they have the exact same shape (although not necessarily the same size). It also means that corresponding angles of the two triangles have the same measure, and that corresponding sides are proportionate.

One way then to find the solution to this problem is to set up a proportion with one corner the unknown value (x), and then to solve the proportion:

$$\frac{12}{10} = \frac{15}{x}$$

This can be read as "12 is to 10 as 15 is to x." The problem can be solved using cross-multiplication. Thus, 12x = 150, leading to the solution x *= 12.5.*

100. (C)

When two parallel lines are crossed by another line (called a transversal*), eight angles are formed. There are, however, only two angle* measures *among the eight angles, and the sum of the two measures will be 180°. All of the smaller angles will have the same measures, and all of the larger angles will have the same measures. In this case, the smaller angles all measure 50°, so the larger angles (including angle y) all measure 130°.*

101. (A)

There are two things one must know in order to answer the question. One is the meaning of the small square at the vertex of angle BXC. That symbol tell you that angle BXC is a right angle (one with 90°.) You must also understand that a straight line can be thought of as an angle that measures 180°. This is a straight angle.

Therefore, the sum of the angles DXC (42°) and BXC (90°) is 132°. This means that the remaining angle on the line must have measure 48° (180° – 132°).

102. (C)

If you know the measures of two angles of any triangle, you can compute the measure of the third angle. (The sum of the three angles is always 180°.) So the measure of the third angle in both of the triangles is 50°, and statement III is correct.

If two triangles have the same degree measures (as established above), then they are similar *triangles. (This means that they have the same shape.) Statement I is therefore correct.*

Triangles are congruent only if they are exactly the same shape and *size. One triangle is larger than the other, so statement II is false.*

Because the second triangle is larger than the first, and they're the same shape, there is no way that sides BC and YZ could be the same length. Statement IV is thus false.

103. (D)

This is a problem of deduction. That is, the answer can be deduced from the information given. One solution to this problem is to make a list of the boys' names based on what you know. You could start by taking the very first bit of information, "Fred beat Matt." This allows you to stack those two names like so,

Fred

Matt

with Fred at the top because he was the faster of the two boys.

Then, instead of just taking the next piece of information ("Curt beat Dwayne"), you could instead look for information that tells you more about the boys already listed. You read, for instance, that Dwayne beat Fred. This allows you to add Dwayne to the list:

Dwayne

Fred

Matt

By filling in the other boys' names based on the information given, you should produce the following list:

Pat

Curt

Dwayne

Fred

Matt

Ivan

This shows that Ivan was last in the race.

104. C

When simplifying algebraic expressions, always work from left to right. First, perform all multiplications and divisions. Once this is done, start again from the left and do all additions and subtractions.

SUGGESTION: It can be helpful to translate the algebraic statement to English. For example, $6 + 2(x - 4)$ is "six plus two times the quantity x minus 4." The word "times" indicates multiplication, so we must first perform $2(x - 4)$ by using the distributive property $a(b - c) = ab - ac$:

$6 + 2(x - 4) = 6 + 2 \times x - 2 \times 4 = 6 + 2x - 8.$

Then we perform the subtraction to combine the terms 6 and 8:

$6 + 2x - 8 = 2x + (6 - 8) = 2x - 2.$

Note that we did not combine the 2x term with the other terms. This is because they are not like terms. Like terms are terms that have the same variables (with the same exponents). Since the terms 6 and 8 have no variable x, they are not like terms with 2x.

105. A

[NOTATION: $m\angle PQR$ will represent "the measure of angle PQR."] The sum of the measures of the interior angles of a triangle is 180°. Therefore,

$m\angle A + m\angle ABC + m\angle C = 180°.$

We also know that $m\angle C = 20°$, so if we substitute this into the previous equation, we have

$m\angle A + m\angle ABC + 20° = 180°.$

Subtracting 20° from both sides of this equation gives us

$m\angle A + m\angle ABC = 160°$ or $m\angle A = 160° - m\angle ABC.$

Therefore, if we know $m\angle ABC$, we are done! To find $m\angle ABC$, notice that ABD is a straight angle and, thus, $m\angle ABD = 180°$. But

$m\angle ABC + m\angle CBD = m\angle ABD.$

So, using the facts that

$m\angle CBD = 36°$ and $m\angle ABD = 180°$, and substituting, we have

$m\angle ABC + 36° = 180°$ or $m\angle ABC = 180° - 36° = 144°$. Hence,

$m\angle A = 160° - m\angle ABC = 160° - 144° = 16°.$

106. D

Let x be the cost of one can of beans. Then 6x is the cost of six cans of beans. So 6x = \$1.50. Dividing both sides of the equation by 6, we get x = \$.25 and, hence, since 8x is the cost of eight cans of beans, we have 8x = 8 × \$.25 = \$2.00.

107. A

Let t_1, t_2, t_3 represent Bonnie's scores on tests one, two, and three, respectively. Then the equation representing Bonnie's average score is

$$\frac{t_1 + t_2 + t_3}{3} = 71.$$

We know that $t_1 = 64$ and $t_2 = 87$. Substitute this information into the equation above:

$$\frac{64 + 87 + t_3}{3} = 71.$$

Combining 64 and 87 and then multiplying both sides of the equation by 3 gives us

$$3 \times \frac{151 + t_3}{3} = 3 \times 71 \text{ or } 151 + t_3 = 213.$$

Now subtract 151 from both sides of the equation so that

$t_3 = 213 - 151 = 62$

108. D

Let s be the length of each side of square ABCD. Since triangle ADC is a right triangle, we can use the Pythagorean Theorem to solve for s. We have $AD^2 + DC^2 = AC^2$ or $s^2 + s^2 = 8^2$. Simplifying the equation, we get: $2s^2 = 64$. Now divide both sides of the equation by two:

$$s^2 = 32 \text{ so } s = \sqrt{32} = \sqrt{16} \times \sqrt{2} = 4\sqrt{2}.$$

Therefore, the perimeter of square ABCD is

$$P = 4s = 4 \times 4\sqrt{2} = 16\sqrt{2}$$

109. C

Let r be the length of the radius of each of the small circles and let R be the length of the radius of the large circle. Then, R = 3r. The area of each of the small circles is $\pi r^2 = 9\pi$. Now divide both sides of the equation by π:

$r^2 = 9 r = 3$. Then,

$R = 3r = 3 \times 3 = 9.$

Therefore, the circumference of the large circle is

$C = 2\pi R = 2\pi \times 9 = 18\pi.$

110. C

Note that the numbers 4, 8, 12, 16, and 20 are the only numbers from 1 through 20 that are evenly divisible by 4. The probability that a ball chosen from the jar has a number on it that is evenly divisible by 4 is given by

$$\frac{\text{total number of balls with numbers that are evenly divisible by 4}}{\text{total number of possible outcomes}} = \frac{5}{20} = \frac{1}{4}.$$

111. B

To solve the equation $2x^2 + 5x - 3 = 0$*, we can factor the left side of the equation to get* $(2x - 1)(x + 3) = 0$*. Then use the following rule (sometimes called the Zero Product Property): If* $a \times b = 0$*, then either* $a = 0$ *or* $b = 0$*. Applying this to our problem gives us*

$2x - 1 = 0$ *or* $x + 3 = 0$.

Solve these two equations:

$2x - 1 = 0 \rightarrow 2x = 1 \rightarrow \frac{1}{2}$ *or* $x + 3 = 0 \rightarrow x = -3$.

But $x > 0$*, so* $x = \frac{1}{2}$.

112. B

$\angle AOB$ and $\angle COD$ are central angles, meaning that their vertices are at the center of a circle. The measure of a central angle is equal to the measure of its intercepted arc. Hence, since arc AB and arc CD are the intercepted arcs of $\angle AOB$ and $\angle COD$, respectively, $m\angle AOB = 65°$ and $m\angle COD = 21.4°$. So,

$m\angle AOB + m\angle COD = 86.4°$.

Therefore, since one revolution of a circle is 360 °, the shaded portion of the circle is represented by the following:

$$\frac{86.4}{360} = 0.24 = 24\%$$

113. D

First find the total sales for each year by reading the graph for the sales of (i) black and white televisions and (ii) color televisions. Then combine these numbers:

1960	*$20,000,000 + $5,000,000*	*= $25,000,000*
1970	*$10,000,000 + $20,000,000*	*= $30,000,000*
1980	*$15,000,000 + $25,000,000*	*= $40,000,000*
1990	*$10,000,000 + $45,000,000*	*= $55,000,000*
2000	*$5,000,000 + $45,000,000*	*= $50,000,000*

The greatest total sales occurred in 1990.

114. (A)

The probability that first card is a diamond is $\frac{13}{52} = \frac{1}{4}$. There are now 51 cards remaining, of which 12 are diamonds; thus $\frac{12}{51} = \frac{4}{17}$ is the probability that the second card is a diamond. Finally, $(\frac{1}{4})(\frac{4}{17}) = \frac{1}{17}$ is the probability that both cards are diamonds.

115. (C)

The area of the shaded region is equal to the area of the large circle (which has $\overline{OB}$ as a radius), minus the area of the smaller circle (which has $\overline{OA}$ as a radius). Because the area of a circle with radius r is $A = \pi r^2$, the area of the shaded region is:

$$\pi(OB)^2 - \pi(OA)^2 = 36\pi - 16\pi = 20\pi.$$

116. (D)

To solve this inequality, we shall use the following rules:

(i) If $a \leq b$ and c is any number, then $a + c \leq b + c$.

(ii) If $a \leq b$ and $c < 0$, then $ca \geq cb$.

The goal in solving inequalities, as in solving equalities, is to change the inequality so that the variable is isolated (i.e., by itself on one side). So, in the equation $8 - 2x \leq 10$, we want the term $-2x$ by itself. To achieve this, use rule (i) above and add -8 to both sides, obtaining $8 - 2x + (-8) \leq 10 + (-8)$ or $-2x \leq 2$. Now we use rule (ii) and multiply both sides of the inequality by $-\frac{1}{2}$ as follows: $-\frac{1}{2} \times 2x \geq -\frac{1}{2} \times 2$ or $x \geq -1$.

117. (B)

In 1 hour, John will have painted $\frac{1}{4}$ of the fence and Linda will have painted $\frac{1}{3}$ of the fence. Then $\frac{1}{4} + \frac{1}{3} = \frac{7}{12}$ of this fence will be painted in 1 hour. To complete the entire fence requires $1 \div \frac{7}{12} = 1\frac{5}{7}$ hours.

118. (D)

For either 1, 2, or 3 nights, the cost is still \$100. For a 4-night stay, the cost is \$150; for a 5-night stay, the cost is \$200, and so on. Each additional night is an extra \$50.

119. (D)

Car J will cost the same as car L, because they lie on the same vertical line. J lies higher than L, so it is more fuel efficient.

120. (D)

When x is close to zero, the value of y is relatively large. As x increases, the value of y shows a pattern of decreasing initially, then appears to remain constant.

Detailed Explanations of Answers: Writing

121. **B**

The presence of "the" before "Westown's" means that the reference is to **the** *council, not to a council belonging to Westown. The other choices are all currently correct, and changing them would make them nonstandard.*

122. **A**

The editorial is suggesting that the population loss is a bad thing and that proposed changes would be a good thing. Thus, population loss is something the author wants stopped, or at least lessened, so **alleviate**, *which means to lessen, is the only possible choice.*

123. **D**

The subject of the first clause is "each," which is singular, so the verb should be "has."

124. **B**

Choice A is wrong because it makes no sense within the sentence; the zoning regulations cannot be easy to change. Choice C makes sense, but its use of "them" is ambiguous—does it refer to the authors or the regulations? Choice D is wrong because, if the authors **said** *the regulations would be hard to change, the word* **apparently** *earlier in the sentence would make no sense. Thus Choice B is the best answer.*

125. **C**

*This sentence includes a remark about the "lack of spark" in DeMarco's writing, which makes a contrast with the previous sentence, where his potential reading competence is regarded as positive. The rest of the paragraph supports this observation. Choice B is also supported by the rest of the paragraph, but it contains no transition of contrast (***moreover** *rather than* **however***).*

126. C

The best answer here is sentence 6, with its "grasps and comprehends." These two words mean exactly the same thing in this context, so one of them is unnecessary. The phrase "all of the class" in sentence 3 is somewhat wordy (it could be "the whole class"), but it is not redundant.

127. D

Sentence 13 contains a **dangling modifier**. *The verbal phrase at the beginning of the sentence should modify a person ("answers" cannot be asked a question), but the only choices are "his" and "answers." Thus the phrase modifies nothing and is a dangling modifier.*

128. D

Sentence 12 refers to journals of all classmates, so the apostrophe should follow the s. Choice A is wrong because **Sideways Stories from Wayside School** *is a book, not a story, a fact which prospective elementary teachers should know. If you didn't, you should get to know some of the more popular authors for elementary school.*

129. C

The phrase "comings and goings" could possibly fit into this sentence, but it is slightly off, whereas the other choices have little or nothing wrong with them. One problem with "comings and goings" is its informal tone: a case study in a textbook usually does not use slangy terms like this one. In addition, the sentence refers to **all** *the students' accounts, not just their travels.*

130. B

Sentence 7 begins with "Although"—used for mentioning the scientists' public statements—and refers to the "hazy" benefits derived from the study. Thus the sentence has to deal with speculation about the "uncertain" benefits. Choice D fits in with the paragraph's development fairly well, but it not the best answer because the pejorative word "racist" would not generally be used to characterize someone in a textbook. (There is little doubt that the author considers the experiment itself to be racist, but he or she does not otherwise characterize any of the individuals involved in this passage—and should not do so without offering evidence.)

131. A

The word should be "affected"; see the discussion of **effect** *and* **affect** *in Chapter 2. The other words are used in standard ways and, even though "whereas" may sound out of place, it is not as obviously wrong as "effected" and is therefore not the best answer.*

132. C

Sentence 7 contains a comma splice. The sentence has two independent clauses, and they are not joined by a coordinating conjunction. They must therefore be separated by a semicolon, not a comma. Part 3, which contains several commas, is correctly punctuated (except for the period at the end, which will be discussed in Answer 13), but they are all necessary to separate the two nonrestrictive phrases: (a) author of the excellent history on the subject and (b) Bad Blood.

133. D

By convention in American English, periods and commas are always placed inside of quotation marks.

134. D

The verb **learn** *should clearly be in past tense, not present, because it concerns something that happened in 1972. Incidentally, the word "media" is technically plural, so the verb form should be "learn" rather than "learns" even if present tense were correct.*

135. A

The last phrase of the sentence—"that chaotic period"—could refer to either the guerilla war mentioned in sentence 12 or the period of relocation mentioned in sentence 13, meaning that the sentence would have to be inserted after sentence 12 or 13 (choices A or B). However, the sentence about the Church's individual members providing support cannot just sit beside a sentence about the church itself providing support: the two thoughts would have to be joined in a logical way. Thus choice B is not as good as choice A. With choice A, sentence 12 would be explained by the new sentence, and then sentence 13 would describe the circumstances under which the support was provided.

136. B

The second paragraph proceeds in from the 1500s to 1975, and the third paragraph describes the cause for the effect mentioned at the end of the second paragraph: the embrace of Catholicism by the Timorese.

137. B

Sentence 4 is a fragment: because "being" is a verbal rather than a standard verb form, it does not act as a verb for "exceptions." (Note: Substituting "were" for "being" would fix the fragment but would not produce an effective sentence—"the exceptions" to what?) Sentence 7 does contain a punctuation error (discussed in the answer to question 18), but the question specifically asks for nonstandard "sentence structure." Be sure to read each question thoroughly.

138. **A**

Sentence 7 begins with a subordinate clause, and a comma should separate that clause from the independent clause that follows. The "who" in sentence 8 is correct even though it refers to "missionaries," which is the object of a preposition, because it is the subject of its own clause—"who were posted." The "its" following East Timor in sentence 9 is correct because the pronoun refers to the country as a whole, not to all the people of the country. The word "government" in sentence 11 is not capitalized even though it occurs with the proper adjective "Indonesian."

139. **D**

Because the first blank must show a contrast with the previous thought, choice B is not possible. Because a comma rather than a semicolon precedes the first blank, "however" is not possible, either. If "however" were inserted, the sentence would have a comma splice, because "however" is not a coordinating conjunction ("but" is).

140. **A**

The first sentence has a plural subject—"animism **and** *spirit worship"—so it should have a plural form of verb as well.*

141. **B**

The adjectival form "second," not the adverbial form "secondly," is appropriate here, since it modifies a noun not a verb.

142. **B**

The opening verbal phrase is a dangling modifier. "Prevention" is not "faced" with anything; Lincoln is. All the other choices are standard English sentences.

143. **C**

"With the outbreak . . ." is a prepositional phrase that is stopped with a period[.]. It has no subject or verb and is not a standard English sentence. All the rest are correct English.

144. **A**

The phrase "at one time . . ." is a nonrestrictive unit that is not necessary to the basic meaning of the sentence; consequently, both commas are needed. The commas for B and D are necessary to set off introductory or qualifying phrases. No commas are needed in B since the phrase that follows is a direct adjectival qualification of what kind of rockets they are as we know them today. Thus, no comma of separation is needed.

145. B

This is just a long phrase; it has no subject or verb. C is an atypical but rhetorically correct and standard English sentence. Many sentences in English begin with "And." The other choices are standard subject/verb independent sentence units.

146. A

This word is too general for such a specific informational context. B should remain because it is the exact, or first, phrase the writer discusses. C need not be changed because only a synonym such as "real" would be needed, but the meaning would remain the same. D is all right because the writer points not to any specific study, research, or development done, but to all that type of "work" in general.

147. C

It is not the work force that is "for the better," but the situation for men. This is also supported by the rest of the evidence offered in the paragraph. The other sentences have their modifying phrases directly related to the idea they qualify.

148. C

The writer is comparing before and after the appearance of women in management; only two things—therefore the comparative form, not the superlative, is correct: "greater." A, B, and D are all incorrect responses; they have no comparative adjectives, just adverbs used as qualifiers, e.g., "overly." These are used in a standard way.

149. B

Sentence 15 is a run-on sentence, incorrectly punctuated with a comma after "families" instead of a period or a semicolon (i.e., it's a comma splice). The rest of the choices are all standard sentences.

150. D

Part 12 has an incorrect agreement between "kids" and "does." Kids [they] do *[something] is correct. All the other sentences use standard English syntax.*

151. D

The sentence is a rhetorical clause that begins with a subordinating conjunction, "because." Consequently, it cannot stand alone as a complete standard sentence. The rest are standard.

152. B

Unless the writer specifies with the correct noun who exactly is drinking the orange juice, it could be either the mother or the baby: both are female. The rest are standard without correction.

153. C

Choice C is a prepositional phrase, "About 25,000 years ago," which is followed by a subordinate clause. This part should be linked to the previous sentence as it is integral to the migration of the Anasazi. Choices A, B, and D are all complete sentences.

154. C

Choice C has to do with the later history of the Mesa Verde area, after the Anasazi had abandoned it. Because this is so far removed chronologically, sentence 7 should be deleted or further developed in a third paragraph. Choices A and B discuss the very early history of the Indians. Choice D follows the chronological time order from A.D. 500 and leads into a discussion of the height of the Anasazi civilization.

155. C

Choice C unnecessarily repeats the words "basis," "based," "founding," and "foundation." These forms need not be repeated and the sentence should be condensed. Choice A repeats the phrase "board of regents," found in the previous sentence, but it is needed for transition of thought. Choice B and choice D are well-worded sentences.

156. B

Choice B fits between sentence 4 and sentence 6. Sentence 4 mentions the topic of dissenting opinion, and sentence 6 elaborates by stating the position that English professors have always been outspoken. This idea is continued in sentence 7. Choice A changes voice to "we," which is out of place in this letter. Choice C is too casual. Choice D directly contradicts the thesis of the letter.

157. B

Choice B contains an inappropriate use of words. The contraction for "who is" should be used to make the sentence correct. The possessive "whose" is not correct in this context. Choice A correctly uses the comparative degree. Choice C correctly uses the superlative degree. Choice D does not make a needed change.

158. C

Choice C, delete sentence 4, is the correct choice. Sentence 4 introduces a new topic—the fact that some companies are not committed to a day care program. Since the paragraphs are both discussing companies that have already made this decision, and the advantages of having made this decision, sentence 4 is out of place. Choice A would make a contradictory statement. Choice B would delete a needed phrase. Choice D would destroy the parallelism created with sentences 6 and 7 that lead naturally as a transition into the next paragraph.

159. A

Choice A is needed for correct subject and verb agreement. The plural subject "companies" should be followed by the plural verb "make." Confusion is caused by an intervening phrase, "showing special initiative in building company loyalty of each employee." Because the phrase ends with a singular noun, it is a common error to make the verb singular also. Choice B, present progressive, and choice C, future, are incorrect tenses for the context of the sentence and the paragraph. Choice D needs a helping verb and cannot stand alone.

160. D

Sentence 9 begins with the transition word "Therefore," so it is best placed after a sentence that would state a reason for building company loyalty and morale. Sentence 11 gives a compelling reason—the company's personal interest in each employee. Choice A would remove the topic sentence to a less prominent position, as well as have sentence 9 clearly out of order with no idea before it in the paragraph. Choice B does not place a sentence with a clear reason before the transition "therefore." Choice C would weaken the paragraph.

161. D

Choice D discusses the tool-making abilities of an otter, not man, so it should be deleted. Choice A would delete the topic sentence from the paragraph. Choice B is incorrect because sentence 2 begins with "During this time," and there would be no antecedent for "this" if the two sentences are reversed. Choice C is incorrect because the suggested addition does not pertain to the development of man during this time period.

162. C

Sentences 8 and 9 need to be reversed. Sentence 8 begins with the transition word "Also," which clearly introduces a second feature, not a first as the position would indicate. Choice A would delete the topic sentence from the paragraph. Choice B would put the second factor after the topic sentence which introduces it. Choice D is the concluding sentence and should not be eliminated.

163. A

Choice A eliminates the fragment in the second half of sentence 4. The subject is "the use of speech," so the verb should be "facilitated" and not the infinitive "to facilitate." Choice B would delete the necessary transition word "other," needed to link developments discussed in the first paragraph with developments discussed in the second paragraph. Choice C changes the comparative degree "less," needed to compare two items in sentence 9, to the superlative degree needed to compare three or more things. Choice D changes the present participle "ensuring" to the past participle "ensured." This change is incorrect because the present participle is necessary to show that survival is still going on; the past participle would indicate that survival has stopped.

164. C

Choice C contains irrelevant information, so it should be eliminated. Choice A contains a phrase essential to the sentence. Choice B would create a fragment after the semicolon because the clause beginning with "although" is a subordinate clause, and only an independent clause would be appropriate after the semicolon. Choice D would create a misplaced modifier; "except for their breath" would be taken to modify the layer of fat on polar bears.

165. C

Choice C is correct because "between" should be used to compare two things, whereas "among" should be used to compare three or more things. Since there are five countries, "among" is the correct form. Choice A would create an error in comparison, since there are more than two types of land-based carnivores. Choice B makes no improvement. Choice D deletes the necessary idea of contrast shown by "but" in contrasting the two levels of polar bear population.

166. C

Choice C is a type of run-on sentence. The technical name for this sentence is a comma splice because two independent clauses are joined by only a comma; they should be joined by a semicolon (as in this explanatory sentence). The comma after "treated" should be a semicolon. Choices A, B, and D are correctly punctuated compound sentences because they contain a comma followed by a conjunction to link the two independent clauses.

167. C

Choice C is the correct answer. The comparative degree is used for comparing two things, so "larger" should be changed to the superlative degree, "largest," because more than two caves were discovered containing scrolls. Choice A correctly uses "between" to indicate something falling between two dates; "among" is used for more than two things. In choice B. the use of "lay" is correct; the past tense is required for a condition no longer in effect. In choice D "who" is correct as the subject of the subordinate clause with the verb "wants." "Whom" is the objective case and cannot be a subject.

168. D

Choice D should be revised to eliminate unnecessary repetition of "photographic" and "copies." Choices A., B., and C. are concise sentences.

169. C

Choice C is the correct answer. The comparative degree is used for comparing two things, so "larger" should be changed to the superlative degree, "largest," because more than two caves were discovered containing scrolls. Choice A correctly uses "between" to indicate something falling between two dates; "among" is used for more than two things. In choice B the use of "lay" is correct, the past tense of "lie" is required for a condition no longer in effect. In choice D, "who" is correct as the subject of the subordinate clause with the verb "wants." "Whom" is the objective case and cannot be a subject of a clause.

170. D

Choice D should be revised to eliminate unnecessary repetition of "photographic" and "copies." Choices A, B, and C are concise sentences.

Writing Assignment 1–Persuasive

WRITING SAMPLE WITH A SCORE OF 4

The Literature of the Past

The direction of modern literary scholarship points toward an alarming conclusion. The depreciation of the literary study of bygone periods is a sign of two disturbing trends. First, scholars are avoiding more difficult study in preference to what seems light or facile. Furthermore, the neglect of the literature of former eras is a denial of the contribution that past authors have made toward modern literature. This is not to suggest that all scholars who study modern literature do so because they are either intimidated by past literature or do not appreciate its value. However, the shrinking minority of past literary scholarship is a clear indication that intimidation and awe of past conventions are deterrents to many students of literature.

The dread associated with past literature reflects poorly upon our society. The attempts to simplify literature to accommodate simpler audiences has resulted in a form of literary deflation. The less society taxes its audience's minds, the less comprehensive those unexercised minds become. Information and ideas are now transmitted to the average man through the shallow medium of television programming. Modern students are evolving from this medium, and the gap separating them from the complexity of the classics is continuing to grow.

Once more, it is important to stress that this essay does not seek to diminish students of modern literature. The only demand this argument makes upon modern students is that they supplement their study with significant portions of the classics from which all subsequent literature has been derived, whether consciously or unconsciously. Failure to do so is an act akin to denying the importance of history itself. Like history, literature exists as an evolutionary process; modern literature can only have come into existence through the development of past literature.

Concerning the relative complexity of the classics to modern literature, the gap is not so great as one may think. Surely, one who glances at the works of Shakespeare or Milton without prior exposure will be daunted by them. However, a disciplined mind can overcome the comprehensive barriers erected over the past few centuries through persistence and perseverance.

Unfortunately, the ability to overcome the barriers to past literature may eventually become obsolete. The more frequently students select their courses of study through fear rather than interest, the wider the literary gap will become, until the pampered minds of all future readers will prove unequal to the task of reading the literature of our fathers. The more frequently students deny the usefulness of the literature antedating this century, the more frequently they deny their own literary heritage, the more probable it will become for modern literature's structure to crumble through lack of firm foundation.

FEATURES OF THE WRITING SAMPLE SCORING 4

Focus and Appropriateness

The paper's topic and the writer's viewpoint are both well laid out in the first paragraph. The two trends described by the author in the topic paragraph are explored in deeper detail throughout the essay. The language and style fit the writer's audience. The style is formal, but possesses a personalized voice.

Unity and Organization

The essay follows the course presented in the topic paragraph, reemphasizing major points such as the writer's reluctance to condemn all modern scholars. This emphasis is not straight repetition, but carries different viewpoints and evidence for the writer's argument. The digression on television in the second paragraph neatly rounds off the writer's overall concern for cultural consequences of historical literature's depreciation.

Many transitional conventions are utilized. "Once more . . ."; "Concerning the relative complexity . . ."; "Unfortunately . . ." The examples throughout the paragraphs have a pointed direction. The concluding paragraph completes the argument with a premonition of future calamity should its warning go unheeded.

Development and Rationale

The writer follows the suggestions of the writing assignment closely, structuring his essay around the reflections and discussions listed therein. Each paragraph bears an example to lend authority to the writer's argument. The second paragraph uses the theory of television's vegetative influence. The third paragraph utilizes the evolutionary equality of history. The fourth paragraph evokes names that the reader can relate to in terms of comprehensive difficulty.

Sentence Structure and Usage

The sentences are standardized and vary in form, although some passive constructions ("will be daunted," "the more probable it will become") might have been avoided. The repetition of "the more frequently" in the final paragraph is particularly effective and pointed.

Words are chosen to offer variety. "Past literature" is supplemented by "literary study of bygone days" and "the literature of former eras." Phrasing is consistent and standard, although the third sentence of the second paragraph ("The less society taxes . . . the less comprehensive") is slightly awkward, though the repetition does achieve some effect.

Mechanical Conventions

Spelling and punctuation are mostly standard throughout the essay. The sentences in the final paragraph might be divided and shortened, although this may diminish their effect.

WRITING SAMPLE WITH A SCORE OF 3

Modern Literature

It doesn't matter whether or not we read past literature. Past literature has been converted into what we now know as "modern literature". The elements of the past are therefore incorporated into the body of what we now have.

When we read a work of modern literature based upon the classics, such as Joyce's *Ulysses*, it doesn't matter whether or not we've read Homer's *Odyssey*. What matters is what Joyce made out of Homer's epic; not what Homer started out with.

When we see *West Side Story* in the movies, it doesn't matter whether or not we've read *Romeo and Juliet*: the end result is the same; therefore, we do not need to know the original source. I don't think it makes a difference whether or not we even recognize Tony and Maria as Romeo and Juliet. Tony and Maria are today's versions of Romeo and Juliet, and they match the culture that they are told in.

It has been said that all of the good plots have been used up by past ages, and that all we create now are variations of those plots. This statement is false. It is rather the case that these plots are universal variables that each age must interpret in its own unique way. I find it rather faseatious to study the interpretation of other cultures. We should be concerned only with our own.

Past literature is not necessary in a modern world that has reformed the mistakes of the past. Anything that hasn't carried over from the past is negligible: what was good for Shakespeare's audience may not be what we need. In conclusion, I would have to strongly conclude that the "trend of studying modern versus past literature" is commendable, and not contemptible.

FEATURES OF THE WRITING SAMPLE SCORING 3

Focus and Appropriateness

The main topic is not supplied directly within the work. Though the reader is aware of the conflict between modern and past literature, there is no sense of scholarly consensus as suggested by the writing assignment. The writer's somewhat informal style is unbalanced throughout the work by his uncertainty with his audience.

Unity and Organization

Though the writer knows the point he is trying to promote, his evidence is presented haphazardly and without a logical design. However, his rather abrupt conclusion is somewhat supported by his points.

Transitions are slight, if any. The repetition of "when we" opening two paragraphs is noticeable. Each point should have been further developed. The writer assumes his reader is quite familiar with *West Side Story* and its characters.

Development and Rationale

The essay does not follow a logical pattern; one premise does not meld fluidly into another. Though the premises loosely support the conclusion, they do not support each other.

Usage and Sentence Structure

Most sentences follow standard sentence structure, although some are very irregular. The first sentence of paragraph three expresses two or three independent thoughts and should be separated accordingly. The final sentence of the fourth paragraph contains an unclear modifier: "own" should read either "own interpretation" or "own culture."

Most words are used in their proper context, and an attempt has been made to use some erudite words. "End result" is redundant; "end" should have been excluded. The declaration "this statement is false" in the fourth paragraph is not supported by logical evidence. In this case, the writer should have asserted that this was his own opinion. However, in other cases it is recommended that the writer be bold with assertions. A degree of proof is all that is required to make those assertions. "In conclusion" is redundant with "conclude" in the final sentence of the essay. Contractions such as "we've" and "don't" should be written out in their long forms.

Mechanical Conventions

Most words are spelled properly, although "faseatious" should be spelled "facetious." (The period in the second sentence of the first paragraph should lie within the quotation marks.) The comma after "commendable" in the final paragraph should be eliminated because it does not introduce a new clause.

WRITING SAMPLE WITH A SCORE OF 2 OR 1

Literature

Modern literature is no better than past literature, and vice-versa. It is interest that matters. If people aren't interested in the past, then so be it. A famous man once said "To each his own". I agree.

For example, you can see that books are getting easier and easier to understand. This is a good thing, because more knowledge may be comunicated this way. Comunication is what literature is all about: Some people comunicate with the past, and others with the present.

I communicate with the present. I'm not saying we all should. It's all up to your point of view. When a scholer chooses past over present, or vice-versa, that's his perogative. It doesn't make him better or worse than anybody else. We should all learn to accept each other's point of view.

When I read someone like Fitzgerald or Tolkien, I get a different feeling than Shakespeare. Shakespeare can inspire many people, but I just don't get that certain feeling from his plays. "The Hobbit," "The Great Gatsby," "Catcher in the Rye," and "Of Mice and Men." These are all great classics from this century. We should be proud of them. However, some people prefer "The Trojan War" and "Beowulf." Let them have it. Remember: 'To each his own."

FEATURES OF THE WRITING SAMPLE SCORING 2 OR 1

Focus and Appropriateness

The writer misconstrues the topic and writes about the relative worth of modern and past literature. The topic does not call for a judgment of period literatures; it calls for a perspective on the way in which they are studied. Her personal style is too familiarized; it is unclear to whom the essay is addressed.

Unity and Organization

The writer seems to contradict her own points at times, favoring modern literature rather than treating the subject as objectively as she had proposed. It is clear that the writer's train of thought shifted during the essay. This was covered up by ending with the catch phrase, "to each his own."

There is neither direction nor logical flow in the essay. One point follows the next without any transition or connection. All three persons are used to prove his argument: the writer resorts to "I," "you," and "a famous man." There is no clear overall thesis guiding the essay.

Development and Rationale

The writer attempts to angle her argument in different ways by presenting such concepts as "communication" and "point of view." However, her thought processes are abrupt and underdeveloped.

Sentence Structure and Usage

Some sentences follow standard formation. Sentence three of the final paragraph is a fragment. The sentences are short and choppy, as is the thought they convey. Too many sentences are merely brief remarks on the preceding statements (e.g., "I agree," "Let them have it," etc.). These are not appropriate because they do not evoke new thought. The reference to Shakespeare in the first sentence of the final paragraph implies more than the writer intended. It should read: "than when I read Shakespeare."

Many words are repeated without any attempt to supply synonyms (e.g., "communication," "past"). Colloquial expressions are widespread and should be avoided. *The Trojan War* is evidently an improper reference to Homer's *Iliad.*

Mechanical Conventions

There are many mechanical errors. Punctuation and spelling are inconsistent. "Comunication" and "comunicate" are spelled improperly in paragraph two, while "communicate" is spelled correctly in paragraph three. "Scholer" should be spelled "scholar." "Perogative" should be spelled "prerogative." In the fourth sentence of the first paragraph, the period should lie within the quotation marks, as it does in the final sentence of the essay. The book titles in sentences three and six of the final paragraph should be underlined and not quoted.

Writing Assignment 2–Expository

WRITING SAMPLE WITH A SCORE OF 4

When I think of what specific characteristics a person must possess in order to be an effective teacher I think of these characteristics: upstanding values, compassion, and a thorough knowledge of their subject matter.

First, a person who becomes a teacher must keep in mind that they are a role model to the children in their midst. Their private and professional life must be beyond reproach. A teacher is responsible for setting values as well as teaching values. A teacher has a big influence on a child's life; therefore, a teacher must be careful about the kinds of signals he sends out to the children in his environment. Today, it is hard to tell teachers from students because they dress alike, wear their hair alike, associate together, and act the same. A teacher should set himself apart if he is to be a positive influence on the students he comes in contact with. Once a teacher loses his credibility and/or self-respect, he is no longer effective in the classroom.

Compassion is a quality that allows a teacher to have a sense of humor, get to know students' qualities, and be supportive of students' efforts. A teacher must be able to laugh with his students. This creates a relationship between learner and teacher, and shows the students that the teacher has a human side, and tells the students that the teacher is approachable. A good teacher will get to know each of his student's learning abilities and styles. This will allow the teacher to get the most from each student. Compassion allows the teacher to empathize with the students who are having problems in school or at home by being supportive and by providing a positive direction. Students can be turned off if they perceive that a teacher does not care.

Finally, if a person is going to be an effective teacher, he must have a thorough knowledge of his discipline. This gives the teacher a sense of confidence and allows the teacher to be well organized. An effective teacher knows and likes what he teaches, and the enthusiasm will show and will become a part of the students. Without a good mastery of the subject matter, a teacher is unable to make well-informed decisions about objectives to be covered.

In conclusion, by possessing and demonstrating upstanding values, showing compassion, and exhibiting a thorough knowledge of his subject area, the right person can make a good teacher. If students are to learn, they must be influenced by persons who have all three of these characteristics.

FEATURES OF THE WRITING SAMPLE SCORING 4

Focus and Appropriateness

This essay, even though it contains minor errors in punctuation and pronoun-antecedent agreement, is clearly written, with a solid thesis sentence and solid support. Note that the introduction and conclusion are not at all creative. Given more time, the writer might have come up with something better—something that drew on her own experience—but she came up with a solid outline instead, which helped her maintain her focus throughout.

Unity and Organization

The writer adequately introduces the topic "Characteristics of an Effective Teacher" by outlining the three characteristics to be discussed. Each of the three paragraphs of the body contains a characteristic as the main idea and details to explain and/or support it. The conclusion is a summary of the essay and an explanation of why these characteristics are important. The reader should have no difficulty understanding the message the writer is conveying.

Development and Rationale

Each body paragraph contains adequate development of its topic. For example, detailed reasons for why a teacher should be compassionate are given in the third paragraph. The reasoning slips a bit in the fourth paragraph, in which the writer mainly talks about a teacher liking his subject area, as if "liking" naturally flowed from "knowing." (Perhaps, given more revising time, the writer would have demonstrated that knowledge usually does flow from enthusiasm, or would have changed the thesis from "thorough knowledge" to "enthusiasm for.") A slip like this might occasionally knock a grade down to a "3" from some graders, but most would give it a "4."

Sentence Structure and Usage

The sentence structure is varied. The second paragraph, for example, opens with a complex sentence, goes to a simple sentence with a compound verb, followed by another simple sentence and then a compound sentence.

There are minor errors of usage, but not enough to lower the score for most graders. The opening sentence is also a complex sentence. Therefore, a comma should have been used to separate the dependent clause ("When I think of what specific characteristics a person must possess in order to be an effective teacher,") from the rest of the sentence (the independent clause). Also, in the first sentence, the pronoun *their* (plural) is used to refer to a *person* (singular). This a pronoun-antecedent disagreement. The pronoun *his* or *her* should have been used. This problem appears once again, then disappears later, suggesting that the writer may have been careless. Always save enough time to proof your essay. When writing hurriedly, it's very easy to make careless mistakes: *their* for *there*, *a* for *an*, *no* for *know*.

Mechanical Conventions

The one mechanical error—the use of *student's* when the writer meant to use *students'*—was not serious enough to lower the score from most graders. Again, however, it is best to save adequate time for proofreading, because some graders may have prejudices (against, say, misuse of apostrophes) that will cause them to see flaws in the rest of the essay.

WRITING SAMPLE WITH A SCORE OF 3 OR 2

A teacher must have the following characteristics in order to be effective: dedication, knowledge of the subject matter, and versatility. A dedicated teacher is one who is always willing to go that extra mile to help a student to learn. A dedicated teacher is not one who is just looking for a paycheck every other week. This type of teacher will find the students' weaknesses and start building on those points day-by-day. A dedicated teacher is also a caring person who will help build confidence in students' ability to learn. Without this type of dedication, there will be a decrease in effective teaching because if the teacher does not show his dedication and concern for the students to learn the material, then the students will not reflect that initiative to learn.

Teachers must be knowledgeable in the subject areas that they are teaching. Teachers with more formal education, teaching experience, and hours of training are more successful in helping students achieve educational goals. Now, without this knowledge and education, you will have a reduction in the effective teaching method. Teachers who do not know the academic subject that they are teaching cannot make clear presentations or use effective teaching strategies. They cannot answer questions fully and must be very evasive in their answers.

Another characteristic that a teacher must possess is the versatility to teach slower and advanced learners in a manner that both will be able to receive and retain the given information. A teacher must be able to make the subject matter come alive, demanding quality work meeting personal as well as academic needs of students and adding humor to the classroom. With the absence of this versitility, a teacher will only reach a small number of students in the classroom.

All of the above characteristics are important. Teachers who do not possess them will have difficulty reaching their students, and the drop-out rate will continue to climb.

FEATURES OF THE WRITING SAMPLE SCORING 3 OR 2

Focus and Appropriateness

The writer of this essay addresses the topic well, and he does not stray from the stated characteristics.

Note that the writer introduces a slightly new idea in the conclusion, as he is supposed to do in the typical organization of an essay. However, he brings up the idea of a "drop-out rate," which hasn't been shown to be increasing, and even though its connection to teachers' effectiveness is intuitive, there should have been at least a mention of the drop-out problem in an earlier paragraph.

Unity and Organization

No introductory paragraph exists. This is very important because the introductory paragraph sets parameters for the remaining parts of the essay. The writer, in this case, combined the introduction and the first paragraph of the body. The introduction should have read like this: "A teacher must have the following characteristics in order to be effective: dedication, knowledge of subject matter, and versatility." The thesis is, however, followed throughout the next three paragraphs.

Development and Rationale

The body paragraphs are well developed. Each is introduced by a characteristic (the main idea), and that characteristic is explained and supported by adequate details. However, a bit of ambiguity exists in paragraph three: "A teacher must be able to make the subject matter come alive, demanding quality work meeting personal as well as academic needs of students and adding humor to the classroom." For purposes of clarity, there should have been a comma after work and a comma after students.

Sentence Structure and Usage

Sentence structure is somewhat varied, but three sentences start with "A dedicated teacher." Some awkward expressions exist throughout the essay, but considering the time factor, this essay is considered adequate.

The only serious usage issue is the nonparallel structure used in this phrase in the third paragraph: "a manner that both will be able to receive and retain the given information." It should read "a manner that will be able both to receive and to retain the given information."

Mechanical Conventions

The essay is without major errors in mechanics of grammar. An example of a minor error is the misspelling of *versatility* in the third paragraph, but the use of this word displays a vocabulary that will usually win more points than the misspelling of it will lose.

WRITING SAMPLE WITH A SCORE OF 1

If you pick up a newspaper, turn on your raidio, you will hear, see, and read about the declining of education. Discepline is a problem, test scores are down, and the teacher is being slained. Society has asked the perplexing question: What makes an effective classroom teacher?

First, to become an effective classroom teacher, there has to be an internal love within self, along with external love of the art of teaching. Secondly, devotion, dedication, and discapline among self and the enviernment in which you are entering will demonstrate the first procedure of effectiveness in the classroom and set up the essential elements involved in teaching. Thirdly, carrying the three "P's" in your heart will produce an effective classroom teacher, being "Proud" of what you are, being "Patient" with whom you are teaching, and being "Persistent" in what you are teaching. Finally, living beyond the classroom, I think, is the most effective in an effective classroom teacher, staying beyond your paid time, getting emotionally involved with your students after your paid time and setting up the ability to cope with the stress of the educational process before your paid time. In order to endure effectiveness, there is long-suffering, perservance, and understanding any situation at any given moment to entitle all children to a worthwile education of an effective classroom teacher.

FEATURES OF THE WRITING SAMPLE SCORING 1

Focus and Appropriateness

The writer of this essay partially addresses the topic, but the essay itself is totally unacceptable. The initial paragraph, which should have outlined the characteristics to be discussed, leads one to believe that the essay will address "declining of education," "test scores," and "slained teachers." To identify problems that demand effective teachers is an acceptable way to introduce the topic, but the writer of this essay does it very poorly.

Unity and Organization

The writer does present the characteristics of an effective teacher, but these characteristics are all contained in one paragraph, and they are very unclear due to poor word choice, ambiguous expressions (awkward), and poor sentence structure. Three paragraphs should have been used, one for each characteristic, and each should have contained details to explain and support the characteristic.

Development and Rationale

Of the four characteristics of an effective teacher, the writer develops only two; the first two are merely started, without any explanation of *why* they are desirable.

Sentence Structure and Usage

The word *endured* is misused as though the writer does not know what it means. In fact, this essay is filled with awkward expressions that suggest an inability to use the language effectively: "declining of education," "internal love within self," "external love of the art of teaching," "demonstrate the first procedure of effectiveness in the classroom," "set up the essential elements," "Finally, living beyond the classroom, I think, is the most effective in an effective classroom teacher," "staying beyond your paid time," and others.

Mechanical Conventions

The writer excessively uses "you" and "your"—second person. Essays should be written in the third person—he, she, or they. For example, the noun *teacher* or *teachers* should have been used as well. Additionally, the past participle of *slay* is *slain*, not *slained*. The few misspellings do not necessarily lower the score, but they do not help.

Index

S

T

NOTES

NOTES

NOTES

NOTES